Interview Skills Consulting

D1589951

# MEDICAL SCHOOL INTERVIEWS

### A practical guide to help you get that place at Medical School

### Over 150 questions analysed

**George Lee MA (Cantab), MB BChir (Cantab), MRCS(Ed), FRCS (Urol), FEBU** Consultant Surgeon

**Olivier Picard BSc (Hons), MSc**
Communication Consultant

**ISC**MEDICAL
Interview Skills Consulting

Published by ISCMedical
Suite 434, Hamilton House, Mabledon Place, London WC1H 9BB
Tel: 0845 226 9487

First Edition: Oct 2006
Reprinted: Dec 2006 / May 2007
ISBN13: 978-1-905812-04-2
ISBN10: 1-905812-04-3
A catalogue record for this book is available from the British Library.

**ISC**MEDICAL
Interview Skills Consulting

# INTRODUCTION

When preparing for the medical school interview, it is tempting to spend a considerable amount of time rehearsing "model" answers to hundreds of questions in front of the mirror. This strategy is very time consuming and yields very little. It only reinforces your weaknesses and does not allow you to consider your answer more thoroughly within a framework. You will also find it difficult to regurgitate pre-prepared answers when you are under pressure.

### Balancing content and structure

Most people worry only about what they "should" say but not so much about how to make the answer effective. As well as concentrating on producing good content, you should ensure that the content is not wasted by being delivered in a bland or confusing manner that would make it ineffective. There is no point having good arguments if the interviewers are not perceiving their full value. Those who get a place at medical school are not necessarily those who deliver 100% of the "ideal" content. Often, they are people who deliver maybe 80% of that content but do so in a personal and structured manner that makes them stand out in the crowd.

### Preparing for the interview

To produce a good performance, you will need to spend some time thinking and preparing for different styles of questions, whether they are of a personal nature, testing your knowledge of the medical environment or attempting to determine your lateral thinking abilities. In our experience, preparing for a medical school interview takes a minimum of 20 hours. This ensures that you have adequate time to study each style of question in depth. This book will give a number of tools, techniques and formats that will help you focus your attention on the important aspects of the process, thus saving you valuable time.

Good luck with your preparation.

George Lee & Olivier Picard

3

# CONTENTS TABLE

**ISC**MEDICAL
Interview Skills Consulting

ISCMEDICAL
Interview Skills Consulting

**ISC**MEDICAL
Interview Skills Consulting

125   A young woman presents with rheumatoid arthritis. She has tried    260
all the conventional treatments but is still having problems.
Unless her symptoms improve, she will have to give up work in
the near future. There is a new but very expensive treatment
available. Treatment for a single patient costs as much as
conventional treatment for 10 patients. The drug is not effective
in all patients and in some cases gives rise to a worsening of the
symptoms. What do you do?

126   You are the Health Secretary and you have a budget of £10m    262
available to you every year. With that budget, you will be able to
make a treatment or procedure available on the NHS. You have
been given the choice between only two options: a treatment that
will considerably alleviate the pain of arthritis sufferers and a
surgical procedure designed to repair a hole in the heart of
neonates. Both treatments/procedures have exactly the same
overall annual cost. What would you do?

127   A 14-year-old girl presents to you asking for a termination of    264
pregnancy. What are the issues?

128   An elderly lady refuses to take her medication for heart failure    266
following a recent heart attack. Not taking the medication
exposes her to serious risks, including possible death. She
presents to your surgery with her husband who wants you to talk
some sense into her. What are the issues?

129   What would you do if a patient came to you asking for advice    268
about a non-conventional treatment that they had found on the
Internet?

130   What would you do if a patient offered you a £50 voucher as a    271
gift at Christmas?

131   Do you think it is right for doctors to have conferences, training    274
sessions and study material sponsored by pharmaceutical
companies or other corporate sponsors?

132   What is your opinion about euthanasia and assisted suicide?    276

133   A patient comes to see you and requests an HIV test. What do    278
you do?

134   You are a physician looking after a patient who was diagnosed    280
with HIV a few months ago. You have encouraged him to
disclose his diagnosis to his wife, which he has refused to do.
What do you do?

**ISC**MEDICAL
Interview Skills Consulting

# MEDICAL SCHOOL INTERVIEWS

# TECHNIQUES
# &
# FRAMEWORKS

# FORMULATING YOUR ANSWERS

Throughout this book, we will demonstrate how individual questions may be approached in order to deliver a strong answer. There are a number of factors that you should bear in mind and that should underline every answer that you give:

**Keep track of time:** no longer than 2 minutes for most questions, 3 minutes if the subject is broad (any longer and you will put the interviewer to sleep).

**No one-liners:** you need to explain what you say, back up all your statements appropriately and generally provide a well-developed answer. This is what this book will teach you to do. Your answers should be sufficiently long to be interesting. A minimum length of 1.5 minutes would be appropriate.

**Keep to the point and use a sound structure/framework:** always directly answer the question at the start of your answer. Do not waffle or have a lengthy introduction. You can diverge slightly afterwards if you want (providing it is relevant). Make sure that your answer follows a well-defined structure or framework. Most structures/frameworks will consist of 3-5 main points (this is as much as anyone will be prepared to listen to). Raising too many points will simply make you lose your audience. If you have more than a handful of points to make, try to see if you can reorganise the information into bigger headings.

**Substantiate and personalise:** use facts to substantiate your answer. Facts bring credibility to your answer. You can draw from your work or academic experience to discuss who, what, when, why and how, and to personalise your answers. Using 'I' rather than 'we' gives more credit to your actions.

**Be positive:** keep the answers positive. Sell yourself. There is no need to volunteer the negative facts. When discussing negative situations, use your answer to explain how much you have learnt from your experience.

**Conclude:** always conclude your answer. Keep it brief. Whenever possible, make sure that the conclusion relates back to you and your future role as a doctor.

# "I DON'T LIKE SELLING MYSELF. IT MAKES ME FEEL ARROGANT"

Feeling arrogant when attempting to sell oneself is a common and natural feeling, which even the shyest candidates have. If you feel arrogant, it is often because you are trying to sell yourself by making bold statements along the lines of "I am a good communicator", "I am a good team player", "I am very organised", etc.

Essentially, all you are doing is giving the interviewers your own opinion of yourself without explaining what you mean. There are three main ways in which you can get around that problem and, with a bit of practice, you will be able to build complete answers that present you as a balanced individual:

1.  Express your strengths in an objective manner by mentioning the fact that other people think that you are good (e.g. "I have often been complimented by my teachers for being a good team player").

2.  Justify your skills by talking about the impact they have or had, and by giving representative examples (e.g. "I have good organisational skills which really helped me in making the College's summer ball a success at the end of last year": you can then go into more details about what the event involved). This helps dilute the bold statement.

3.  Stay practical and talk about your experience rather than what you think you are good at. For example, "I have a lot of experience of working with teams both as a leader and a simple team member" is a lot more effective and down to earth than "I am a really good team player and team leader". Of course, once you have made a statement about your level of experience, you will need to go on describing that experience and your role within it.

Throughout this book, we will show you how this can be achieved in individual questions.

**ISC**MEDICAL
Interview Skills Consulting

# SELLING YOURSELF
# THE "TAGS" FRAMEWORK

A number of questions are designed to make you talk about yourself, to describe why you feel that you are a suitable candidate for Medicine and what your aspirations are. To answer such questions successfully, you will need to address a wide range of issues, thereby demonstrating a broad knowledge of the medical environment and what being a doctor entails. You will also need to deliver your answer in a clear and structured manner, for which the following framework should assist you. Where necessary, we will refer to this framework throughout our explanations.

## **T**raining & Experience/Clinical

- The exams that you have passed
- The extent of your technical knowledge and of your training
- The extent of your experience
- The courses and seminars that you have attended

## **A**cademic

- Teaching others
- Carrying out research activities
- Ensuring that your practice is up to standard by doing regular audits

## **G**eneric skills

- Communication skills (listening skills, caring approach, empathy, etc.)
- Team playing
- Leadership
- Management and organisational skills

## **S**ocial

- Social life, hobbies, volunteer work, etc.

## "ISCMEDICAL
Interview Skills Consulting

# QUESTIONS ASKING FOR EXAMPLES

Questions asking for examples are popular at interviews. This form of questioning, called "behavioural", stems from the fact that your recruiters are likely to learn a lot more about you by getting you to talk about your past experiences than by asking you how you might behave in hypothetical situations. Typical questions are likely to be of the form: *Describe a situation where you played an important role in a team, where you used your communication skills effectively, where you made a mistake, where you failed to communicate effectively, where you had to deal with conflict, etc.*

### The Rules
Although most candidates find such questions difficult, they are in fact relatively easy once you have identified a good example to discuss, providing you follow a number of important rules.

### Rule 1: Make sure that you choose a specific example
Many candidates prefer to address vague situations or to speak about their experience in general. For example, "Describe a situation where you played an important role in a team" often leads to answers of the type "I work in teams all the time, at school, in my summer job or at the local youth club". Giving such an answer would be missing the point of the question. If you read the question correctly, it is asking about a situation, i.e. a specific case or project that you handled. You would therefore need to be very specific.

### Rule 2: Take some time to identify all the skills that you need to demonstrate
In a question such as "Describe a situation where your communication skills had a positive effect on a situation", it is obvious that the question is testing your ability to communicate. In other less obvious questions, such as "Give an example of a situation where you had to deal with a complex situation", there are many skills that you can demonstrate such as:

- Your ability to take the initiative and to work within your own limits.
- Your ability to identify the resources you need to resolve this problem.

- Your ability to seek help from others whenever required.
- Your ability to work with your team to achieve the best possible result.
- Your ability to communicate with all parties involved.

### Rule 3: Ensure that your example is relevant and addresses as many of the required skills identified as possible

Many candidates are so happy to have found one example that they rush into their explanation without thinking whether they are maximising their chances by using it. A bad example will be difficult to explain in detail and will leave a bad impression on the interviewers.

### Rule 4: Do not be tempted to make things up

It does not require much training to recognise a liar. Interviewers will be able to spot fairly easily whether you are making things up simply by the lack of detail that you are providing and the vagueness of your answers.

### Rule 5: Be personal

Describe what you did, not what everyone else did (unless it is absolutely relevant to the situation). Too many candidates waste their time discussing what the team did and how the team worked, giving little information about what they, themselves, did. You must always remember that the point of the recruitment process is to find out about you, not about anyone else. Concentrate on the "I" rather than the "We" and don't be afraid of going into detail, providing it is relevant.

### Rule 6: Follow the "STAR" technique

The STAR technique, described in the following chapter, provides an easy way to give a focused and organised answer. Take some time to apply it to as many examples as you can so that it becomes second nature. See p.18.

### Rule 7: Prepare suitable examples before you go to the interview

It is notoriously difficult to come up with good examples at an interview if you have not done any preparation. Without that preparation, you will come up with examples that are lame and do not allow you to show your full potential.

The range of questions relating to examples is limited and you should therefore be able to prepare adequately without wasting too much time. By preparing examples of good communication, good teamwork, leadership, initiative and creativity, a mistake that you have made, dealing with a complex situation and with a conflict situation, you will have covered 99% of the example questions normally asked.

If they are suitably complex, some examples can be used to illustrate different skills. For example, dealing with a difficult customer in your summer job may enable you to show good communication, good leadership and good conflict handling skills. Preparing complex examples will therefore enable you to kill several birds with one stone and will help you minimise the number of examples that you need to remember.

**ISC**MEDICAL
Interview Skills Consulting

# THE "STAR" TECHNIQUE

The acronym "**STAR**" stands for Situation Task Action Result. It is a universally recognised communication technique designed to enable you to provide a meaningful and complete answer to questions asking for examples. At the same time, it has the advantage of being simple enough to be applied easily.

Many interviewers will have been trained in using this structure. Even if they have not, they will recognise its value when they see it. The information will be given to them in a structured manner and, as a result, they will become more receptive to the messages you are trying to communicate.

### Step 1 – Situation or Task
Describe the situation that you were confronted with or the task that needed to be accomplished. Set the context. Make it concise and informative, concentrating solely on what is useful to the story. For example, if the question is asking you to describe a situation where you had to deal with a difficult person, explain how you came to meet that person and why they were being difficult. If the question is asking for an example of teamwork, explain the task that you had to undertake as a team.

### Step 2 – Action
This is the most important section as it is where you will need to demonstrate and highlight the skills and personal attributes that the question is testing. Now that you have set the context of your story, you need to explain what you did. In doing so, you will need to remember the following:

- Be personal, i.e. talk about you, not the rest of the team.
- Go into some detail. Do not assume that they will guess what you mean.
- Steer clear of technical information, unless it is crucial to your story.
- Explain what you did, how you did it, and why you did it.

## What you did and how you did it

The interviewers will want to know how you reacted to the situation. This is where you can start selling some important skills. For example, you may want to describe how you used the team to achieve a particular objective and how you used your communication skills to keep everyone updated on progress etc.

## Why you did it

This is probably the most crucial part of your answer. Interviewers want to know that you are using a variety of generic skills in order to achieve your objectives. Therefore you must be able to demonstrate in your answer that you are taking specific actions because you are trying to achieve a specific objective and not simply by chance.

For example, when discussing a situation where you had to deal with conflict, many candidates would simply say: "I told my colleague to calm down and explained to him what the problem was". However, it would not provide a good idea of what drove you to act in this manner. How did you ask him to calm down? How did you explain the nature of the problem? By highlighting the reasons behind your action, you would make a greater impact. For example:

"I could sense that my colleague was irritated and I asked him gently to tell me what he felt the problem was. By allowing him to vent his feelings and his anger, I gave him the opportunity to calm down. I then explained to him my own point of view on the matter, emphasising how important it was that we found a solution that suited us both."

This revised answer helps the interviewers understand what drove your actions and reinforces the feeling that you are calculating the consequences of your actions, thus retaining full control of the situation. It provides much more information about you as an individual.

**Step 3 – Result**

Explain what happened eventually – how it all ended. Also, use the opportunity to describe what you accomplished and what you learnt in that situation. This helps you make the answer personal and enables you to highlight further skills.

# DEALING WITH ... , COPING WITH ...
# THE FOUR 'R'S

Interviewers sometimes ask how you would deal or cope with a particular situation (e.g. stress, a difficult person). They are not asking for a specific example (in which case the STAR framework would apply), but the approach that you would take generally.

Such questions are very hypothetical because, in practice, your reaction would very much depend on the intensity of the problem, the personality of other people involved and the context. Nevertheless, you need to address these questions fully and the four 'R's framework should help you do this.

**R**ecognise the situation: You must recognise that there is a problem and that you understand its nature.

**R**ecruit information about the situation: Gather facts, identify the cause of the problem and the issues involved.

**R**esolve the situation: Take the appropriate steps to resolve the issues identified.

**R**eflect on the situation: a good answer is always personal. You should demonstrate that you can learn from situations.

# EXPRESSING AN OPINION

There will be many questions where you will be asked what you think of such-and-such concept or situation. These questions are not designed to test whether your ideas match those of the panel. Indeed, you are allowed to think what you want, providing it does not make you an unsafe or bigoted doctor, and provided that you can justify your opinions with sensible arguments.

What the panel will require from you is an ability to think about the topic from different perspectives, to present balanced arguments in a clear, concise and structured manner and to be in a position to discuss the topic in an adult fashion with them. In most cases, this will mean reserving your own opinion on the topic until the end and presenting the various sides of the argument first. Giving your opinion first would not only stop you from addressing the multiple facets of the issue in question, but would also often make you run the risk of appearing one-dimensional.

In most cases, the opinions that you will be required to give will be related to something which is either in the news at the time of the interview (current trial, court case), an ongoing political issue (role of nurses, NHS reforms) or an ethical issue or scenario (abortion, euthanasia, vivisection, liver transplants for alcoholics, etc.).

In order to deal with current issues or political issues, you will need to be familiar with the details and this book will help you a lot in understanding some of the intricacies. However, you would be well advised to spend some time reading relevant news websites and newspapers as they are often a rich source of arguments that you can use in your own answers.

In order to deal with ethical issues, you will also need to have done a substantial amount of thinking and reading in your own time so that you can acquire a good ability to debate. This book will give you many arguments that you can use. However, to complement it, you will need to spend some time discussing them informally with friends and family. You will be all the more equipped for having listened to and argued with your closest friends or relatives. The interviewers will expect you to engage in a similar debate with them.

# MEDICAL SCHOOL INTERVIEWS

# ANALYSIS
# OF
# INTERVIEW QUESTIONS

# QUESTION 1

**Tell me about yourself.**

## Introduction

This question, when asked, will be the first one in the interview and you must use it to your advantage to make the best possible impression. Most people find that it is a difficult question to approach and struggle to find an interesting angle. Consequently, they end up making one of two serious mistakes:

- They want to tell their life story and end up speaking for over 5 minutes, giving a year-by-year account of their studies and interests;

or

- They mention two skills superficially and do not personalise their answer. This results in a 10-second answer of the type *"My name is John, I like science, I am a good team player and I want to be a doctor"*.

Many candidates' first reaction is "What do you want me to talk about: my studies, my hobbies or my work experience?" In reality, you should exploit the vagueness of the question to discuss what you want to discuss (and not what you think they might want to hear), using the opportunity to sell your experience and skills.

## How to approach the question

Essentially, this question is asking you to verbalise information that should already be included in your personal statement. It therefore gives you an opportunity to shine using information that you have already gathered. If there are some omissions in your personal statements, here is a chance to make up for the deficiencies.

In order to provide a complete picture, use the TAGS framework highlighted on page 14 and take the interviewers through each section in turn.

**ISC**MEDICAL
Interview Skills Consulting

### Training & Experience
Provide the highlights of your education so far, your 'A' Levels and career to date. Explain how you developed your interest in Medicine and, as part of this, what you gained from your work experience.

### Academic
Develop your experience and interest in teaching, lab work, research, etc.

### Generic Skills
Highlight your interpersonal skills and other personal attributes. This would include communication skills, team playing abilities, organisational and leadership skills. You should relate each skill mentioned to your life experiences and work experience, giving examples of situations where you demonstrated such skills.

### Social
Talk about yourself as a person. What social life do you have? How do you relax? What are your hobbies? This aspect is important as it presents you as a well-balanced individual. This will be crucial throughout medical school and your life as a doctor to enable you to cope with the pressure of exams and difficult work experiences, and to relieve your stress.

With 2-3 minutes to answer the question, and four sections to address, you effectively have 30-40 seconds per section. You therefore need to be succinct in your answer, while providing enough information to sound interesting. This requires preparation and practice.

### Example of an ineffective answer

> *Hi, my name is John. I am currently taking my 'A' Levels and am really keen to do Medicine. I think Medicine will be a great way to have an interesting life and to make a real difference to people. I am a good communicator, a good team player and I am very dedicated and focused. I enjoy playing football and going out with my friends.*

This example is not "bad". The general structure and approach are fine but the wording is too generic to have a strong impact. Its main weakness is that it contains many statements that are not fully explained and whose interpretation is left to the judgement of the interviewer.

Interview Skills Consulting

In particular:

- What does "a great way to have an interesting life" mean?

- Why is the candidate keen to do Medicine? Perhaps he expects to be asked later on. You should avoid making assumptions. Rather than speculating on what questions you might get, ensure that you answer each question on its own merit.

- The candidate says that he is a good communicator and team player. Should we just take his word for it? What makes him say that? This needs to be backed up by examples and related back to his social activities or work experience.

- The candidate says that he enjoys playing football and going out. Nothing wrong with that but how is that different to someone who enjoys playing the violin and cooking? The statement needs to include a personal reflection on what the candidate gets out of these activities.

By themselves facts are not very interesting unless you explain their significance.

**Example of an effective answer**

*My name is John and I am a very dynamic, adaptable and focused individual. I am currently studying Chemistry, Biology, English and Graphic Arts, all of which I am really enjoying. As well as studying hard to be successful over the past few years, I have become involved in charity work and have organised work experience in hospitals and hospices. During my work experience I have learnt a great deal about the importance of doctor-patient communication. In particular, I had many opportunities to witness the difference that doctors can make to patients by being good listeners and keeping the patient involved at all times. I experienced this myself too when I had to have a discussion with an elderly patient who was reluctant to go into surgery. I particularly found it rewarding that I was able to help him reach his own conclusion simply by discussing the matter with him and by helping him analyse the situation. Seeing how the whole team pulled together to achieve great outcomes also really reinforced in me the desire to pursue my ambition to become a doctor.*

*I am also a very keen learner and I have a natural curiosity for scientific matters. Over the past few years I have been reading journals like Nature or the Student BMJ, where I have really learnt a lot. As well as educating myself, I also enjoy teaching others and, in particular, I have been mentoring a child with learning difficulties at the local school for the past year, with really encouraging results. On the social side, I have always been active in extra-curricular activities such as the Duke of Edinburgh Award. I am also a member of my school's chess club and football committees. I really enjoy all these activities because they give me an opportunity to socialise with different people and to challenge myself to constantly achieve more. They have also given me a good opportunity to use my creative side and my sense of initiative and innovation. Apart from the above, I sing, cook and play piano in my spare time, which helps me relax and cope under stress.*

This is just one example and you will obviously need to adapt your answer to your own circumstances. This answer is effective because the candidate concentrates on a few key messages, using his experience as well as his personal learning and feelings as a backup.

# QUESTION 2

**Take us through your Application Form / Personal Statement.**

Essentially, this question is the same as "Tell us about yourself", though many candidates would be tempted to prepare different answers. In reality, the answer to "Tell me about yourself" should have used most of the information already contained in your personal statement and therefore there is no reason why the answers to both questions should differ widely.

The main danger with this question is to take it too literally and to go through your personal statement line by line. This could take 20 minutes and be tedious. Instead of trying to remember exactly what you wrote and in what order, you should try to convey the meaning of what you wrote, adding an all-essential element of personality. This takes us back to the previous question.

**Why ask this question if they have already read your statement?**
The answer is simple:

1. They haven't actually read your statement and want you to make their job easier. Do not discount this possibility; many schools do not have the time to read the personal statement at shortlisting stage. You should therefore ensure that you can summarise it well at the interview

2. A written statement conveys emotions and personality with difficulty. By asking you to summarise the personal statement verbally, they are giving you an opportunity to present the information in an enthusiastic manner.

3. They are using the question as an ice-breaker, on the presumption that you will find it easier to talk about a topic that you will have prepared before. This is a unique chance to make a good first impression and you should not miss it.

You might also want to use this opportunity to add to the statement anything you might have forgotten to include in it before you submitted it.

# QUESTION 3

**Why do you want to do Medicine?**

**First things first! Why do you actually want to do Medicine?**
Many candidates launch straight into an explanation without having first clarified in their own mind why they actually want to be a doctor. To give a good answer, you must analyse those reasons and recollect the process that you followed to identify Medicine as a career.

There are many reasons why people want to study Medicine. These may include:
- A strong interest in biology and/or sciences
- Wanting to go into a challenging profession
- Wanting to help others
- Wanting a profession that combines intellectual abilities and a strong element of communication
- Being interested by the variety of work involved, from prevention to treatment but also teaching, research, etc.
- Enjoying close contact with people, and making a difference to their lives
- Wanting to work in an environment where there is a strong element of teamwork
- Enjoying constant learning.

All reasons are laudable and you must ensure that your own reasons are clear in your mind. The main problem at interviews is that the reasons above are likely to be mentioned by most people. If you simply list a few of them then your answer will be bland and will resemble 700 other answers. However, this does not mean that the above facts must be rejected. They are an important aspect of the answer and should be addressed too.

**How can you stand out?**
Firstly, it is important to realise that sounding different does not necessarily mean that you have to find a reason that no one else has thought about. In other words, you don't need to present an obscure reason for choosing Medicine in order to sound interesting. Instead, you should identify your true reasons and develop them well.

Secondly, you must make your answer personal and deliver it in an enthusiastic style. Repeating five times in your answer that you are really keen on Medicine will not make your point any stronger. Your enthusiasm will come across through the way you speak and the personal nature of your answers. The following should help you out:

1. *Choose three or four reasons only.*
   It is better to concentrate on a handful of points that you develop well, than to develop 25 different ideas in 2 seconds each.

2. *Introduce an element of personal reflection for each point.*
   Many candidates will say that they enjoy science, but it is hardly a convincing argument by itself. It is also quite difficult to convey your enthusiasm for science through such a simple statement. Instead, try to back this statement up by explaining what you enjoy about science. Is it the intellectual challenge of having to use facts and judgement to resolve problems (in which case you will enjoy diagnosing patients)? Is it the fact that it is both intellectual and practical (in which case, Medicine is definitely a good field to get into)? etc.

   Similarly, it is easy to comment on the fact that Medicine is challenging. What is more interesting for an interviewer to know is why you find that it will challenge you. Is it the fact that you will have to deal with the unexpected? Or maybe the fact that it is a constant learning curve, that you have to keep up to date and that it involves working with many people with different skills and personalities? Whatever the reason, you need to develop it so that the interviewers are not fed quick headlines but a really personal point of view.

3. **Use your work experience and other personal experiences.**
In many cases, the reasons that you chose Medicine as a career will have been highlighted through the personal experience that you have gained of Medicine. In your work experience, you might have seen first hand how medical teams work, you might have had personal experience of the impact of good listening and empathy on particular patients, or had exposure to the wonders of technology. Everything counts and helps in making your answer stand out. To make it personal you will need to go into some detail about what you have seen and experienced, and, more importantly, how this has made you feel and how these experiences have reinforced your career choice.

**Example of an effective answer**

*Medicine is a career that I have had in mind for a very long time and which I have learnt to appreciate even more over the past year during my work experience.*

*I have always been very interested in science, whether this was biology or physics, and I have a very inquisitive mind. I have always been fascinated by the complexities of the human body, the intricate mix of the biological and the chemical and also the manner in which the human psyche can interact with the physical. Over the past few years I have read up on many medical and scientific issues. For example, I read quite a lot about CJD when the crisis broke out and at the moment I am following closely the current debate on euthanasia. I feel that going into Medicine will really give me a good opportunity to work in an intellectually challenging environment.*

*I really enjoy taking care of others. I have been a volunteer for St John Ambulance since the age of 15 and I have spent a lot of time providing first aid at major events. I also recently spent some time working for a helpline for suicidal people. These two experiences have really helped me to understand more about the various pains that people can experience, from the physical to the psychological. I enjoyed both experiences because I could feel that I was making a real difference to those people, if only by offering a reassuring presence. This reinforced in me the desire to get into a profession where I would make a difference at a personal level and that Medicine was really the path that I wanted to follow.*

> As well as all this, I am greatly interested by the vast opportunities and the variety that Medicine offers. As part of my work experience, I had the opportunity to shadow a consultant anaesthetist who shared his time between clinical work and research. This gave me a good insight into the numerous roles that doctors play. As well as managing the care of his patients, he spent time supervising and teaching junior colleagues or carrying out his research. I also had the opportunity to shadow a GP for 3 weeks, and gained a first-hand understanding of how the doctors are not just clinicians but they are also educators and counsellors. I find this range of activities very exciting.
>
> Overall, I feel that Medicine offers everything that I am looking for in a career: an intellectual challenge, an environment where teamwork and communication play an important part, a close proximity to people, and, more than any other profession, a true feeling of being able to make a real difference to my surrounding environment.

### Do you need to have had an interest in Medicine since you were born?

A good way of introducing your answer to the "Why Medicine?" questions is to talk about how your interest in Medicine started. For example, some candidates have had serious conditions themselves and through these they have been exposed substantially to the medical profession, which has prompted their interest. Others may have nursed elderly relatives throughout their youth and discovered their vocation in this way. Others may have had experience of voluntary work with disadvantaged people, whether in the UK or abroad, and developed an interest in "making a difference" from an early age.

If you have been in such a situation, you may find that it is useful to use it to fully personalise your answer. However, most people have not been exposed to such circumstances and, in an effort to be personal, they tend to provide answers with a forced personalisation that could sound corny, such as:

- "I broke my leg when I was ten and I was fascinated by the work that doctors did on it. This really made me want to be a doctor". Maybe so, but it runs the risk of sounding a little weak. It is a bit like saying "My sister does jigsaw puzzles and I really want to do this for a living". We are all exposed to different events in our lives and we are obviously influenced by all of them. However, these days, you see more medical drama on TV

than you would see at the hospital when breaking a leg and the jump from the broken leg to a medical vocation is slightly weak.

- "I used to visit my Nan at the hospital and found it fascinating to see how the nurses cared for her." Again, we all observe events in our lives and you would need to have been strongly influenced and to have been marked sufficiently by that situation to justify its link to your career in Medicine. Many people find the work of firemen fascinating but have never really thought of making a career of it. Observing a situation does not mean that you would be good at working within that setting unless you could demonstrate the extent of your feelings following your exposure. In this example, you would get more mileage out of explaining what you gained from caring for your Nan and helping her through her illness from a physical and psychological point of view than by observing how others cared for her.

There is no real harm in mentioning personal events, but you should make sure that you don't give them an importance that they don't necessarily deserve in reality.

### Should you mention the fact that there are doctors in your family?
A number of applicants have taken the medical route because someone in their family is a doctor and they have gained exposure to the system from an early age. In principle, there is nothing wrong with mentioning it, although you should realise that this will not be sufficient to get you a place. Interviewers will be more concerned about whether you have what it takes rather than whether you were born in the right family. Therefore you should identify in your experience the elements that made you grow as a person and you should avoid dwelling too much on what you have observed or heard from others in your family. The last thing you want is to give the impression that you are only there because your family thought it might be a good idea. Generally speaking, you should be able to put forward a convincing argument without mentioning that your family is full of doctors.

Conclusion: if you can avoid it, then avoid it. At the very least, keep your references to the bare minimum. You will get more credit by talking about the work experience that you have organised by yourself and from which you have personally gained than from a ready-made experience handed to you by relatives. You must show drive and initiative as well as personal will.

**What if you are a graduate?**
There are two main types of graduates: those who have already tried to enter medical school before and those who have not.

If you have already attempted medical school before then you should explain how the past few years have helped you to mature in your decision to become a doctor. As part of that process, you should also address the additional skills that you gained during your degree.

If you have never attempted medical school before, then you will need to explain how the past few years have made a difference. In some cases, it pays to be honest by explaining what your original career intentions were and by setting out how you discovered your vocation for Medicine.


**What if you are a mature student or already have a career behind you?**
A number of candidates go into medical school at a later stage in life. Such candidates are welcome because they bring a range of attributes and maturity that is not always found in younger students. They usually show more motivation as their decision to join Medicine tends to be deliberate rather than impulsive.

In many ways, this should make it easier to explain your motivation towards Medicine because you will have followed a personal journey to reach that decision and therefore should have more arguments than most to explain your new-found vocation.

The only real approach that you can take is to explain how you came to choose your first career and to detail the process through which you changed your mind. There are a number of factors that you should bear in mind:

- *Never be ashamed of your past* and never present the situation in an apologetic manner. No one has a straightforward life and people from very different backgrounds can be good doctors regardless of how they got there.

- *Never criticise your old career.* You do not want to give the impression that you are choosing an alternative career as a knee-jerk reaction. It is likely that there are aspects of your old career that you

will have found less satisfactory than others, but you should try to present these in the context of all the good aspects of that job and the learning and maturity that you have drawn from it.

This answer is on the long side but it develops well each of the arguments brought forward by the candidate. Note how it is made up of three paragraphs (not too many points) framed by an introduction and a conclusion. Each paragraph starts with a message which is then backed up by experience in the text. This provides a clear structure which enables the listener to keep track of the main reasons being highlighted.

In the example above, each point is backed up by two experiences. If your speed of delivery is slow or if you feel uncomfortable with answers on the longer side, then the answer could be made shorter by simply mentioning one experience in each paragraph instead. Whether you take a short or a long approach, make sure your answer fits within a 1.5- to 3-minute window. They need to have time to ask you other questions too!

# QUESTION 4

**Why not nursing? Why not any other healthcare profession?**

This question is often interpreted as a trap when it is merely testing your motivation in greater depth. Do not take such open questioning as a sign that your first answer was not appropriate. Instead, use the opportunity that you have been given to demonstrate your understanding of the roles played by doctors, nurses and other professionals, and how they complement one another.

**Beware of the common traps:**

1. *"Doctors can prescribe"* – True, but so can nurses now!

2. *"Doctors can make decisions"* – Are you saying nurses can't?

3. *"Being a doctor is more interesting"* – Go and say that to a nurse!

4. *"Doctors can make a real difference to patients; nurses merely follow orders."* Doctors often find that nurses can achieve much more than they can in many cases because nurses spend more time with patients and are often better able to communicate and empathise.

5. *"There are better career prospects for doctors."* Given the fact that there are areas where there are 1000 applicants for one post, this is not a very clever argument. In any case, nurses now have new opportunities with the opening of nurse practitioners and nurse consultant posts. In some cases, they may even earn more than doctors.

**ISC**MEDICAL
Interview Skills Consulting

**How to approach the question**
1. Do not criticise nurses. You will have to work with them and there may even be some on the panel. The main problem with the arguments above is that they are too simplistic.

2. You may develop similar arguments but in a more explicit and complete manner. You should also illustrate your arguments with examples. Arguments that may be used include:

   i. Doctors receive a general training, which ensures that they have knowledge and experience of clinical areas beyond their specialty. This aids the management of the patient when matters beyond that specialty are important.

   ii. Doctors have ultimate responsibility for the patient. They are driving the decision-making process. Although nurses contribute greatly to that process, the final decision will rest with a doctor.

   iii. Both nurses and doctors may get involved in research activities. However, doctors are more likely to take a lead in the research projects while nurses may be more involved in the actual practical execution of projects.

   iv. Although nurse practitioners undergo similar training to medical students, for clinical examination for instance, they do not meet the standards of clinical skills that doctors are able to achieve after taking postgraduate examinations (e.g. exams for membership of Royal Colleges).

   v. It is true that, nowadays, some nurses have taken roles traditionally taken by doctors, particularly in the domains of investigation, diagnosis and treatment, and that the gap has narrowed. However:

      ▪ Only a small minority have the opportunity to become involved in these activities, and only in very specialised areas. The activities of these nurses are highly protocol driven, leaving little leeway for discretion (i.e. basically the art of Medicine);

- Nurse specialists have clinical expertise in that specialty only, whereas the doctors, due to their medical training, will have knowledge and experience of clinical areas beyond that specialty. For example, a TB specialist nurse managing a patient with a history of liver problems may run into problems when considering anti-tuberculosis treatment and will require the involvement of a specialist doctor.

3. Somewhere in your answer, make sure that you praise the role of nurses and mention how important they are to the care of patients. Emphasise that it is not a matter of one being better than the other but of people with different levels of responsibility and skills working together towards one goal.

**Why not any other healthcare profession?**
Your answer to this should start with "Indeed, why not?" Many healthcare professions have a lot in common with the role of doctors (close contact with patient, caring patient-centred approach, etc.) and in many respects they are joined by people who have similar personal characteristics to those exhibited by doctors.

In the first instance, you should highlight the similarities between other healthcare professions and being a doctor, thereby showing your understanding that it is not as simple as "them and us". You can then follow this with a highlight of some of the differences. These would include the differences highlighted above between nurses and doctors, as well as the fact that doctors can prescribe and diagnose, which adds to the challenge.

# QUESTION 5

**What would you do if you did not get into Medicine this year?**

The answer to this question will depend on your current situation. The point here is that you should demonstrate drive and motivation to become a doctor while being realistic (especially if it is the fifth time that you are applying!).

**If you are applying for the first time**
In this situation you have no choice but to give the message that you will be trying again. Giving up at the first opportunity would be interpreted as a serious lack of motivation. It is most important that you appear as someone who is motivated and energetic and your answer should also discuss the steps that you would take to gain further experience and maturity while you are waiting to reapply. In most cases, this would consist of a productive gap year. When you describe your planned activities ensure that they bear some relation to Medicine (you would get severely penalised for saying that you want to go wind-surfing for a year).

**Example of an effective answer**

*I have had a passion for Medicine since a young age and I am determined to do everything possible to gain entry to medical school. If I do not get into a medical school this year, I will of course be very disappointed but I know that I will also be able to rely on support from my friends and family.*

*My first step will be to identify the weaknesses in my CV and in my interview skills by getting feedback from the medical school and other people I can trust. This will help me improve my application for next time.*

*I will also organise a gap year. During that time I intend to get involved in healthcare work experience and charity work, such as working for the Red Cross and St John Ambulance. I would also like to shadow doctors at my local hospital for some time in order to familiarise myself further with the*

**ISC**MEDICAL
Interview Skills Consulting

*medical profession and possibly to get involved in working in a scientific lab to find out more about medical research.*

*I would also like to take some time out to go travelling before applying again for medical school next year. I am particularly interested in South America and I may be able to organise a long trip to Chile where I would be able to combine a holiday with an involvement in local charity work.*

The above answer addresses three basic concepts: finding out what went wrong, work experience at home, and travelling (combined with work experience). From a delivery point of view, this simple structure makes the points easy to identify and therefore makes it easier for the interviewers to receive the information.

**If you are not applying for the first time and want to try again**
If this is not your first application then you will need to provide a realistic view of the situation. There is little point in mentioning that you will keep trying until you reach the age of 65! We have seen cases of candidates applying six times in a row, who thought that applying again and again showed that they were motivated. This may be the case for the second or third attempt but there comes a time where you have to show common sense and show an understanding that enough is enough and that you simply cannot put your life on hold for a distant ambition.

In most cases, you will be able to do a degree that will enable you to get back to Medicine at a later stage. Do not forget that the answer to this question should sell your motivation, and not simply admit defeat.

**Example of an effective answer**

*Although I am passionate and determined to pursue a career in Medicine, I understand that this is my third consecutive year in applying for medical school. This year, I have tried my absolute best to enhance my CV in terms of academic achievements, generic skills and experience in the medical field. In particular, I have gained a lot of maturity through my work experience. I really hope this will demonstrate my strength and dedication in a medical career. However, if I fail to get in again, I will apply for a*

40

> *pharmacy degree. I am confident that by practising pharmacy both in a hospital and in the community and by getting exposed to patients on a daily basis, I will have a job that I enjoy. As well as giving me some useful skills and knowledge, this degree will enable me to reapply to Medicine as a postgraduate or mature student entrant later on.*

Obviously, any degree relevant to healthcare would be equally suitable, ranging from biochemistry and biology to pharmacy or even dentistry (whose students often have common lectures with medical students).

**If you are not applying for the first time but have seriously thought about an alternative career**

Many people will mention the fact that, should they fail, they will do a related degree and will try again in a few years' time. This is a good strategy, but with a small risk that the interviewers will have heard it all before. You may also be at a stage where you have already done the degree and another degree is not an option. Remember that the point of this question is to test your aptitude for Medicine and therefore your personal attributes. There are other careers that may look very different to Medicine but in fact have many similarities.

For example, law is a career where you will have contact with people, where you will need to build a strong rapport with your clients, understand issues from their point of view, study a great deal and make use of your knowledge and best judgement to make important decisions (not dissimilar to the art of diagnosing). So, mentioning that you have thought about a career in law would not be a totally absurd idea, providing it is well presented. Other possible alternatives include social services, psychology or generally any professions which are centred around improving quality of life.

This can be a risky strategy but may reap greater rewards if you have the personality to pull it off.

# QUESTION 6

**What steps have you taken to find out whether Medicine is the right career for you?**

**What is the question testing?**
Essentially, this question is designed to test two things:

1. Drive and initiative – to demonstrate this, you will need to talk about the steps that you have taken to test your interest in the medical profession.

2. Enthusiasm and determination – to demonstrate this, you will need to talk about your experiences from a personal point of view, highlighting not only what you did and observed but introducing also an element of personal reflection by discussing what you enjoyed about these experiences and how they contributed to reinforcing your vocation.

Note: quality is more important than quantity. It is often better to have only gained one or two experiences but to be able to discuss them in a personal manner than to discuss ten different jobs superficially.

**What do they mean by "steps"?**
There are several activities that you may have undertaken and the following list should prompt your memory (or give you some ideas if you are planning to gain some experience in the forthcoming months):

- Attending seminars run as an introduction to the medical profession
- Attending open days at a local hospital and at any medical school
- Discussing your aspirations with a doctor
- Work experience in a local hospital or shadowing a nurse or a GP
- Working as a healthcare assistant or a hospital porter
- Working with disabled children or in a hospice
- Working as a temporary medical secretary.

All these give you an opportunity to learn about Medicine in different ways. Seminars and open days can give you a chance to discuss your aspirations with people who work in the field and are therefore very informative. Work experience is a good opportunity to see Medicine from the inside and to understand what being a doctor is about. It also gives you opportunities to experience patient contact.

**How to approach the question**
The list of possible work experiences is limited and most candidates will have made some kind of effort to test their vocation. In order to stand out, you will need to produce an answer that presents your own experience in an interesting manner rather than simply listing the two or three hospitals in which you worked. In practice, this means detailing each experience, how you organised it and, most importantly, what you learnt from it and how it contributed to your decision to get into Medicine.

**Example of an ineffective answer**

*I went to a couple of seminars and also shadowed a doctor for 2 weeks during the summer break. It was really interesting and it really made me realise that I wanted to do Medicine.*

What is wrong with it?
- It lacks detail. What kind of seminars? What kind of doctor did he shadow? What did he observe? And how did he organise the shadowing (the candidate may have missed an opportunity to sell his personal initiative)?

- There is no personal reflection. The candidate should have expanded on some of his key messages: what was interesting and why? How did the experience make him realise that Medicine was a career that he would enjoy?

Generally speaking, you should avoid using words such as "interesting", "fascinating", "enlightening", "excellent", etc. by themselves. Whenever you use one of these words or other words designed to express personal feelings, you should ensure that you provide backup to all your statements by explaining why you felt that way.

**Example of an effective answer**

> *One of my first steps was to arrange a meeting with my school careers adviser, following which I arranged to shadow a consultant anaesthetist at my local hospital. I spent 2 weeks observing the consultant both in his clinics and in theatre. It was very exciting to see a patient being given general anaesthesia before undertaking a major ENT operation. It really gave me a good insight into the different roles played by doctors, ranging from communicating with the patient before the operation to obtain consent and to reassure them about the procedure, all the way to actually carrying out the anaesthesia and the clinical knowledge and judgement that this requires. I also found the teamwork aspect of the job very inspiring, particularly the fact that the team was very well coordinated and worked well together to benefit the patient. From a personal point of view, I had the opportunity to have a chat with the patients that we managed both before and after their operation and I could see the impact that our discussions had on them, if only as a means of reassurance.*
>
> *I have also worked with disabled children for a local charity, helping them with their homework and helping the carers during day trips. It was hard work and could sometimes be disheartening, but I have always found it very rewarding. It really taught me the importance of being patient with the children and to involve them as much as possible in resolving the issues that they faced. Although it was evident from the beginning that not all these children would manage by themselves, it was really rewarding to see the progress that they all made, however little this was.*
>
> *Overall, I feel that my work experience has been really useful and has really reaffirmed in me the fact that Medicine is a career that I will thrive in and through which I will most benefit others.*

Note the depth added by having two experiences of a different nature (one geared towards observation and one geared towards personal experience) and the manner in which personal feelings are described and explained, which helps make the answer personal and interesting to an interviewer's ear. The simple two-point structure contributes greatly to the clarity of the answer.

Interview Skills Consulting

# QUESTION 7

**Tell me about your work experience.**

### The importance of work experience
Although this may not have been necessary in the 1990s, nowadays you will find it difficult to enter medical school without some kind of work experience. If you have none, you would be well advised to contact your careers or education adviser or a local hospital/hospice to gain some exposure. Alternatively, your local GP or a nurse may be willing to let you shadow them if you ask politely. Failing this, your CV may look a little depleted and you will find it nearly impossible to answer interview questions such as this one.

### How to approach the question
This question is similar in nature to the previous one ("What steps have you taken to find out whether Medicine is the right career for you?") and the approach to answering it should be nearly identical, the only difference being that the question is asking you to concentrate on work experience rather than any other activities such as attending relevant seminars or open days.

### *Do not make assumptions about how much the interviewers know and how much they might have read or not read about you*
Interviewers will normally have read your personal statement, either at shortlisting stage and/or just before the interview itself. However, they will also have read personal statements from many other candidates and may therefore need you to refresh their memory. It is your job to make sure that they get the right message. That means banning phrases such as "As you have seen in my personal statement" or "As you know". Build a personal answer from scratch.

### *Be descriptive and personal*
Refer to the previous question for a full explanation of how to approach this type of question. In your answer you need to describe the extent of your experience: if possible, how you organised the work experience, what you observed and what you gained from a personal point of view.

Explain what you enjoyed and, most importantly, why you enjoyed it and how it helped you decide in favour of a medical career.

**Example of an ineffective answer**

*Last year, I shadowed an anaesthetist and an A&E consultant, which I enjoyed tremendously. I also did my summer job at my local hospital as a healthcare assistant and now I know what it is like to work in a hospital. I have also done some work experience at the local GP practice.*

What is wrong with it?

- Good mix of experience but we don't know whether the candidate was just making cups of tea and watching TV during that time, or whether he actually learnt a lot from these experiences.
- "I know what it is like to be working in a hospital." What is it like then?
- No details and no personal reflection on each of these experiences.
- Knowing what it is like to work in a hospital does not mean that he liked it. How did this experience contribute to reinforce Medicine as a career for him?

**Example of an effective answer**

*I have done work experience both at my local hospital and my local GP practice and I found that it really helped me in identifying and thinking about the challenges that I will face as a doctor.*

*At the hospital, I observed a busy team in the oncology department, which showed me the practical side of dealing with patient care. One of my main learning points has been that being a doctor is a lot of hard work, which I feel I am prepared to take on, but that it can also be very rewarding. The team had a number of good successes with some of their patients and the efforts that the team put in really paid off. During my time there, I had the opportunity to attend some team meetings as well as some multidisciplinary meetings. Through this, I gained a good insight into how doctors and other health professionals pull their expertise together for the good of patients and I found this particularly enriching. I also gained a lot from my personal experience in dealing with patients and, through this,*

*about the importance for doctors to be skilled in many areas and not just in terms of clinical skills.*

*When I worked in the community at the local GP surgery, I observed the holistic approach of the GP. I have learnt the importance of good communication and demonstrating empathy. I particularly liked the way patients are treated for all their physical, psychological and social needs.*

*I feel that I have learnt a lot from my work experience and I am looking forward to starting Medicine as soon as possible so that I can continue to experience the feelings and the buzz that I experienced during these assignments.*

**"ISC**MEDICAL

Interview Skills Consulting

# QUESTION 8

**Tell me about your gap year.**

## What is this question about?

This question is similar to previous questions about work experience or how you prepared for a career in Medicine. Its main purpose is to determine not only your determination to enter a career in Medicine by looking at the medical experience that you gained during that year, but also your organisational skills and initiative by looking at how you went about organising your gap year.

There is no harm in discussing time taken off for a holiday providing it did not last the entire year, but this will need to be done in an appropriate manner, i.e. always trying to emphasise personal learning or selling personal attributes such as initiative and organisation skills.

Similarly to the questions discussed previously, the recipe for a good answer lies in the following:

- A good mix of experience, with a brief description of what it entailed
- Drawing attention to what you gained from that experience rather than simply describing how interesting it was
- Emphasising how this helped you towards a career in Medicine.

## Example of an effective answer

*My gap year was a valuable experience in many respects. I travelled with my friends to South America in the first 2 months after the exams. This gave me a good opportunity to relax and condition myself for the rest of the year. I really enjoyed preparing for the trip, having to plan our itinerary, finding suitable accommodation and working to save money so that we could afford it. Once there, it was good to experience a different culture and we saw some really fantastic places.*

48

*I then spent 6 months working with disabled children in Chile. I found the experience very humbling and enriching from a personal point of view. I learnt a lot from working there and, in particular, how important teamwork is when you have to deal with both day-to-day and complex issues. Because we had few resources, we needed to use whatever resources were available and to use one another's skills to succeed in helping the children out. It also really taught me that, when all else fails, communication is very important. Although we knew that some of the children would never really have a very good life, it was amazing to see what difference we could make simply by listening to them and showing generosity and empathy.*

*After a fantastic 6 months I came back home to work as a healthcare assistant at my local hospital in Colchester. As well as helping me out financially to finance the trip to South America, it gave me an excellent opportunity to work in a UK medical environment. During that time, I had many opportunities to have close patient contact and to observe how doctors and nurses work closely together in a very busy environment.*

*During my gap year, I learnt an awful lot from a personal perspective. In particular, I feel that I have leant to be more mature, responsible and organised. It has really reinforced in me the desire to become a doctor.*

If your gap year is not yet over at the time of the interview then you should also talk about the projects that you have for the remainder of the year, emphasising what you are hoping to get out of it.

**If you have not had a gap year**
Obviously, if you have not had a gap year (for example, because it is the first time you have applied to medical school), then this question will not apply directly to you. Nevertheless, you may still get a question of a similar nature, such as "If you failed to get into Medicine now and wanted to take a gap year, how would you spend it?" Essentially, your answer would be following similar principles to those outlined above. You should give examples of activities that you would like to get involved in and emphasise what you would hope to gain from that year from a personal perspective.

# QUESTION 9

**What have you read or experienced to prepare you for Medicine?**

This question is very similar to Q.6: "What steps have you taken to find out whether Medicine is the right career for you?" and you may choose to use a similar answer. Since the question asks explicitly what you have read or experienced, you will need to address both aspects. You could divide your answer between essential and desirable preparation.

**Essential preparation**
- 'A' level subjects such as Biochemistry, Biology and Mathematics
- Saw career advisers and enquired about the various medical schools
- Read the medical schools' prospectuses
- Visited the medical schools (open days or by yourself)
- Spoke to the medical students
- Organised work experience in GP practice, hospital or hospice.

**Desirable preparation**
- Attended introductory course or seminar for Medicine
- Read relevant medical journals (*Lancet*, *BMJ*, etc.)
- Read articles from the *studentBMJ* or other magazine/paper
- Read about healthcare issues, such as postcode lottery, in national newspaper on websites, newspapers or other media
- Read and researched ethical issues posed by current court cases
- Worked for charities such as Oxfam and Hospice
- Summer jobs in a hospital such as porter or healthcare assistant.

Summarise the extent of your experience. Select the main activities that you have undertaken and describe what you did and observed there. Ensure that you bring an element of personal reflection on each activity, describing why you enjoyed each experience and how this made you understand Medicine and/or the role of doctors. When talking about what you have read, explain what you learnt from it and why it made an interesting read.

# QUESTION 10

**What does a doctor do apart from treating patients?**

This question is often regarded as a trick question, though, in actual fact, there is nothing to be feared from it. Overall, it is designed to test your understanding of the role of a doctor in its entirety and, in a sense, the effort you have put into gaining that understanding.

Most candidates have a fairly limited understanding of all the activities undertaken by doctors in the course of their working day and therefore fail on a question where the answer should be obvious to any motivated candidate. Doctors do a few more things than paperwork!

**How to approach the question?**
To give a thorough answer, you will need to use the TAGS approach described on page 14 as it will prompt you for different ideas.

*Training & Clinical Experience*
- Doctors need knowledge in order to treat patients. This is gained by attending regular teaching sessions and courses. They also take relevant exams and attend relevant seminars and conferences.

- As well as treating patients' illnesses, doctors are involved in prevention work (advice on lifestyle, vaccination, etc.).

- In relevant cases, doctors can also be involved in counselling patients and helping them deal with the consequences of their illnesses, whether by themselves or by involving other professionals.

## Academic

- Doctors spend time teaching medical students and other doctors (either junior doctors or doctors from other specialties).

- Most doctors have some involvement in research, although the degree of involvement varies depending on their specialty and the post in which they work.

- Doctors also spend time looking at the quality of their work and set up audits to measure the quality of the care that they provide against guidelines or standards.

## Generic

- Organisational and managerial: doctors must organise a wide range of activities, whether they are managing busy clinics, dealing with a wide range of paperwork or organising teaching sessions for others. They are also required to attend meetings for a variety of reasons, whether this is about discussing clinical governance issues (see Q.102) or reviewing patient cases to identify how care could be improved.

- Leadership: doctors must be able to make important decisions, motivate their team, anticipate and resolve conflicts, deal with patient complaints and team issues effectively, etc.

## Social

- Since this question relates to the work of doctors, this section is not so relevant here. However, if you wish you can talk about the need for doctors to relieve stress and therefore the importance of a good social life and a few hobbies.

## Formulating your answer

The answer is fairly straightforward to formulate by following the above structure. Avoid listing these activities with no explanation. To give more body to your answer you should spend 10-15 seconds on each of them, explaining why they are important as part of a doctor's role.

# QUESTION 11

**Where do you see yourself in 5 to 10 years' time?**

This question is a mystery to most candidates since what they will be doing is fairly obvious: *"I will be a doctor of course, but I am not sure what kind yet."* Such an answer reveals very little about the candidate him/herself and therefore it is unlikely to have any kind of impact at an interview. Not mentioning the fact that it is almost telling the interviewers that they have asked a stupid question, which can't help much.

### Example of an ineffective answer

| *I see myself being a final year medical student finishing my medical training in 5 years' time and becoming a doctor in a busy teaching hospital treating sick patients in 10 years' time. I hope I can achieve these goals.* |
| --- |

As well as stating the obvious in several places, the answer does not provide any information that would help the interviewers grasp the candidate's motivation. Also, the end is not very encouraging. One would think that a candidate would more than "hope" and would instead take control of the situation to maximise their chances of success.

### How to approach the question
If you read the question carefully, it does imply that you should limit yourself to your broad career aims. This is a perfect opportunity to outline the objectives you set for yourself using the TAGS framework (see p.14), which will enable you to address your ambitions from different perspectives: training & experience, academic goals, generic skills and social.

A good answer will show that you have an interest in developing yourself in a multidimensional fashion and that you have some sense of direction. By using the TAGS framework, you will also show a good understanding of the different aspects of life as a doctor (see Q.10: "What does a doctor do apart from treating patients?" for ideas).

**Example of an effective answer**

Medical school will have given me a good background and a solid base on which to build a career as a doctor. During my work experience, I have really enjoyed my time shadowing a surgeon at my local hospital and it is something that would interest me as a career; though, obviously, my medical training over the next 5 years may open my eyes to other opportunities.

Throughout my work and my training I will have learnt to deal with difficult clinical situations. I will have become more organised and will know how to manage my time effectively. I think I will also be a more sensitive and empathic doctor and will have gained good communication skills. As I progress through the different grades, I would also like to gain more management responsibilities and to build upon the good leadership skills that I have demonstrated so far, both during my school years and during my work experience.

From an academic perspective, I am very interested in teaching. I have already built some good teaching experience by mentoring two children at my local school and by being a football coach on Wednesday evenings over the past 2 years. It is something that I enjoy very much and I would like to think that teaching others will form a central part of my future job as a doctor. Besides teaching, though, I have not had much experience of research so far. I have read many articles based on clinical research and this is an activity in which I would like to get involved at some stage.

Finally, I am a keen cyclist in my spare time and would like to think that I will still have some time to pursue this as a hobby. I would also like to start a family once my career path is more settled.

I am very motivated and focused on my goals and I am confident that all the hard work that I am putting into succeeding will reap some great personal rewards and will enable me to have a career where I can make a big difference to my patients while also giving me an opportunity to build a successful personal life.

Note that there is little difference between 5 and 10 years' time. After 5 years, you will have just left medical school and in 10 years you will be in the middle

of your specialisation. Ultimately, the skills that you would like to develop are the same.

Note also the attempt to personalise the answer by bringing past experiences of teaching and hobbies into it. The answer could possibly be personalised further by bringing examples of past leadership experience in the second paragraph, though it is a trade-off between providing enough information and having a short enough answer to remain interesting.

# QUESTION 12

**If you had the choice between being a GP, a surgeon or a physician, which would you choose?**

At first, it is tempting to sit on the fence and, in an effort to upset no one and to give a "one-size-fits-all" answer, to simply answer that you have no idea at this stage and that you will use your time at medical school to find out about the different specialties before you can make a choice. In reality, you should bear in mind a number of important facts:

- The vast majority of candidates will give the answer written above. Giving the same one may seem like playing it safe but you are not really adding value or trying to stand out. Without being definite about your career choice, you can still find a way to sound a bit more determined and aware of the different medical careers that suit you.

- If you have already made your choice, it is okay to show that you have a good idea of what you want to do. It shows that you have thought about your career and it will make you appear more motivated than the "sitting-on-the-fence" candidates. However, since your experience of the medical environment is fairly limited at this stage, you should ensure that you remain open-minded, at least for the sake of the interview. In particular, you do not want to give the impression that you will study your preferred specialty at medical school and that you will neglect the rest.

- GPs, surgeons and physicians tend to have personalities that are adapted to the type of work that they do ("tend to" because of course there are plenty of exceptions). Your personality may be more adapted to one or two of these three choices.

- You will not get better marked for choosing one option or another. The key in this question is your motivation and the reasoning behind your answer.

**ISC**MEDICAL
Interview Skills Consulting

**The facts**
To help you, we have summarised below some of the more commonly accepted work- and personality-related characteristics of each of these three career choices.

*General Practitioner (GP)*
- Holistic approach to patient care (i.e. looking after not only the clinical aspect but also the psychological and social aspects)
- Continuity of care – GPs can follow their patients from "cradle to grave" and deal with all aspects of their care. Effectively GPs can be seen as Health Managers
- Work in the community rather than in a hospital
- Enjoy variety in their work including:
  - ❖ Dealing with different specialties
  - ❖ Dealing with varied patients (age, social background, etc.)
  - ❖ Dealing with different activities (prevention, treatment, practice management and administration, home visits, etc.)
- More flexibility to accommodate work-life balance
- Early contact and responsibilities with patients as training is quicker than for hospital doctors
- Provides many opportunities for people with an entrepreneurial drive (as GP practices nowadays operate as businesses)
- Usually attracts more friendly, caring doctors who enjoy communication and working in broad teams.

*Physician (sometimes also called "Medic")*
This is the term used for doctors who have a preference for the diagnostic and medical treatment of patients (as opposed to surgical treatment).

- Usually specialised. More thorough in their approach because they have in-depth knowledge and experience of one specialty
- Enjoy intellectual challenge of dealing with complex conditions
- Approach is more pathology orientated
- Approach requires more investigations and is often empirical (try it and see)
- Attracts doctors who are good communicators, who enjoy working in teams, are conscientious and enthusiastic.

*Surgeon*
- Enjoy immediate results
- Increased patient satisfaction due to more immediate and "dramatic" results of surgery
- More procedure orientated. Surgery attracts doctors who have good dexterity (obviously!) and have a keen eye for detail
- Requires patience and endurance, while maintaining quality at all times
- Being a more competitive environment, people who do well in surgery tend to be more dynamic and decisive.

## How to approach the question
Essentially, you must use your own experience of Medicine to explain your point of view. Whatever preference you have will have originated from your work experience or from other settings. You should also ensure that you describe what made you interested in that particular section of Medicine, rather than simply quote that you found it "interesting, fascinating, enlightening or enriching".

Finally, make sure that you have a sentence that presents you as broad-minded and that you have set your heart on a realistic career. If you go too strongly for one aspect of Medicine or, even worse, one of the many specialties (e.g. cardiology), they will simply counter you by saying: "How do you know you will like it for 40 years when you have observed it for 2 weeks?!"

## Example of an effective answer
*During my work experience, I was fortunate to observe a cardiologist, a GP and a urologist. During that time, I observed a lot of similarities but also some differences in the approach to patient care. I must say I enjoyed my surgical attachment more than the other two. I was particularly motivated by the competence with which the surgeon treated the patients. Also, although the ward rounds were very busy, he took time to teach both the nurses and me. I observed the way he communicated with his patients and the rest of the team. His approach was clear and decisive. More importantly, I was very encouraged by how quickly the patients recovered after the surgery and that really inspired me to think about a career in surgery as I feel I would get personal satisfaction out of my job. Having said that, I do recognise that I still have plenty to learn about the system*

*and my time at medical school will give me a good opportunity to learn about and reflect on each career option so that I can make a fully informed decision once I have graduated.*

## Another example of an effective answer

*Most of my work experience was spent in a hospital shadowing a cardiologist. It really taught me a lot about the manner in which physicians approach their patients. I was particularly impressed by the wide range of skills that the consultant and his colleagues possessed. Having a very analytical mind, I enjoyed observing their problem-solving approach when they had to diagnose a patient. I also witnessed the crucial role that communication plays in a physician's day. Not only did they have to explain complex conditions to patients who had no medical knowledge, they also acted as counsellors and, in some cases, needed to show a lot of care, attention and empathy. As someone who enjoys working in close contact with people, I found this proximity to the patient very appealing and, in that regard, I feel that I would enjoy being a physician. Obviously, my time at medical school will give me many opportunities to become familiar with other career options and at this stage I would like to keep an open mind.*

## And another...

*One of my main motivations for getting into Medicine has been the work that I did in Southern India, working for 2 months in a rural community, helping women give birth in really difficult conditions. Although it was sometimes difficult to deal with, I really enjoyed the obstetrics work and this is something that I would really like to do as a career. Back in the UK, I had the opportunity to shadow an Obs & Gynae consultant for 2 weeks and this has only reinforced my desire to get into an obstetrics career. As well as the extreme feeling of satisfaction that I got from helping a baby being delivered, I enjoyed enormously the buzz of working on busy labour wards when I was there. Having said that, my current choice of career is only based on my experience so far and I am sure that medical school will give me lots of opportunities to experience the good sides (and maybe the not-so-good sides) of other specialties. Therefore I might be better placed to answer this question in a more definite manner in 5 years' time once I have graduated.*

# QUESTION 13

**What do you want to achieve during your career in Medicine?**

Essentially, you need to look at the TAGS framework (see p.14) to give you some ideas and provide you with a strong structure.

*Training & Experience:* you will want to develop a strong career where you can excel from a clinical point of view. Maybe you already have some idea of the type of specialty that you want to pursue (see previous questions). Undoubtedly, you will want to ensure that you are fully up to date and that your career included a good mix of clinical experience and training (courses, conferences, reading up on matters, etc.).

*Academic:* you may have an interest in research that originates from previous experience or exposure. You may also be interested in teaching others and will want to ensure that you develop good teaching skills during your training and beyond with the aim of playing a substantial part in the training of future doctors. You may even have thought about becoming a lecturer.

*Generic Skills:* being a doctor is more than just being a clinician (see Q.10). You will want to build confidence in dealing with conflict, and managing and leading teams, which may include playing a substantial part in helping your hospital develop new services. You will also likely want to build on your existing communication skills to learn the art of dealing with people at all levels and in all circumstances.

*Social:* you will want to make sure that both you and your team are happy in what they do, by promoting a healthy work-life balance. Maybe there are activities that you enjoy greatly (hobbies, voluntary/charity work) and that you would like to pursue (don't spend too long on this; it is a slight tangent as not strictly Medicine-related, but still okay to mention).

**Example of an ineffective answer**

> *I hope to become a doctor in a busy teaching hospital treating sick patients. I want to make a difference to those patients who are in need, especially the children.*

Apart from the fact it only has two sentences and will hardly fill a 2-minute slot, the above answer is ineffective for many reasons:

- It starts well by giving a clear aim, but the candidate does not explain his reasons. Why does he want to work in a busy teaching hospital rather than a District General Hospital or even become a GP? Is it because he has ambitions to be a specialist in an environment that provides many academic opportunities? Or because he wants to teach at a high level? Whatever the reasons they must be explained, for this is where the real value of his answer lies.

- "I want to make a difference to patients who are in need" is a fairly bland statement by itself. You could do many other jobs and still fulfil that criterion. A porter would make a difference to a patient in need. Also, he declares an interest in children, but does not really explain why he has such an interest. Has he worked with children before? Has he got any other personal experience with children in general? How is he proposing to achieve this? By specialising in paediatrics? By becoming a GP? By being a doctor in some completely different specialty but doing volunteer work for a local orphanage?

The answer needs to be explained and personalised a lot more.

**Example of an effective answer**

> *There are many things that I would like to achieve during my medical career and I am really looking forward to taking on all kinds of challenges. From a clinical point of view, I would like to build strong medical background knowledge with a view to specialising either in Paediatrics or Oncology. I have developed an interest in these two specialties through some of my reading as well as my work experience and I feel that working in those specialties would provide me with a career in which I can make a real difference to people's life by showing a caring and empathic approach,*

*and adopting a way of working which is more holistic than, maybe, other specialties.*

*I have also always liked teaching and training others, and have had many opportunities at school to become involved in tutoring other students. This is an interest that I would like to develop further throughout my career, and I would like to think that I could play a substantial role in the training of junior doctors both during my training and once I am fully specialised. I have also been involved in research projects in the past, including a recent one which included some lab work. I have thoroughly enjoyed the challenges that this project presented, including the setting up of the project and having to handle the unexpected and I would hope to be able to continue to do some kind of research as a doctor to participate in the advancement of Medicine.*

*As an individual, I feel that I have good communication skills and, in particular, that I am very caring and empathic, as well as a good listener. However, these are skills that can always be improved and I would like to use my experience to build on these strengths, thereby making a greater impact on patients.*

*Overall, I am a good team player, very organised and conscientious, and, above all, someone who you can rely on to deliver a quality service. I therefore think that I will be able to make a good contribution to any team or unit in which I will be working, which in turn will enable me to provide my patients with the best possible care. Outside Medicine, but still related, I want to make full use of my organisational skills to make sure that I can carry on working with the Red Cross, with which I have been involved for the past 3 years.*

# QUESTION 14

**What impact do you hope to make in the field of Medicine?**

This question is very similar to Q.13 ("What do you want to achieve during you career in Medicine?") and the answer should be approached in a similar manner. However, you need to phrase your answer so that it presents a tangible impact rather than simply personal achievements. Whatever you say, make sure that you explain why you feel that you can make an impact and, in particular, what skills you would use to achieve this. Again, this will use the TAGS framework (see p.14) as a useful prompt for content and as a possible structure.

**Example of an effective answer (reworking the answer to question 13)**

*There are many areas where I can make an impact in Medicine at my own level.*

*I am interested in specialising either in Paediatrics or Oncology. I have developed an interest in these two specialties through some of my reading as well as my work experience and I feel that I have much to offer to these specialties in many ways. My friends and teachers have always commented on my good communication skills and particularly the fact that I am a good listener. I am generally a very patient and attentive person and this will really help me in building a good rapport with patients and good relationships with my colleagues. Having spent 3 weeks working in a hospice this summer, I could see how much difference my personal approach made to the daily comfort of the patients.*

*I am also a very proactive person and, in particular, I tend to regard problems as challenges rather than hindrances. For example, I was involved in organising last year's summer ball at my college and had to troubleshoot many unexpected issues ranging from financial problems to logistical problems with the catering. I feel that I have a lot to contribute to Medicine in that regard and could play an important role in any team in*

*terms of helping to improve standards, procedures, and the general quality of care of patients.*

*I have always liked teaching and training others, and have had many opportunities at school to become involved in tutoring other students. This is an interest that I would like to develop further throughout my career and I would like to think that I could play a substantial role in the training of junior doctors during my training and once I am fully specialised. I have also been involved in some research projects in the past, including a recent one which included some lab work. I have thoroughly enjoyed the challenges that this project presented, including the setting up of the project and having to handle the unexpected and I would hope to be able to continue to do some kind of research as a doctor to participate in the advancement of Medicine.*

*Overall, I am a good team player, very organised and conscientious, and, above all, someone who you can rely on to deliver a quality service. I therefore think that I will be able to make a good contribution to any team or unit in which I will be working, which in turn will enable me to provide my patients with the best possible care.*

This answer, based on that written for Q.13, demonstrates that once you have clarified the ideas in your mind, you can use them at will to answer many different questions. It is therefore crucial that, when you prepare for your interview, you think about the different themes that you will need to address rather than individual questions.

Note that the answer above is based loosely on the TAGS framework. We have swapped the Academic and Generic modules to improve the general flow of the answer. This illustrates the fact that frameworks are useful to organise your ideas but that you also have to demonstrate some flexibility in order to ensure that everything hangs together. The main message is that you must have a strong structure, with key points being highlighted and dealt with in turn (and not in one long confusing paragraph).

In the answer above, we have also left out the social part as we felt that it would add little value to the answer. Depending on the information that you wish to convey, you may wish to include one example or not.

# QUESTION 15

## Why have you chosen this medical school?

For the purpose of this question, we will assume that you have chosen this particular school for a number of reasons, and not just because it is the only one that you feel will have you; or because you can't be bothered to move away from home since that would mean eating spaghetti bolognese every day for 5 years and living in a house with other people who can't be bothered to wash up. If that is the case, then you will just have to pretend.

The mistake often made by candidates is to massage the ego of the interviewers by telling them that there is nothing better in the world than their school, that it has a superb reputation and that it is a well-known centre of excellence. Say that in Cambridge and they will ask you why not Oxford. Say that in Manchester and they will ask you why not Leeds. You can't win.

In truth, medical schools often have similar features to others and all think that they are really good. So, if you want to have an answer that sounds different to the other candidates you will need to back up your arguments with a few facts. And that means... doing some homework! Ultimately, as ever, what really matters is that you have a handful of well-chosen and well-explained reasons rather than a long list of superficially addressed bullet points.

### The different components of your answer

Although you may not have thought in depth about it, in reality there will be a wide array of reasons behind your choice of medical school. The TAGS framework (see p.14) should help you think about these in a systematic manner.

### *Training & Experience /Clinical Environment*

- Medical school and the associated hospital have a good reputation both clinically and teaching-wise (if you can, explain where you got that from. Have you talked to people who are studying there?)

- The type of patients and conditions met in the area provides a good variety (particularly true in bigger cities)
- The style of teaching suits you: problem-based learning (PBL), traditional, both (you need to explain why they suit you).

## Academic

- You will have opportunities to get involved in teaching others and in doing research.

## Generic

- Opportunities to work in teams (e.g. if PBL) and workshops. Opportunity to develop other skills such as communication (e.g. if there is an early contact with patients) or leadership (e.g. if the school encourages students to get involved in certain activities)
- You liked the people that you met when you visited the school, both consultants and students. They were friendly and encouraging.

## Social

- You have friends who will be studying there. You have family links nearby and need to study in the area (caring for a relative, children, husband works locally)
- You know the area and enjoy it for a particular reason (big city, rural, mix of the two, access to international airport if you are foreign, easy access to areas of natural beauty, proximity to London but still in the countryside, proximity to the sea)
- You have social commitments that you want to continue during your studies (charity work, flexible part-time job to finance your studies)
- The school offers social activities that you enjoy such as sports or music clubs, rowing, choir, trekking and rambling, drama, flower arranging and macramé, Sudoku (only joking). The beer at the university bar is cheap (only joking too)
- You will be with people from outside Medicine at the residence hall.

**Example of an effective answer**

*There are several reasons why I want to study here.*

*First of all, I have done a lot of reading and attended the open day a couple of months ago. One of the things that really attracted me to the school is the fact that it uses a dual approach to teaching, with a nice mix of PBL and traditional teaching. This means that we can learn about the same topics in different ways, both systemically and globally and also that we can have an early involvement with patients. I also liked the fact that there are regular workshops that are organised, which will really provide good support to ensure that we assimilate the information. This was one of the features that the current students that I met at the open day preferred. Obviously, it matters a lot to me that the school is located near XXX hospital, which is a large tertiary centre of great renown as it will create good opportunities for me to see many different types of conditions and patients.*

*From a social point of view, one of my great passions in life is singing. I am currently a member of a good classical choir in my home town and I was attracted by the range of musical options that the school offers in its list of clubs. Finally, I also enjoy the region. Having spent a few days in the area since I applied, I have had the opportunity to visit both the town of XXX and its region. I really enjoyed the nice mix of small historical market towns, big city centres and the easy access to the sea.*

*All in all, I think that the YYY medical school provides an excellent setting to study Medicine for 5 years and I am sure that I will enjoy it greatly.*

# QUESTION 16

**There are other universities with the same teaching methods. Why this one in particular?**

If you are pushed in this way, it is because they are trying to test your resilience and your motivation. If you say "You are right, I don't know", this would mean that your arguments are weak and that you lack confidence in your choice. The best thing to do when you are being placed on the defensive or pushed into uncomfortable territory is to retain your cool and look at the situation rationally. Of course there are other schools, and of course no real university is unique. There is no point digging yourself into a hole, but in the end you have to apply somewhere!

**Example of an effective answer**

*It is true that there are other schools which may match my criteria, and in fact I have applied to some of them. Ultimately, what I am looking for is:*

*1 – a school that has a good training programme with a good mix of teaching styles and that supports its students. From the feedback that I got, from the syllabus and from my discussions with current students at the open day, YYY medical school offers this.*
*2 – a school where I will be involved with patients early on and you offer this.*
*3 – a school where I will be able to get involved in activities that I enjoy and through which I will be able to meet good friends. YYY medical school has a good range on offer and is also in a setting that I will enjoy, being close to the sea and with good proximity to interesting towns and landscapes.*

*Out of all the schools that I applied to I feel that YYY medical school is probably the best match to all these and I feel very confident that I will enjoy my time here and that I will reward the school with good success in my studies and in my professional life once I qualify.*

# QUESTION 17

**What attracts you the most and the least about our medical school?**

The first part of the question ("the most") should be easy to answer if you have worked out an answer to Q.15 ("Why have you chosen this medical school?"). The second part ("the least") is a bit trickier because they are effectively asking for any points that you may regard as negative. You will therefore need to be tactful. Once you have mentioned a number of positive aspects about the school in accordance with the answer to Q.15, there are several ways in which you can address the negative points.

**Sitting on the fence**
This is an easy but not necessarily a bad way out. You could provide an answer such as "Obviously every school has some less attractive aspects and I will probably come across them along the course of my studies; but, judging from all the literature that I have read and the feedback that I have obtained from students here, I think it will be a very productive and exciting experience and I am looking forward to joining the school next year."

Note that, although the answer is sitting on the fence, there is an effort to justify the answer (rather than simply saying "I can't think of anything negative", which could indicate that you simply couldn't be bothered to think about anything in particular). With this answer, you are signalling to the interviewers that you have done your homework (and you give some detail of that homework). You are also showing realism in pointing out that everything has negative aspects. Finally, you are demonstrating your enthusiasm with the final part of the answer.

This answer's only disadvantage is that it is not terribly original and will not help you stand out a great deal. However, you might not want to stand out too much on this one anyway and, if you deliver it with great enthusiasm, you could have a fairly strong impact regardless. Hopefully, the good answer that you will have provided for the features that you enjoy the most will be

sufficient to allow you to sit on the fence for the features that you enjoy the least.

**Identifying something mildly negative that will not cause a real problem**
Easy targets include the teaching methods used in the school, which have both positive aspects (which you find attractive) and negative aspects (which you have to put up with if you want to benefit from the positive aspects). For example:

- if the medical school you apply for has a PBL training structure, the obvious drawback is the lack of background knowledge such as anatomy, physiology and biochemistry prior to patient contact.

- if the medical school of your choice is traditional, i.e. it has pre-clinical and clinical curriculum, then the obvious thing to point out is the lack of patient contact in the first 3 years.

Whatever negative aspect you want to mention, you must make sure you tell the interviewers that it also has many advantages and that therefore nothing will cause you a real problem.

# QUESTION 18

**What challenges do you think that a career in Medicine will bring you?**

This question can be answered using the TAGS framework (see p.14), which will enable you to think about different aspects and will provide you with a good structure. The key to a successful answer lies also in the way in which you describe why each item presents some form of challenge (i.e. do not simply list a few issues but show your understanding of those issues).

### Training & Experience/Clinical

- You will need to have robust background knowledge and to continually update your skills. This is challenging because it takes time and you will need to be organised. You will also need to study and pass exams, while maintaining your clinical duties. All this takes endurance and hard work.

- You will need to recognise your own limitations so that you can ask for advice and assistance if required. In some cases, this means trying to determine what you don't know, which can be challenging.

- You may need to make difficult decisions at very short notice, for example when dealing with acute emergencies. Some of your decisions may be a matter of life and death.

### Academic

- You will be required to audit your practice. This can take time and can be tedious, though necessary.

- You may need to be involved in research. As well as taking you away from clinical commitments, there is pressure to make your research public by publishing it in well-known medical journals.

- You will need to spend time training others, which will test your communication skills.

*Generic*

- Communication is an art rather than a science. As a doctor you will communicate with many people at all levels. Showing empathy can sometimes be difficult. You may also face patients who are violent, vulnerable, distressed or otherwise difficult to communicate with, which will be challenging.

- You will need to work as part of different types of teams. To achieve good results, you will need to make sure that your teams function well.

- You will need to negotiate with other colleagues (negotiations, for example, between GPs and hospital doctors to admit patients). This can be a real communication challenge.

- You will need to deal with conflict, both within your teams and with patients. This includes managing complaints from patients and relatives, with, in some cases, the danger of being sued.

- You will need to learn to manage people and resources. Some of these people may be more experienced than you (such as senior nurses).

- You will be exposed to difficult situations. For example, patients may die. You may also encounter patients in vulnerable situations, which you may find difficult to manage.

*Social*

- You will have to work in busy environments and during unsocial hours. This can be tiring. It requires stamina and good organisation. You will need to be able to cope under pressure and to deal with stress.

- You will need to maintain a good work-life balance.

**Delivering your answer**

Once you have set out the challenges that a career in Medicine will bring you, you need to reassure the interview panel that you are the right person for the post. Explain why you feel that you are up to it, bringing a few examples from your work experience and other activities.

# QUESTION 19

**What are the pros and cons of being a doctor?**

This question tests your general understanding of the role of doctors and how realistic your view of Medicine is. Again, you can use the TAGS framework (see p.14) to generate ideas.

**Pros**
- Opportunity to use your skills to treat patients and make a difference
- Dynamic subject which requires regular updating of knowledge
- Rewarding to teach the next generation of doctors
- Opportunities to get involved in activities such as research where you can contribute to medical advancement
- Opportunities to use a wide range of skills at a high level (communication, team playing, management, leadership, organisational skills)
- Respected by the public.

**Cons**
- Can be stressful, particularly if exposed to long hours, changing shift patterns, difficult patients, or having to make difficult decisions on your own
- May become too involved emotionally with patient care
- Some aspects of Medicine can be fairly routine (paperwork, etc.)
- Need to manage with limited resources
- Constantly under public scrutiny. Also exposed to danger of complaints
- Patients may have unreasonable expectations
- Compromise on work-life balance because of on-calls and possible unsociable hours
- Often dealing with uncertainty.

In this question, you either come up with ideas or you don't. All you need are four or five ideas for each section that you can explain and develop briefly.

# QUESTION 20

**How would you dissuade someone from going into Medicine?**

Many candidates are either stalled by this question or fail to understand its multiple facets. The knee-jerk reaction would be "Why would I want to dissuade someone from going into Medicine?" This is obviously one of the avenues to explore and developing it enables you to sell your own motivation and ambition for a medical career. However, there is another side to the question which is really to test your understanding of some of the more negative aspects of Medicine. Therefore the answer to this question should combine some of the arguments developed in Q.19 and other questions addressed in the previous pages. The key here is to present a realistic understanding of the medical environment while reassuring the interviewers of your own unequivocal commitment.

**Example of an effective answer**

*Fundamentally, I would not seek to dissuade someone from going into Medicine unless I really felt that they could not cope with medical school or with a medical career in general. In particular, there are aspects of Medicine that may not be suitable for everyone. For example, it takes a long time to train and in fact training never stops, even when you become a consultant. Medicine can sometimes be stressful as we deal with difficult or sensitive situations, with angry patients or with cases where we feel powerless, and work-life balance can also sometimes suffer.*

*However, from my own perspective, I think that Medicine is a fantastic discipline which offers a unique opportunity to combine my love of science, my analytical skills and my interpersonal skills in a truly altruistic environment. Far from putting me off, life-long learning is a real challenge that I am looking forward to. I will also greatly enjoy the teamwork that Medicine involves as well as the research and teaching opportunities that it offers. So, rather than trying to dissuade someone, I feel that I would do a much better job at recruiting others.*

# QUESTION 21

**What are you looking forward to the most and the least about becoming a doctor?**

This is a similar question to Q.19 ("What are the pros and cons of being a doctor?") but this time with a slightly more personal slant. Therefore, although the answer to Q.19 could be delivered in a factual manner, you will need to deliver the same material in a more reflective manner for this one. Also, note the following:

- Because the answer will be more personal, it will take longer to address each point. Therefore you will need to deal with fewer points but in more depth.

- The question is asking for the "most" and the "least". However, it does not mean that you will have to limit yourself to just one positive and one negative point.

**Example of an effective answer**

*I am passionate about the opportunity to use my skills to treat patients and make a difference. I think this is the most rewarding part of being a doctor. The ability to treat an ill patient and to watch them recover from the illness is a priceless gift. I am also keen to continue to learn new skills in Medicine since it is a dynamic subject which requires regular updating in my knowledge. Using this knowledge, I am keen to teach the next generation of doctors. I have also got strong communication skills and people management skills. I am looking forward to applying these skills in treating patients.*

*I do understand that there are difficulties in being a doctor too. I am a caring person and I guess that I will need to ensure that I do not get too involved emotionally in treating patients. I have also observed that doctors do not always have enough time or resources to attend courses to update their knowledge and to teach others, and that they are sometimes being*

*rushed around, and I guess that this can make the job harder. Also, there has been a lot of negative publicity about doctors and doctors are constantly under public scrutiny. This is a type of pressure that I do not particularly look forward to. However, overall I feel that there are many more advantages than disadvantages in being a doctor.*

*Medicine is something that I feel very passionate about and I look forward to starting my training as soon as possible so that I can experience its good sides and learn to deal with its less attractive features.*

Note how the positive aspects are handled in a personal manner: "I am passionate…", "I am keen".

On the other hand, the negative aspects are handled in a detached manner: "I understand …", "I have observed…" This helps reduce the impact of the negative points and ensures that they are not perceived as being a problem for the candidate. The positive conclusion also helps in leaving a positive final impression.

# QUESTION 22

**What are the different aspects of communication?**

There are a number of areas of communication in which a doctor must excel. They would generally fall under one of the following two categories:

**1. Active Listening Skills**
This is closely linked with empathy, which all doctors are required to demonstrate. Empathy is characterised by a personal ability to see a situation from the other person's point of view and relates to the following behaviours:

- Being attentive and acknowledging
- Reflecting the other person's feelings and experiences
- Probing in a supportive manner
- Providing feedback, being supportive, showing warmth and being caring
- Checking with the other person whether your interpretation of a situation is accurate
- Knowing when to stay quiet and simply give the other person the time they need.

This applies equally to your dealings with patients, colleagues and friends. The impact of good active listening skills is a better relationship, and an ability to build a rapport and to generate mutual trust, which is crucial in your dealings with everyone. This results in better care for patients and a better working relationship with your colleagues.

**ISC**MEDICAL
Interview Skills Consulting

**2. Conveying messages in a clear and effective manner**
The skill involved in conveying messages effectively resides principally in your ability to adapt your communication style to your audience. This includes:

- Using clear and unambiguous language
- Checking the understanding of your audience and adapting your message to it
- Having a clear idea of what you are trying to communicate
- Taking account of prior knowledge and personal circumstances of your audience
- Using the appropriate level of jargon
- Choosing the most appropriate medium to communicate (written / face-to-face / email / telephone / diagrams / posters / models, etc.).

**Handling the question at the interview**
At an interview, this question calls for a simple factual answer. There is no need to remember all of the above by heart. Try instead to understand how they apply on a day-to-day basis to a doctor. Most of it is common sense.

All you need to do is remember the two main aspects and be able to discuss how they contribute to making a good doctor by using some of the arguments and giving practical examples. For example, rather than simply "Communication involves using the appropriate level of jargon", you can develop the concept by saying: "As a doctor, you need to communicate with patients of different backgrounds as well as with colleagues who have varying depths of knowledge of Medicine and you need to use the appropriate level of jargon so that everyone understands at their own level".

# QUESTION 23

**How would you rate your communication skills?**

This question is slightly tricky for several reasons:

- You need to rate your own skills and must remain relatively realistic while also selling yourself appropriately.
- It looks like it calls for a one-word answer when in fact you really ought to explain why you are rating yourself at that level.

**Rating yourself – How to start the answer**
There are several answers that are commonly given but could actually count against you. Here are a few:

- **"I would give myself 8 out of 10"** – the question I would have is "What does 8 mean? Why not 9 or 10? A number by itself is meaningless. Since you will have to provide an explanation to back it up anyway, you might as well find a more effective manner to describe your level of communication skills.

- **"I would say that my skills are average (or okay)"** – if your skills are just average or okay, there are plenty of other candidates whose skills will be better than yours and who will get the place instead. Even if this is true, you simply <u>must</u> present a more positive image.

- **"My communication skills are excellent"** – other than the fact that it sounds a little arrogant, it simply cannot really be true. Even if it were true, you would want to appear a little more humble (you are applying to become a doctor after all).

Ultimately, you will need to give the feeling that your communication skills are good. You can achieve this in many ways:

- Make a simple statement pitched at the right level: **"I think that my communication skills are good"**

or
- Talk about the skills that you have developed rather than how good you are: **"Over the past few years, I have developed some good communication skills"**

or
- Talk about what other people think of you rather than what you think of yourself: **"I have always had good feedback from my colleagues and teachers about my communication skills, and during my work experience I was often complimented by the patients at the hospice about my listening abilities."**

**Developing and finishing your answer**
Once you have made your opening statement, you need to explain what you mean by it, i.e. what communication skills you have, how you developed them, what they help or helped you achieve, etc. Provide concrete examples to make the answer interesting. To give a complete answer that shows an in-depth understanding of communication within the medical context, you need to convey that communication is a constantly evolving skill and that, as a doctor, you will constantly improve your communication skills through your experience and formal training.

**Example of an effective answer**

*I have always had good feedback on my communication skills both at school from my teachers and also in all the summer jobs that I have done. One of my main strengths is my listening ability, which enables me to get on well with people in all kinds of circumstances. For example, I spent quite a long time with elderly people at my local nursing home and I felt that I made a real difference to their quality of life simply lending an empathic ear to their problems and reacting in a caring and patient manner. I have also developed a good ability to discuss ideas with people at all levels. In one of my summer jobs I was in charge of dealing with customer complaints and, although it was challenging, I found that I could avoid conflicts simply by communicating at the right level with them and explaining complex financial issues in a way they could understand. I was also at ease teaching young children in a deprived area last year, where I needed to remain patient and explain facts several times in different ways. Being a doctor requires a wide array of communication skills. I feel that I have acquired some good foundations in that respect, which I am looking forward to developing further throughout medical school and later on through my medical career.*

# QUESTION 24

**How have you developed your communication skills?**

This question is very similar to previous questions on communication skills albeit in a different format. You will need to discuss the various elements of communication, adding information about how you developed those skills.

**How are communication skills developed?**
Like any skill, you develop communication skills through exposure to various people and situations involving these people, either by direct involvement or by observation. This includes:

- Parents
- Friends
- Teachers at school

- Teachers at specialised courses
- Doctors from work experience
- Clients during summer jobs

**Example of an effective answer**

*I have gained some of my communication skills from my father, who is a businessman and who I observed when I worked at his company during the summer when I was younger. He always communicated well with his employees, always listened to them attentively and with respect, and conveyed his instructions with clarity. He was also very good at ensuring that there were good records by following up on his instructions by email to confirm the details. In a sense, I have learnt to be conscientious from him.*

*Apart from my father, I also learnt communication skills from the career adviser at school. He was approachable, sensitive and always had time to listen to my concerns. This gave me the opportunity to learn about some of the key communication skills such as active listening and empathy. In my Duke of Edinburgh expeditions, we always worked in teams. There, I developed essential skills in communicating within a team so that we could work effectively together to achieve our common goal. This included being upfront about problems and making sure that everyone was being kept up to date with what everyone else was doing.*

*These are just a few examples and in reality I learn about communication skills throughout my daily life by observing others and by interacting with them constantly. Communication is a difficult skill to master but I feel that I have great strengths in this area, which I am sure will contribute greatly to making me an effective doctor.*

# QUESTION 25

**Can you learn communication skills?**

This question is a more generic variant of Q.24: "How have you developed your communication skills?" However, while Q.24 related to your past experience and skills development, this question is asking you to debate on a generic principle.

Do not make the mistake of providing a basic answer to the question such as "Yes, of course you can". Why would they bother asking the question if the answer was so obvious? This question is not about giving the right or wrong answer, but about how you use the opportunity to explain how you have learnt and how you are planning to develop further your communication skills.

### Example of an effective answer

*Although, to some extent, some people are born better communicators than others, I believe that a lot of our communication skills are acquired through experience by observing and interacting with other people. This could be at home with your parents, at school with your friends and teachers, or even at work with your colleagues. For example, no one has an innate skill for breaking bad news and you have to observe and make your own mistakes in order to develop your own understanding and your own style.*

*From my own point of view, I have gained some of my communication skills from my father, etc. – (see example from Q.24, which can be simply inserted here to discuss your own personal experience of acquiring communication skills).*

Note how the answer starts by addressing the question straight away, by developing a couple of essay-type arguments, but then quickly diverges into your personal experience. This is crucial to make the answer interesting. It helps the interviewers visualise what you are trying to say by placing it in a concrete context.

# QUESTION 26

Are you an empathic person?

## Can you say "no" to this?

Empathy is the ability to put yourself in other people's shoes (virtually, not physically of course). It is a crucial skill that is required of all doctors. The answer therefore has to be "yes". Again if it were as simple as this, then there would be little point in asking the question for the sake of ticking the right box. What makes you say that you are empathic? Can you give some examples?

## Example of an effective answer

*Empathy is a crucial part of communication and I feel that it is a personal attribute that I possess and that I have also learnt to develop over the course of my life and of my education. Empathy is something that I have demonstrated on many different occasions. I have spent time listening to friends who were discussing their personal problems with me. As well as being an attentive listener, I always try to be non-judgemental and to view the situation from their own perspective.*

*Also, recently, I did some work experience in a hospice. I came across a mother of two young children who was dying of cervical cancer and I will never forget the opportunity that I had to talk to her. I spend a lot of time at her bedside and with her relatives, listening to her concerns. I sensed through what she was saying and through her body language that she was scared of dying, scared of leaving her children and her husband behind and that she was also feeling very lonely. I put myself in her shoes and really felt how difficult this must be to deal with. Through this, I began to understand her loneliness, her anxiety and her fears. One week after she passed away, I received a letter from her relatives thanking me for my time and understanding. This really gave me a strong sense of achievement and of having made a difference.*

# QUESTION 27

**Can you think of a situation where your communication skills made a difference to the outcome of a situation?**

This question is asking for a specific example of a situation and you should therefore use the techniques described in the first section of this book, including the STAR framework (see p.18-20). Your first task is to identify a situation where your communication skills may make a difference. This could be, for example:

- When you were part of a team organising an event and had to negotiate with your team or third parties.

- When you had to deal with a group of people that you needed to bring round to your point of view.

- A teaching experience which was particularly challenging.

- An experience with a patient during your work experience, with whom you had to show empathy, demonstrate listening skills and discuss their problems in an appropriate manner.

This list is non-exhaustive and everyone will have had some experience at some stage, even if it is not necessarily at high level. What matters is not so much that the example is totally fascinating but that you are able to extract the full potential out of the situation by explaining how you behaved and the impact that your behaviour had on others.

**Example of an effective answer**

The example used in Q.26 can be used as it is to answer this question.

---

*Situation/Task*

*Recently, I did some work experience in a hospice. I came across a mother of two young children who was dying of cervical cancer and I will never forget the opportunity that I had to talk to her.*

*Action*

*I spent a lot of time at her bedside and with her relatives, listening to her concerns. I sensed through what she was saying and through her body language that she was scared of dying, scared of leaving her children and husband behind and also feeling very lonely. I put myself in her shoes and really felt how difficult this must be to deal with. Through this, I began to understand her loneliness, her anxiety and fear.*

*Result & personal reflection*

*One week after she passed away, I received a nice letter from her relatives thanking me for my time and understanding. This really gave me a strong sense of achievement and of having made a difference.*

---

Interview Skills Consulting

# QUESTION 28

**What makes a good team player?**

As you will be studying with other people and working in teams both within and outside the hospital during your career, team playing is an essential quality of a doctor and is often tested at interviews. In essence, a good team player is someone who:

1. **Understands his role in the team and how it fits within the whole picture**
   In order to get on within a team, team players must have a thorough understanding of what they need to achieve and what is expected of them. They must also understand what is expected of others so that they can work with them effectively. In Medicine, all team members must be well coordinated in order to ensure the best care for patients and it is therefore essential that everyone in the team knows what they have to do and who else is involved.

2. **Treats others with respect. Is supportive**
   Team players treat fellow team members with courtesy and consideration. They show understanding and provide the appropriate support to other team members to help get the job done. Effective team players deal with other people in a professional manner. Medicine is not something that you do by yourself. There will be times when you will have problems to resolve and when you will require assistance from other colleagues at all levels and it is important that you show willingness to involve others at the right time.

3. **Is willing to help**
   Good team players go beyond any differences that they may have with other team members and find ways to work together to get work done. They respond to requests for assistance and take the initiative to offer help. As a doctor, you will get requests for help from all directions (juniors, seniors and even people who are external to your place of work).

**ISC**MEDICAL
Interview Skills Consulting

4. **Is flexible and adaptable**
Good team players adapt to ever-changing situations without complaining or resisting. Flexible team members can consider different points of views and compromise when needed. They do not hold rigidly to a point of view especially when the team needs to move forward to make a decision or get something done. They must strike a compromise between holding on to their own beliefs and convictions while respecting and taking on board other colleagues' opinions. Medicine is a teamwork environment. You may have your own views about how to proceed in a particular situation and you should be prepared to defend them. However, other people may disagree and you should be prepared to at least consider their arguments. Also, you will need to constantly question your own practice (e.g. through the audit process) and you should therefore be prepared to change your ways accordingly if necessary.

5. **Communicates constructively and listens actively**
Teams need people who speak up and express their thoughts and ideas clearly, directly, honestly, and with respect for others and for the work of the team. Good listeners are essential for teams to function effectively. Teams need team players who can absorb, understand, and consider ideas and points of view from other people without debating and arguing every point. Such a team member can also receive criticism without reacting defensively. Finally, a good team member shares information with colleagues and keeps them up to date about progress on his or her assignments. Communication is key to good medical practice. With several doctors and nurses working on the same patients, there is a great need for a coordinated approach, which is only made possible through good communication.

6. **Is reliable. Takes responsibility and ownership of his role**
A good team member should do everything possible to deliver his assignments on time and with the level of quality expected of him by the rest of the team. He should get things done and do his fair share to work hard and meet commitments. Others can count on him to deliver a good performance all of the time, not just some of the time. He should also be relied upon to admit his mistakes and proactively sort them out.

## How to approach the question

Note that the question is asking generally about team playing and not directly about you. The main part of the answer will therefore be spent giving the attributes of a good team player and explaining why these attributes are important in Medicine by giving an example of a situation where they play an important role. For example:

> *A good team player is someone who is supportive of others and willing to help. In Medicine, you work with people at different levels of knowledge and experience and, in the interest of patient safety and of their own development, it is important that we all cooperate and help one another.*

and

> *When you work in a team, everyone has their own opinions and it is important to recognise that you are not always right and that others may have a point. Part of being a good team player is to be able to show respect for other people's skills and ideas so that you can combine your strengths to provide a better service for patients.*

## How to finish your answer

Do not forget that you are there to sell yourself and not just to theorise about team playing. You should conclude by explaining briefly why you feel that you make a good team player. There would be little value in simply stating "This is what the qualities of a good team player are and I feel that I am a good team player because I satisfy all of them." If you say so ..., but prove it! A short paragraph describing the extent of your experience of teamwork and some of your learning will do.

## Example of a suitable ending

> *Over the past few years, I have personally been involved in working in different types of teams. I was involved in organising major events at my school such as a fund-raising dinner for 300 people and a summer ball. I am also part of the coaching team at the local football club, for children aged 1012, and I have also done a lot of summer jobs where I worked with*

*various groups of people ranging from secretarial staff in the City of London to medical staff during my work experience at the local GP practice.*

*I have learnt a lot about myself and about teamwork during those experiences and, in particular, the importance of communication in ensuring that problems are anticipated and resolved at an early stage, as well as the importance of helping others and seeking help when necessary. Wherever I have worked, people have always regarded me as a good colleague and someone who was approachable. These are two qualities which will help me be a good doctor.*

# QUESTION 29

**Give an example where you played an effective role as a team member.**

As with all questions asking you to describe an example of a situation, you should use the STAR framework (see p.18-20) to narrate a specific situation in which you were involved, highlighting the role that <u>you</u> played.

For the purpose of this question, you should make sure that you highlight skills that are relevant to team playing as described in previous questions. You do not have to discuss all aspects of team playing but developing one or two of them well would be good.

### Example of an effective answer

*I was recently allocated the role of marketing and selling the tickets for a school concert performance. Since there were other fund-raising events happening at the same time, this proved a difficult task and I felt that it was crucial to involve the team in making important decisions in order to avoid a disaster on the day. I contacted the project manager and asked him to set up a meeting with the rest of the team. I chaired the meeting and explained in detail to my colleagues the work that I had done, the nature of the problems that I had encountered and the initiatives that I had taken to resolve them. I encouraged my colleagues to share any ideas that they had and ensured that everyone could contribute. As a group, we came up with creative ideas in selling the tickets in the local town hall and I organised for this to take place. As a result, we managed to have a successful concert with a full audience and raised a lot of money for charity. By being upfront with the team and encouraging a good exchange of views, I ensured that we could maximise our revenue for the event.*

Note the description of the scenario, of the action and the result with a final sentence on personal learning.

# QUESTION 30

### What are the attributes of a good team leader?

Leadership is about setting objectives and ensuring that the team is on board to achieve those objectives, which itself involves many different skills. There are many definitions of leadership. One popular definition is that a leader is someone who tells people what to do but not how to do it. In other words, a leader sets a sense of direction and purpose for the team and then ensures that the team finds its own way of working and achieves the objective with the appropriate level of supervision and support. Whatever definition you wish to adopt, a good leader must be able to demonstrate that he:

1. **Has clear objectives and communicates them effectively to the team**
   In order to lead a team, a leader must have a clear sense of direction, and clear objectives. A good leader is able to communicate those objectives clearly to the rest of the team so that they can take responsibility to achieve their own goals.

2. **Leads by example**
   A good leader is effective only if he is being followed by his team. He must engender respect from his colleagues by showing a good example. A leader needs to be enthusiastic, competent and confident. He needs to demonstrate that he works at least as hard as he expects others to do.

3. **Understands and motivates his team**
   A good leader must understand the strengths, weakness and aspirations of each team member. This enables him to share responsibilities accordingly. He motivates his team towards achievement by:
   ▪ Praising and encouraging others
   ▪ Rewarding colleagues (This could be through financial incentives, promotion, or by involving team members in specific projects)
   ▪ Empowering people and giving them responsibilities and freedom
   ▪ Making himself available.

4. **Communicates and interacts well with his team**
A good leader should listen to the input and ideas of the team and take them on board. Communicating constantly with the team is also important for the leader to have a good idea of how the team functions, of grievances, etc. which makes it easier to anticipate and to resolve conflict.

5. **Recognises the need for change and implements it. Is a decision maker**
A good leader is not static and constantly seeks new ways of working and improving. A good leader is able to take on board all the input he receives and to make a decision on that basis. He does not seek short-term popularity at the expense of achievement.

6. **Is flexible**
A good leader will adapt his leadership style to the demands of particular situations and the individuals involved. Some situations or individuals will require him to take a hands-on approach while others may require him to take a step back and be more hands off.

**How to approach the question**
In order to provide an effective answer, you need to describe the main qualities of a leader as explained above. You also need to bring a personal element to the answer by giving a few brief examples of situations where you have exercised leadership.

# QUESTION 31

**Tell me about your leadership skills.**

This question is asking about your skills and not about a specific situation. Therefore the best way to address it is to identify a few situations where you have been a leader, to describe those situations and identify for each how you acted as a leader. To do this, you can base yourself on the leadership qualities described in Q.30.

You might have noticed that there were some similarities between the attributes of a good team player and those of a team leader. Being flexible and willing to help others belongs to both, and so does communication. Do not forget to mention the attributes that are common to both as it will soften the answer a lot. If you keep talking about making decisions, setting objectives and making others work to achieve those objectives, you run the risk of appearing a little authoritarian. Balance is what you need to show.

**Example of an effective answer**

*I have learnt a great deal about leadership in my sixth form college, where I have been given numerous opportunities to lead in sports and Duke of Edinburgh expeditions, and to play an important part in various committees. One of my strengths is the fact that I have a clear idea of what I am trying to achieve and am able to bring people on board through my own enthusiasm and by involving them at an appropriate level. I find that it is important to involve people in making important decisions so that they can give more of themselves to achieve the team goals. For example, I had to lead a cricket team through inter-school competitions and, rather than trying to impose what I felt was right, I spent time discussing various techniques with my team so that they would all buy into the final decision.*

*I am also an approachable person and am open to suggestions and criticism. Not only does this make people comfortable in approaching me with their own ideas but it also enables me to identify any potential issues at an early stage. One good example is when I was part of a Duke of*

*Edinburgh expedition during which we got lost. By remaining open to suggestions, I quickly identified that a number of team members had found a suitable alternative which the team agreed upon and which eventually got us out of the trouble we were in.*

*There have also been occasions where I have needed to make important decisions by myself, either because there was no consensus amongst the team after much discussion or because there was little time to act. For example, when I was a member of the social committee of my school, I had to allocate a small budget between different activities. Obviously, everyone in the team wanted as much money for their activity as possible and I needed to be fair while remaining firm at the same time. This forced me to make decisions that were sometimes unpopular but with suitable communication I was able to avoid any real conflict and to manage my colleagues' expectations.*

*I really enjoy working with people. Being approachable, determined and a good communicator has really helped me succeed as a leader in many situations in the past and will be a great asset for me throughout my medical career.*

# QUESTION 32

**Are you a leader or a follower?**

This question is easier than it looks. At first glance, the word "follower" appears fairly negative and suggests that you would just follow orders and not take any initiative. But if you think about it carefully, there are many occasions where you are just a follower, with someone else taking the lead. Being a follower does not mean that you are totally passive, it simply means that, although you may be playing an important role in the team, you are not the one leading it. In that respect, more or less everyone has a boss and therefore follows someone else's lead. Being a follower certainly does not preclude you from being a good team player.

Conclusion: rather than take offence and give a defensive answer of the type "I am a leader of course" with a view to pleasing the interviewers, think about the different occasions where you have been a leader and where you have not. Within that experience lies the answer to this question.

### Example of an effective answer

*I am a hardworking, dynamic and enthusiastic person and I always put in the maximum effort to help my team achieve the highest performance. This is something that I have achieved as a team leader but also as someone who is ready to follow someone else's lead while retaining an important role as a team member.*

*I have learnt a great deal about leadership in my sixth form college, where I was given numerous opportunities to lead in sports and to play an important part in various committees. One of my strengths is the fact that I have a clear idea of what I am trying to achieve and am able to bring people on board through my own enthusiasm about the project and also by involving them at an appropriate level. I find that it is important to involve people in making important decisions so that they can give more of themselves to achieve the team goals. For example, I had to lead a cricket team through inter-school competitions and I spent a lot of time discussing*

*various techniques with my team so that they would all buy into it, rather than trying to impose what I felt was right.*

*As a team member following someone else's lead, I have always been an active and enthusiastic colleague, and all my "leaders" have always regarded me as a valuable asset in their team. I have learnt a lot from observing other people's lead and, in that respect, it is essential to know how to be both a leader and a follower.*

**ISC**MEDICAL
Interview Skills Consulting

# QUESTION 33

**What makes a good team?**

This is another question that tends to stall many candidates at medical school interviews. There two components in a team: team members and a team leader. To have a good team, you must therefore have good team members and a good team leader who can ensure the cohesion of that team. The answer to that question is therefore a summary of the previous questions on team playing and leadership.

One word of warning though: you could write books about team playing and leadership. At an interview you only have a couple of minutes to make your case, so try to be selective about the aspects of team playing and leadership that you want to present, bringing in appropriate examples to make the answer interesting. Do not worry too much about the detail.

**Example of an effective answer**

*A good team should have both a good team leader and good team members. Essentially, you need a team of people who are enthusiastic and motivated in the work that they do, and who can take responsibility to manage their own work and achieve the results that are required from them. They should also be people who are able to show some initiative.*

*Team members also need to be flexible in their approach so that they can adapt to change and a range of circumstances. They need to communicate well with one another to exchange information, to identify problems and to ensure continuity in the work that they do.*

*On top of that, a good team will require a good leader who can make sure that the team members remain motivated, and who encourages the sharing of ideas and discussions to resolve problems and anticipate potential areas of conflict. A good team leader will also be able to make some of the more difficult or controversial decisions and will keep the team focused on the tasks at hand.*

**ISC**MEDICAL
Interview Skills Consulting

> Recently, I was involved in setting up the sixth form farewell ball. I was elected President of the ball committee, which proved very successful thanks to everyone's efforts. Everyone had contributed to setting out the goal that we had in mind and therefore supported it. Everyone was also very enthusiastic and extremely hardworking. Each had a specific role in the project but everyone was able to help others out when needed. We had regular meetings to troubleshoot any arising issues and everyone really put in a lot of effort. As the leader, I delegated the work in a fair manner and I was able to make quick decisions when needed. We had the most amazing ball and the whole college was proud of our achievement.

**ISC**MEDICAL

Interview Skills Consulting

# QUESTION 34

**What are the advantages and disadvantages of working in a team?**

**Advantages**
- Able to spread the workload through delegation to others
- Easier to gather ideas to deal with issues as everyone can contribute
- Can learn from others
- Able to rely on the support of others if you require assistance
- Achieve more by using everyone's strengths appropriately than if you do everything by yourself
- More social environment.

**Disadvantages**
- Too much input can be confusing; it can lead to conflicts and hinder the decision-making process
- May be more difficult for some individuals to shine if the work and rewards are shared with others
- Breeding ground for office politics
- Not everyone is a team player. Some elements may be disruptive
- Will only function well if there is a strong leader
- Can be distracting to have too many people around and could affect collective performance (too many coffee breaks and gossip!).

**How to conclude your answer**
Overall, you do not want to give a bitter feeling about teamwork and you should try to remain objective. Here is a possible example for a neutral ending: "Overall, there are as many advantages as there are advantages. However, a good team is really what the individuals within it make it, which is where the role of the leader becomes important in making sure that everyone is aware of and fulfils their personal responsibilities."

# QUESTION 35

**How do you manage your time?**

Working as a doctor will require you to multitask. Not only will you have to deal with your clinical work but you will also need to find time to study and keep up to date, to teach others, to carry out other activities such as research and audits, to attend meetings, to have your own life and to deal with emergencies when required. All this requires good organisational and time management skills, hence the question.

Bringing your experience into play, you should be able to demonstrate that you:

- plan your work properly
- prioritise your work in order of urgency
- maintain appropriate communication to ensure that you know what is happening and that you can allow for any changes
- anticipate potential problems
- allow for the unexpected if you need to
- allow for some time to rest.

You can also talk about tools that you use to help you with your time management. This would include:

- a diary (paper or electronic such as a PDA)
- making task lists (paper, word processor, spreadsheets)
- using other resources (e.g. secretaries) to give you reminders or manage your diary if you are already working or if you have done summer jobs where this applied.

**Example of an effective answer**

*I have always been efficient at organising my time so that I can fit in everything that I need to do within a busy day. During the past few years, I planned my revision carefully by looking at the amount of work that I would*

*need to do in relation to the syllabus. I also allowed some time for outside activities, which enabled me to relax and be more efficient in my work.*

*Over the past few years, I have also become involved in organising a number of events within the school, all of which had tight deadlines that had to be met. This required careful planning and coordination with other members of the team. In order to meet the deadlines, I had regular discussions with my colleagues so that we could identify any potential problems and find solutions to minimise their impact.*

*Overall, I like to be punctual, to deliver my assignments on time and to complete my projects within a comfortable margin. To do so, I find it useful to keep a list of tasks that I need to do, either on my electronic diary or, in the case of a larger project, on a spreadsheet that I can update at regular intervals depending on developments. When I was responsible for social events at my school, I also made full use of the college's secretaries, who helped a great deal to ensure that everything ran smoothly and freed up some of my time when there were fires to be fought.*

Note how each idea is backed up by a practical application and is not simply part of a long list.

# QUESTION 36

**How good are your organisational skills?**

**What are organisational skills?**
Organisational skills are closely linked to time management skills. As well as time management, they also include the ability to:

- multitask
- anticipate needs
- identify the right resources
- plan effectively to get things done on time
- prioritise
- delegate/use the team effectively
- adjust to unfolding events and reprioritise appropriately
- stay focused on the task at hand.

Essentially, the example will be very similar in nature to that set out in Q.35.

**Example of an effective answer**

*I have always enjoyed being busy and getting involved in several projects at the same time. For example, over the past year, I have studied for five 'A' Levels, worked at weekends at a local charity shop and spent some time gathering some work experience in preparation for medical school. I have also kept up with my sporting activities and music commitments at the local music school. To achieve all this, I needed to be very organised and I feel that I have demonstrated good organisational skills.*

*In particular, it was essential that I planned my weeks reasonably early so that I could identify what I would need to prepare in anticipation. I allocated time slots in my schedule which I would protect for my homework. I would also allocate proper time where I could relax and practise my hobbies. In terms of my academic work, I analysed on an ongoing basis how much work I would need to put in for the following week, taking account of planned examinations and assignments, and I arranged for suitable*

*preparation time. I also arranged time with my friends so that we could revise some important topics together and go out afterwards. Being meticulous and organised has really helped me minimise stress by enabling me to achieve everything I needed to achieve; as a result I feel more than equipped to deal with the pressure of studying Medicine.*

Interview Skills Consulting

# QUESTION 37

**Tell me about your IT skills.**

This question is very factual and all you need to remember in answering such a question is to ensure that you present a complete picture. IT is crucial in Medicine to speed up the transfer of information, to consult databases in order to access research literature, and to communicate between doctors. X-rays are being sent via online connections to be read by specialists away from the place where they were performed. IT is an integral part of Medicine and your interviewers will want to be reassured that you are IT-literate and IT-minded.

In answering this question, you could content yourself by simply listing a few pieces of software but that would not be very interesting to listen to. Instead, try to be a bit more descriptive about how you use each type of software.

**IT skills**
- **Word processing**: used for essays, writing reports for extra-curricular activities, general correspondence. If you are able to design complex documents with it then mention it.

- **Spreadsheet**: used for your private finances, to resolve issues, statistical and data analysis in one of your projects.

- **PowerPoint®**: an important piece of software to mention as all doctors are required to present topics and use this as a presentation tool. You might have used it at school to present a topic to your class or in your extra-curricular activities, for example if you are part of a team organising events or some charity.

- **Digital imaging**: now more and more fashionable as it has become easier to use. If you can talk about using specialist software needed to manipulate images, this is a plus. In any case, talk about how you integrate digital imaging within your presentations.

**ISC**MEDICAL
Interview Skills Consulting

- **Web design**: may not seem directly relevant but many doctors have potential web requirements. Having some knowledge of how web pages are constructed and what can or can't be achieved is a bonus. For example, GP surgeries have their own websites. A number of doctors run their own educational websites for colleagues in their own specialties or even for patients. Also, hospitals have intranet sites which are used to present the most recent guidelines as well as hospital protocols and policies.

- **Email:** used to keep in touch with friends and colleagues, both casually and for work purposes.

- **Search engines:** very useful tool to find information. A great educational resource. Doctors consult online research databases such as Medline & Cochrane to find out about the latest research-based evidence. There are also numerous educational medical websites.

- **Palmtop organisers:** handy to carry information with you, that you can consult at any time. Some doctors use them to carry their to-do list, their calendar (with reminders for appointments and results to check), information about dosage, etc.

There is no real technique to answer this fairly straightforward question other than:

- Quoting a range of IT skills
- Explaining how you use each piece of software and how proficient you are at using it
- Concluding by explaining that you know IT plays an important part in the daily work of a doctor and that you enjoy finding out about new products to develop your own skills.

**isc**MEDICAL
Interview Skills Consulting

# QUESTION 38

**How important is IT in Medicine?**

This question calls for a little bit of lateral thinking and some awareness of changes that are taking place in the NHS, rather than for any particular technique. In order to produce a complete answer, you must avoid thinking about the question randomly (or panicking because IT is not your forte), and you must start thinking about the topic in an orderly and logical fashion, using the different settings in which IT may be used.

**Daily work of doctors**
Doctors use word processing to send referral letters, produce reports or prepare educational material. Doctors use spreadsheets to analyse data for research or audit purposes. Some doctors also use spreadsheets to organise and plan their work as they are easy to set up and manipulate. Doctors use Microsoft PowerPoint® software as an easy tool to produce presentations to peers. Some doctors use palmtops to store and retrieve information.

Some specialties also embrace IT at a core level. For example, the development of teleradiology means that radiologists can have X-rays and scans sent to their home or secondary place of work electronically for reporting. The need to be on-site is greatly reduced, which makes the process more efficient.

**NHS projects**
The NHS launched a new project called National Programme for IT (NPfIT). If you are interested, full details can be found on the following website: www.connectingforhealth.nhs.uk. This programme's aims are:

- To create a unique electronic record for each patient; this will be made available electronically and securely to health professionals.

ISCMEDICAL
Interview Skills Consulting

- To implement the Choose and Book system, allowing GPs to book appointments on behalf of their patients straight into the diaries of the relevant hospital clinics and to send referral letters electronically.

- To allow the Electronic Transmission of Prescriptions: a system enabling easier prescribing and collection of prescriptions.

- To set up Picture Archiving and Communication Systems, designed to enable the storage of fixed and moving images (X-rays, CAT scans, MRI scans, ultrasound scans, etc.).

- To facilitate the analysis of the quality of care provided by GPs through the Quality Management and Analysis System.

Such a system will enable easier access to information, a safer way of storing it, an easy way of retrieving information for analysis through audit and a faster service for patients.

The project had been delayed due to several problems. It has a number of disadvantages including the fact that it is expensive. It is also proving difficult to persuade some doctors to become IT literate and, from a logistical point of view, to enable the relevant pieces of software to work well together on such an ambitious scale. Finally, there is an obvious potential problem with patient confidentiality and security will need to be at its tightest.

**Patients**
There has been much talk in the press about the possibility of allowing patients to carry a chip card containing their data. This has an obvious link to the above programme, and is another example of how IT could play a major part in the care of patients within the NHS.

This should have given you an idea of how important IT is in Medicine. IT will in future be driving the whole system. IT will be responsible for ensuring that contact is maintained between doctors, that patients' records are well maintained and that the system works more efficiently.

# QUESTION 39

**What are your hobbies?**

The purpose of this question is to establish whether you have ways of relaxing and whether you take an interest in things other than your work. There are several points that you should bear in mind when discussing your hobbies:

- It is not a competition about who has got the most interesting hobby out of all the candidates, or who has got the weirdest hobby of all. You don't need to go cart-racing on Mount Everest every weekend to be an interesting candidate.

- What really matters is the range of activities that you have, what they bring you and what you find interesting about them. You will get a place at medical school if you enjoy reading novels and cooking for friends, providing you are able to explain in a personal way why these things matter to you.

- If most of your hobbies are solitary (such as reading and playing the piano), mention them but try to counterbalance them with other aspects of your life that present you as a sociable person. It is not to say that you have to present yourself as a party animal, but a sociable human being would be good enough.

- Do not try to lie about your hobbies or present, as hobbies, activities that are no more than just routine. For example, there is no point pretending that you like cooking if all you do is defrost pizzas, or that you enjoy photography if you only take holiday pictures of your boyfriend, girlfriend or dog. They might dig further into your answers and you run the risk of being found out.

- You may extend the definition of "hobbies" to include other personal interests such as charity / voluntary work. It all helps to sell yourself!

**ISC**MEDICAL
Interview Skills Consulting

**Hobbies that you might mention**

*Music:* Listening to opera, jazz, classical and ethnic music. Playing an instrument, singing, dancing. Be specific about what you do. Do you belong to an orchestra or a choir or do you play at home? Did you achieve certain grades or have particular achievements you want to talk about?

*Culture:* Modern and classical arts, wine tasting and cooking, etc. Again be specific, but avoid mentioning wine tasting if you only do this on Friday evenings in a pub with your mates after five pints of beer! Cooking for friends and socialising is can be an enjoyable thing to do.

*Leisure:* Travelling, stamp collecting, pottery, etc. Discuss where you travelled and what you enjoyed about it. Stamp collecting can be sociable if you belong to a club. If you do it by yourself, you can always go on about how you find it useful in teaching you patience, but you will need to counteract it with something more sociable to strike the right balance.

*Sports:* You can include team sports such as football, netball, hockey, etc. or individual sports such as skiing, cycling, walking and mountain climbing, (most of these are sociable activities too).

*Languages* are good to demonstrate your commitment to learning, patience and a logical mind. Don't pretend you are an expert at Portuguese or Russian if you are not. You want to avoid being asked a question in Russian!

**Example of an effective answer**

*I have many interests outside school. I enjoy team sports such as football, which I play regularly with my friends. It is a great way to de-stress at weekends after a hard week. I also love going to the opera and museums. I get very passionate about Mozart's operas and I regularly make the effort to go and watch them live at the Royal Opera House. I noticed on the medical school website that there are hundreds of clubs on offer at the university and I am looking forward to trying new interests such as culinary clubs and dancing clubs. As you can see from my statement, I also learned French and German at GCSE level. I am hoping to consolidate my modern languages when I travel with my friends to Europe before starting medical school.*

# QUESTION 40

**Tell me about a non-academic project in which you were involved.**

This question is a test of your drive and initiative. It asks for a specific project/example and therefore the STAR framework (see p.18-20) will help you structure your answer. Through this question, you should sell yourself in terms of communication skills, teamwork and leadership as much as you can.

### What kind of projects are they talking about?
Non-academic projects can be for example:

- Sporting events such as football or netball tournaments (note that if you only played, you won't have much to talk about. Use this if you actually helped organised part of a project/event)
- Duke of Edinburgh Award Scheme
- Committee activities such as balls, charity events, cultural events
- Business projects you have set up.

### Example of an effective answer

*The non-academic project that I am most proud of is an online business that I recently set up and which is selling Italian gourmet products online. I started by doing a lot of market research by talking to customers in shops, as well as friends and family, and I identified a gap in the market. One of the main problems was that I needed some capital in order to purchase some preliminary stock. My first approach was to contact several friends to help raise the £2000 that I needed as initial capital. I also involved my friends in the business and we worked hard as a team. Everyone contributed in accordance with their strengths. I delegated to one of them the task of setting up the website; others were better at negotiating and I involved them in purchasing the goods. Others helped with packing and shipping the items. Some members of my family are helping too when I am busy studying. The business is expanding and we are also making a small profit. I am hoping the money will help to fund my gap year.*

# QUESTION 41

**How do you cope with stress?**

This question frightens many candidates. Everyone thinks about mentioning a few hobbies, though few provide an explanation about why they enjoy those hobbies and their personal importance. Few actually go beyond the "hobbies" approach.

**Why this question?**
Stress is something that you will experience throughout medical school and your career as a doctor. You will be stressed for many reasons, including:

- Work overload and lack of resources
- Not being confident about your own abilities
- Making mistakes or fear of making them
- Working with difficult colleagues
- Unexpected events, both work and family related
- Unsociable hours
- Dealing with difficult patients
- Experiencing the harshest aspects of Medicine (seeing a patient die for the first time, seeing a sick child)
- Taking on difficult assignments such as breaking bad news to a patient
- Having to make a presentation in front of a large audience
- Having to find a good job that suits both your career and your social ambitions.

Stress is omnipresent and you simply cannot resolve every situation by playing football or playing the piano after work.

Interview Skills Consulting

**How to deal with stress?**
The way that you will deal with stress depends on its origin and the means available to you. You do not deal with long-term stress due to burning out in the same way that you deal with the immediate stress caused by a mistake that you have made. The easiest way to approach the question is to follow the four 'R's structure which helps you deal with any questions where you are asked how you deal or cope with something.

**Recognise**
You must become aware of your stress if you want to be able to address it properly.

**Recruit information**
You need to gain a greater understanding of the causes of stress in order to identify a solution. To achieve this, you need to take a step back, remain calm and analyse the situation.

**Resolve**
You can resolve stress in many ways, including:

- Organising yourself (better planning and time management, prioritising tasks, taking tasks one at a time)
- Delegating tasks to others
- Taking breaks/time off
- Anticipating future problems and taking proactive steps to prevent them and minimise their impact
- Seeking advice from friends and colleagues. In Medicine you can also get independent advice from legal helplines often run by defence organisations, charities or even the GMC
- Having a healthy lifestyle, hobbies and activities.

**Reflect**
Spend time to reflect on events at the end of the day and make sure that you draw lessons from your experience. Place events in perspective.

**Example of an ineffective answer**

> *I can cope with stressful situations such as exams. I always meditate and keep calm. I find this is very useful. I also play football and tennis to help me cope when I am stressed.*

This example mentions a few basic ideas and does not present any information about how the candidate copes with stress other than by playing sport. This may be useful but not in all circumstances. The answer lacks depth and needs to be a bit more detailed in its approach (e.g. by quoting examples) and to encompass different aspects of stress.

**Example of an effective answer**

*I always find that a bit of stress keeps me focused and gives me the adrenaline that I need to do well in my work. However, too much stress can potentially be destructive and I have learnt to deal with it in many different ways. I always try to keep calm, take a step back and evaluate the reasons behind the stress. Depending on the cause of the stress, I will react differently. For example, during my exam revisions, I had to deal with many topics at the same time, which put a lot of pressure on me time-wise. Having drawn a revision plan at the start, I took some time to review my plan halfway through to make sure that I could remain on target. I also found it important to take regular breaks as it helped me relax and ultimately helped me concentrate better. On a different note, a few years ago I had to deal with stress caused by illness in my family and I coped with that stress by talking to a few trusted friends about the situation, which helped a lot.*

*Generally speaking, I try to maintain a healthy lifestyle so that I am fully prepared to handle stressful situations whenever they arise. It also helps me to minimise my ability to get stressed in the first place. I try to eat healthily and I am involved in extra-curricular activities. I find running and playing football extremely helpful. They help to keep me calm and to release my frustrations. I also love listening to jazz; in particular, I find Miles Davis' music extremely calming. Finally, whenever I have had a difficult time, I find it useful to reflect on the situation and see how I can prevent something similar happening in future. I find that by doing this I grow more confident in being able to handle the unexpected.*

# QUESTION 42

**How do you feel that your hobbies have contributed to your studies?**

This question is very similar to Q.39: "What are your hobbies". Do not make the mistake of discussing your hobbies without addressing the second part of the question. You would be missing the point. Whether you enjoy hockey or flower arranging is not really where the difference will be made at the interview (although unofficially some interviewers may have a subconscious preference for candidates who do sport or music). One thing is certain: the marks with be higher for candidates who bring a personal reflection into their answer. If you have specific achievements (prizes, competitions), present them.

## Example of an effective answer

*I have always been interested in competitive sports such as rugby. I find competitive sports keep me focused and motivated. They also help me to push myself to the limit. I am now in a team which has won a number of cups. I hope to continue to pursue my passion for rugby when I am at medical school.*

*I find that rugby has contributed a lot to my studies. In the same way that a game is not won or lost until the last second of play, I always work hard and try my best in coursework to achieve my goals. I always stay focused and don't give up easily. Of course, rugby is also a team sport. I have made some brilliant friends at school through the club and I intend to continue to meet new friends in the same way. It contributed greatly to my studies in helping me appreciate the impact of good teamwork and good communication.*

ISCMEDICAL
Interview Skills Consulting

# QUESTION 43

**What makes a good doctor?**

This is a question that you should expect in one form or another. Ultimately, you cannot go into medical school without knowing what would be required of you. Even if you have not thought in great depth about this question, there are a number of points that should come to mind in view of the issues discussed so far in the book.

Do not be fooled by the generic aspect of the question. Despite the fact that it asks about "a good doctor", it is also a bit about what would make you a good doctor. And if you are short of ideas, think about what makes your own doctor a good one.

Since this question deals with personal skills, we will use the TAGS framework as a structure (see p.14). You would be well advised to read the *Good Medical Practice (2006)* issued by the GMC (see their website at www.gmc-uk.org) as it contains important information about the behaviour expected of doctors both within and outside their clinical practice.

**Characteristics of a good doctor**

*Training & Experience/Clinical*
- Good knowledge of Medicine
- For a surgeon, good dexterity
- Confident in his clinical abilities and decision making
- Keen to keep up to date, develops new skills and improves standards
- Keeps abreast of developments
- Able to recognise his limitations and when to seek help from other more experienced colleagues
- Evidence-based approach (See Q.107 for more details on Evidence-based Medicine)
- Good patient-based approach.

Interview Skills Consulting

**Academic**
- Interested and proactive in teaching others
- Involved in regular audits to check how his practice matches standards and implements necessary changes to improve patient care
- Interested in research activities. Either carries out research himself or takes an interest in research being carried out.

**Generic skills**
- Good communicator (See Q.22)
- Good team player (See Q.28)
- Good team leader (See Q.30)
- Good organisational skills (See Q.36)
- Able to handle stress effectively (See Q.41).

**Social**
- Friendly, sociable and approachable
- Caring and selfless
- Objective
- Honest and trustworthy
- Personal and professional integrity
- Respects patients and colleagues.

**How to deliver an effective answer**
Most candidates have a fairly good idea of what to say and will mention at least half of the above. It is therefore difficult to compete on content alone. With so much information needing to be communicated across to the panel, you must make sure that your answer is well organised so that the interviewers can follow your thread.

Avoid listing these items at random; it will not get you very far. Hence the importance of the TAGS framework (or any other framework that you feel works well for you). You should list the main points one by one, stopping on each of them to explain why that particular point makes a good doctor.

For example, for teamwork, you can phrase your module as follows:

> *Doctors work in a wide range of teams: their immediate team of colleagues, doctors from other hospitals or surgeries, social workers etc. and a good doctor will therefore be a good team player, who invites and respects other people's points of view, keeps others informed, offers his help when required and remains approachable.*

For communication skills:

> *It is crucial for a doctor to be a good communicator. Not only do you need to extract information from patients but you also have to reassure them, educate them and sometimes counsel them. All this requires a lot of patience, tact, good listening skills and a big dose of empathy when necessary. It is therefore very important that a doctor builds a good relationship and a good rapport with his patients.*

You should be able to use the answers to previous questions to assist you in building a good complete answer, bringing in the main characteristics described on the previous page.

**How to finish your answer**
Essentially, you must never lose sight of the fact that you are there to sell yourself. Whenever you have a question addressing global skills, you should use the opportunities to sell your own. Do try to remain humble and do not attempt to suggest that you already have all those qualities (otherwise there would be little value in training you). What you need to suggest is that you have developed a lot of these and are keen to continue.

For example:

> *Over the course of my studies and experiences, I have started to develop a lot of these skills. I have always worked hard at everything I do and have achieved some very good results. I have had opportunities to work in many different teams, whether through my sporting activities or my responsibilities on the social committee at school. I have also learnt a lot about communication, both at school and during my work experience in a hospice and at the GP practice. All this, together with my ability to work well under pressure, has really given me a lot of confidence in the fact that I can have a very successful career as a doctor.*

# QUESTION 44

**What are your main strengths?**

If you think about it, your mains strengths will need to be a close match to the requirements for a good medical student, which should be a close match for the attributes of a good doctor. This takes us back to Q.43 but with an emphasis on your personal attributes – it would be difficult to present an interest in research as a main strength. You need to stick to the more generic skills of a doctor such as:

- Good communication
- Team player
- Good leader
- Organised
- Other personal attributes such as conscientious, hardworking, dynamic, entrepreneurial, honest, caring, approachable, etc.

Rather than present a very long list of attributes, try to concentrate on a few powerful concepts which you can back up with examples. One important aspect of your answer is that it should be rigidly structured so that the interviewers are not presented with a self-gratifying ramble, but with information they can easily digest.

## Example of an effective answer

> *I am conscientious and hardworking and as a result I consistently achieve high grades at school. I am also an enterprising person and I try to read a lot outside the curriculum in order to broaden my knowledge. In particular, I have read articles on scientific research such as the Human Genome Project and I am looking forward to doing some research when I become a doctor. It is also thanks to my entrepreneurial drive that I have succeeded in getting involved in very interesting work experience posts, both in a hospital and in the community.*

ISCMEDICAL
Interview Skills Consulting

> *Another one of my strengths is my communication skills. I am regarded by all my friends as someone who is very approachable and I feel that being a good listener is essential to building good relationships with people. I had the opportunity to test my listening skills and empathy when I did some work experience at a local hospice, where some of the patients told me that I had brightened up their day and helped them through simply by being there and showing some care and attention.*
>
> *I am also a very organised person and I can work well under pressure. I have always enjoyed getting involved in a wide range of activities, whether they are academic projects or social activities. I also enjoy being part of groups where I can use my leadership skills. For example, I sit on the social committee at school. Because I have my hands in many projects at the same time, I have become very good at organising my time and also at using all the resources that I have to make sure that I can do everything on time and with a good quality outcome. I like working under pressure because it gives me a buzz and I feel that it helps me to stretch myself. Luckily, I also find time to fit in a couple of hobbies, which help me deal with all this stress and pressure. I am particularly keen on football, which I play regularly with my friends.*
>
> *All these attributes will really help me during my career in Medicine and I am looking forward to developing them further during medical school and beyond.*

Note the manner in which the strengths are presented. There are three distinct paragraphs, which makes it easier for the interviewers to follow.

Each paragraph deals with a separate idea and each idea is backed up by personal experience. Note also how we have grouped together a number of ideas which are related (for example conscientious, hardworking and entrepreneurial in the first paragraph).

Interview Skills Consulting

# QUESTION 45

**Why are you the best candidate today? Why should we take you on?**

These are both the same question. Essentially, you are the best candidate because you fit all the requirements and more. This question is therefore similar to Q.44 about your main strengths. Make sure that you use a strong structure so that the information passes across to the interviewers effortlessly.

### Example of an effective answer

*I am sure all the candidates today are of a very high standard. However, I think I have many good qualities that make me stand out. Firstly, I have consistently demonstrated my commitment and devotion to Medicine. I have done a lot of work experience both for charities and shadowing consultants and GPs over the past 2 years. This has given me a really good understanding of what being a doctor is like.*

*Secondly, I have a good academic track record. I work hard and perform well in school. My headteacher has predicted straight 'A's in my 'A' Levels. I am very encouraged by that. I am also a keen sportsman who understands the importance of teamwork. I also seize opportunities to enhance my leadership skills. For example, I have been involved in setting up various projects in my school and in organising football tournaments at my local school.*

*I am an approachable person who enjoys working with others and interacting with people at all levels. I have really learnt a lot about communication from my work experience and I feel that I have developed some good listening skills.*

*Finally, I am a dynamic, friendly, conscientious candidate and I believe that my motivation and inspiration will ensure a successful career in Medicine.*

# QUESTION 46

**Give three adjectives that suit you best.**

Again a question very close to "What are your main strengths?" Your answer to this will very much depend on whether you want to cheat by discussing three concepts rather than giving three adjectives. For example, does "being a good communicator" fit the bill? Strictly speaking no because this is not an adjective, but they will probably let you get away with it.

If you want to "cheat" then you can answer the question in the same way that you addressed the "main strengths" question.

If you are more of a purist, then there are numerous adjectives that you can use, which will lead to similar answers:

- Adaptable
- Dynamic
- Friendly
- Confident
- Honest
- Entrepreneurial

- Assertive
- Dedicated
- Flexible
- Conscientious
- Reliable
- Focused

- Approachable
- Decisive
- Dependable
- Hard-working
- Trustworthy
- Motivated

Follow the models set out in the previous answers to highlight three adjectives that allow you to demonstrate wide-ranging qualities.

# QUESTION 47

**How would your friends describe you?**
**What would you like written in your obituary?**

For those who don't know, an obituary is what people write in a newspaper when you have died and it therefore concentrates on your positive attributes and achievements. These two questions are therefore almost the same. They pose many problems to candidates when, in reality, they are no different to the previous questions about your strengths or about the adjectives that would best describe you.

### Example of an effective answer

*I have made friends in all the activities that I have undertaken and I think that they would describe me in a very positive light.*

*From a general perspective, people tend to see me as someone who is easy-going, friendly and approachable. I always try to make time for them if they want to have a chat. I am a good non-judgemental listener, which I think they appreciate.*

*I have also made friends at my basketball club, where I am the captain. People trust me to make good decisions and they would probably say that I am a very inclusive person who takes account of others' ideas and opinions but can also make clear decisions when needed. I think they would recognise that this has really helped the team achieve the success that it has had over the past 2 years. As well as being a good leader and motivator, they also regard me as a good team member, who enjoys socialising and has a good sense of humour.*

*Finally, I think that they would say that I am someone who is very honest and has a lot of integrity. I am the first to recognise when I have made a wrong decision, for example. Overall, they would agree that I am someone that they can depend on in all circumstances.*

# QUESTION 48

**Do you have the personality that it takes to do Medicine?**

If you ever considered answering "no" or "maybe" or "I don't know", you ought to think about an alternative career. There is only one possible answer to this question and it is "yes, of course".

Essentially it is asking: "Do you have what it takes to be a good doctor?" and you will therefore need to establish confidently that you are:

- Knowledgeable, competent, confident
- Keen to learn
- A good communicator and team player
- A good potential leader and well organised
- Able to work well under pressure
- Caring, sensitive, supportive, approachable
- Hard-working, enthusiastic, motivated, disciplined, conscientious
- Trustworthy, honest and have integrity

**Example of an ineffective answer**

> *The personalities that are needed to do Medicine are honesty, motivation, caring for patients and good discipline. I feel that I have all of these and I am ready to go into Medicine.*

This answer does not work well for two reasons. It does not address a wide range of skills (what has happened to communication skills and teamwork?) and it does not really provide any personal backup to the claims made.

**Effective answers**

A good example would be any example derived as per Q.42, Q.43 or Q.44, all of which are similar in nature to this question.

**ISC**MEDICAL

Interview Skills Consulting

# QUESTION 49

**What skills have you gained in your current work that are transferable to Medicine? (Question for graduates)**

Wherever you are currently working, there are many skills that you may have used that are crucial in the day-to-day life of a doctor and therefore that are directly transferable. These skills include your ability to:

- Listen effectively and identify client needs
- Explain complex issues in a simple language
- Organise complex information, summarise and present it
- Identify resources needed to help you reach your goals
- Seek expert advice when required
- Manage third parties
- Negotiate with third parties
- Use your initiative to resolve complex problems
- Identify areas of change and implement corresponding solutions
- Work independently and as part of a team
- Lead a group of people
- Influence others to your point of view
- Work to tight deadlines
- Deal with conflicting demands on your time and on your resources
- Deal with stress
- Handle conflict
- Manage difficult colleagues or clients
- Identify areas for development
- Provide good customer service, beyond requirements
- Develop your own knowledge and skills, and drive your own career.

You simply need to identify a handful of skills which you feel are characteristic of your current position and to present them following the same technique as set out in the previous questions. You should explain in what context you have developed those skills and how relevant they will be to you in Medicine. See Q.42, Q.43, and Q.44 for possible models of answers.

# QUESTION 50

**Do you work better by yourself or as part of a team?**

This is a trick question and many candidates, in their eagerness to appear sociable, come out with "As part of a team of course". Essentially, the short answer is: both.

Of course, as a doctor it is crucial that you are able to work well as part of a team. However, there will also be many opportunities where you will need to make decisions by yourself, or where others will simply expect you to deliver results without necessarily relying on other team members at all times. In other words, you should also be able to demonstrate that you can get on with things and take the initiative.

Working by yourself does not mean that you are antisocial, selfish and a complete loner. It can also mean that you are dependable and can take responsibility to get on with your work. In your answer, you simply need to be able to describe both sides, bringing examples from your experience and explaining how this relates to Medicine.

### Example of an effective answer

*I can work well both as part of a team and on my own. In the past I have been part of different types of teams. For example, I play football and, during the summer, I spent time working as a sales assistant. I have always communicated well with my colleagues and been very supportive. I have always been proactive in contributing in team meetings, in involving others in my work when needed and in showing willingness to help out.*

*At the same time, I can also take responsibility for my work and I am able to deliver results by myself when expected. This is not to say that I work totally independently, but I am able to get on with my work so that I can report back to my team at a later stage. For example, when I was on the social committee at my school, being in charge of the budget for my team, there were times when I needed to interact with my colleagues and others*

*when I simply needed to spend some time on my own so that I could concentrate on the complexity of the problem and deliver a financial solution that made sense in view of all the input that I had received during the consultation process.*

*The same applies to Medicine. Work is agreed as a team and you can draw on the team's resources to help resolve any issues. But there comes a stage where you also have to work independently in order to get the work done.*

# QUESTION 51

**What is your main weakness?**

This is a question that sends shivers down everyone's spine all the way to consultant interviews! Ask anyone how best to address this question and everyone will give you a different answer, telling you that their way is best because one of their friends got into medical school by giving that answer.

Some people got into medical school by saying that they didn't have any weakness and some people got rejected for saying the same thing. Some people got accepted by saying that they were perfectionists and others got rejected because that answer was too corny. Some people even got into medical school by saying that their main weakness was that they liked chocolate ice cream too much.

The truth is that any answer should be viewed in its context, in relation to the person who delivers it, the people who receive it, their sense of humour, what they would themselves have said at an interview, etc. It is extremely difficult to give advice to derive an answer that will guarantee success; nevertheless, there are answers that are safer than others and we seek to explain below how we feel the question should be approached.

### The corny and the unwise answers
Some answers are definitely unwise or very risky:

- "I don't have any weakness" – the aim of this question is really to establish whether you are aware of your negative traits and how you are addressing them. Not having any weaknesses will not make you a better human being or a better doctor. In fact, it may present you as someone who is arrogant and refuses to admit that there are aspects that you could improve.

- "I am not very good at anatomy" or any other topic – not wise. If you are not good at a topic that you have chosen, and which is highly relevant for Medicine, that will be the end of the day for you.

- "I am disorganised" – there are some fundamental requirements for Medicine that you should not consider highlighting as a weakness. Doctors should be organised, keep their cool under pressure, be able to handle stress, etc. If you are disorganised, you will find it difficult to cope. Personal organisation is something that is difficult to change and therefore you would not really be selling anything positive as part of your answer.

- "My handwriting is not very legible" – same as above. Clear and legible handwriting is crucial to ensure accuracy of the notes and the safety of patients (imagine the consequences of a nurse misunderstanding your dosages) and is tested on recruitment all the way to consultant level. If your handwriting is bad, it will never really improve and it may go against you.

- "I eat too much chocolate" – great! We have really learnt a lot about you here. You never know, it has been known to work.

- "I am a perfectionist" – the problem with this weakness is that this answer is probably given by 50% of candidates and therefore you will not go very far with it. So, although the weakness by itself is perfectly fine to mention, it is the wording that causes a problem by being overused. Also, being a perfectionist can have different meanings and, if you really want to develop this concept, you would need to be a lot more specific. More later …

- "I can't say 'no' to people" – the problem is the same as for the "perfectionist" answer. The concept suffers from overuse and is not developed enough to have any impact. More later too …

**ISC**MEDICAL
Interview Skills Consulting

**Presenting a strength as a weakness**
This is a technique often used by candidates and in principle it is probably the best way to handle the question. For example, having high expectations can be a strength because it means you are striving for quality. But it can also be a weakness because it could make relationships difficult with others at times.

Although many candidates are on the right track with this approach, they ruin their chances by taking a light-hearted approach to the question. In an effort to get rid of it as soon as possible because it feels uncomfortable, they become evasive and lose the personal touch that the question calls for. For example, "I have a tendency to focus too much on detail and, although this can be a good thing, it can also be a weakness" may be a good concept in principle but it feels really impersonal and empty of any really meaningful content.

**Suggested approach**
Our suggestion is to take an approach that is both explanatory and personal.

The first thing to recognise is that most weaknesses are actually strengths that have been pushed too far and which, under some circumstances, have become a real weakness. Therefore, rather than pretending that your weakness is really a strength (which may give the impression that you are trying to fob off the interviewers), you can be a lot more accurate by describing a real strength that you have which is sometimes becoming a weakness.

Secondly, you must be descriptive and use your experience to back up everything you say. This is the only way that you can make a real impact on your interviewers. Describe the strength and why it is a strength. Explain how it can become a weakness and how this has affected you in the past. If you can, give a concrete example.

Thirdly, describe how you react to this weakness, how you identify it, and what you are doing to remedy it. Again, be practical.

## Worked examples

### "Perfectionist"

The answer "I am a perfectionist" is only cheesy because the wording has become a common phrase at interviews and because candidates do not often bother to explain what they mean by it. Being a perfectionist can mean many things. It can mean that you have high expectations of others. It can also mean that you do not always see the larger picture and pay too much attention to small detail, particularly when you become stressed.

### Example of an effective answer (high expectations of others)

*I am someone who is constantly striving to achieve the best and I have high expectations of myself as well as others. On one hand it can help me achieve a lot in my work, but there are occasions where it can become an issue, especially if my own expectations do not necessarily match those of others. I can remember one particular occasion where I was part of a group organising a big fund-raising event. My role consisted of organising the catering and I was keen to achieve the best possible quality for the budget available. As a result, I placed a lot of conditions on the caterers and consequently most pulled out of the bidding process. This forced me to review my criteria, which lost us 2 days in the organisation of the event.*

*Ultimately, I was able to recognise where I had gone wrong and worked hard to rebuild contact with the caterers to make the event a success. Part of the issue was that I had only listened to part of the advice that some of the caterers had given me. I learnt a lot from this experience. In particular, I am a lot more aware of the times when I can be too demanding and have learnt to think more carefully before I issue instructions and requests to others. It has also taught me to be more open to suggestions from everyone rather than just a few selected people. In this particular case, although I had taken account of my colleagues' suggestions, I had not fully taken on board the caterers' comments. In many ways, this is something which I can improve further through experience and exposure to different situations and I feel that I have already improved quite a lot in that respect.*

Note that in this answer we have not mentioned anywhere the word "perfectionist". Instead we have defined one of its meanings more accurately. We have also illustrated the weakness through an example, which gives it more realism and helps the interviewers de-dramatise the weakness and understand it in a real-life context. In turn, this enables you to explain how you cope with the weakness from a practical point of view, which helps personalise the answer. Note also how the example presents a personal reflection towards the end, explaining what the candidate has learnt from the situation and how he is working on improving.

### Example of an effective answer (too much attention to detail)

*My main weakness is perhaps that I sometimes pay a little too much attention to detail and, as a result, I can spend more time than I really should on matters that do not necessarily have that much of an impact on the overall result. For example, I spent many hours writing and correcting the personal statement that I have submitted for this university application. It has obviously done the trick because I am sitting here today but I am fairly sure that I could have achieved the same result by spending a third less time on it. I guess that fundamentally it is about wanting to do my very best but that there has to be a trade-off somewhere between the time spent and the result achieved.*

*I feel that this is something that I am getting better at, partly by observing the way my friends work and discussing this issue with them. I am also improving as I gain more confidence in myself and in my capabilities.*

### "I can't say 'no'"

"I can't say 'no'" is also a common answer, which makes it ineffective. Again, the problem is not so much with the concept behind it – this is a good weakness to mention – but more with the phraseology.

It can actually mean different things. On the positive side, it can mean that you are a good team player, willing to get involved and to please others. It could also mean that you are ambitious and are keen to get involved in many activities. Identify the messages that you are trying to put across and make them explicit.

On the negative side, it can lead to overload of work, stress, people taking advantage of you, less time for your family, etc.

With regard to what can be done to resolve the problem, people often state that they have learnt to say "no". You must be careful not to go the other way by presenting yourself as someone who is no longer a team player. The answer is not always to start saying no to others, but for you to become more realistic about what you have the time to do, to work with others to make them understand your situation, to make sure that you understand their situation and for both of you to come to an agreement. You must learn to be more in control and maybe to be a bit more assertive.

Putting all this together and incorporating an example would give:

> *I am someone who is ambitious and I like getting involved in numerous projects in order to achieve a lot and develop new skills. However, sometimes it can get a little too much to deal with. For example, over the past 12 months, I studied for five 'A' Levels, I got involved in running a youth club on Wednesday evenings, I played football with young kids at week-ends, I learnt to drive and spent a lot of time gaining work experience in the evening at the local hospice and at a GP surgery on Fridays. I got involved in some of these social activities because people were asking me to get involved and I did not want to disappoint them. However, in hindsight, I realise that it placed me in a difficult situation where I had rather a lot to handle all at once, which was sometimes quite stressful.*
>
> *This is an issue which has occasionally arisen in the past and I feel that I am getting better at recognising what I can realistically get involved in and what I can't. I have learnt to manage people's expectations by being honest with them about my workload but also by trying to see how I might be able to find a solution without being directly involved every time. This has eased up the pressure on my time and I now feel much more confident in dealing with these requests.*

**ISC**MEDICAL
Interview Skills Consulting

**Other possible weaknesses that you can mention**

Ultimately, there are many weaknesses that you can discuss and which, if illustrated by the right example, are perfectly palatable at an interview. Possible weaknesses include:

- Taking criticism too personally – this is a perfectly normal reaction and provided that you explain how you are changing in that respect by seeing criticism as a way to improve then you will be fine.

- Being over-empathic. Many people go into Medicine because they are caring and empathic. But these attributes, which are real strengths, can become weaknesses when you deal with very ill patients to whom you might get attached. You have to learn to harden your skin and this will come through experience.

- Being direct with people. This is a good attribute as people know exactly what you mean and it avoids confusion. However, there are situations where tact is required and you have learnt through experience to mellow your approach towards more sensitive people.

# QUESTION 52

**If you could change two things about yourself, what would they be?**

This is also a weakness-type question, but this time they are asking for two! People are often reluctant to talk about their weaknesses, understandably so. However, if prepared properly, these answers can make a real difference compared to other candidates who may come up with a bland answer. Remember that discussing your weaknesses shows a good personal insight and a willingness to improve. Use these questions to your advantage. Most of your success will depend on how confident you are in delivering your answer as much as on its content. You can inspire yourself with the previous question to get some ideas about what you can say.

### Example of an effective answer

*One thing I would like to change about myself is learning not to take on too much at the same time. I am always eager to get involved in various projects. For example, last year, as well as having to study for five 'A' Levels I was working weekends at a local charity shop, did some coaching for kids who wanted to play football and took piano lessons. Although I managed to cram everything in, it could sometimes prove quite stressful. Part of the issue was that I did not want to let anyone down when they asked me if I wanted to get involved, so I guess it might just be a case of being a bit more self-confident and assertive when needed.*

*Another thing that I would like to change about myself is to learn to live more healthily. When I am busy I don't tend to have such a healthy diet and I tend to neglect my usual exercise regime. It is something that I have noticed over the past year and that I will need to address as soon as I get into medical school. I guess that having a number of sport clubs on-site will be a great help in that regard.*

# QUESTION 53

**Who has had a major influence on you as a person?**

This question is not so much about who as it is about why. Ultimately, it does not really matter if the person who influenced you most was your father, your older brother, a teacher, the local priest or Lord Nelson. What really matters is how they inspired you and the qualities that they demonstrated that you found attractive. This question is therefore about you, not them. Consequently, in your answer you will need to detail what qualities you found inspiring in that person and how you incorporated those qualities within your own life.

The qualities that you may wish to demonstrate through your answer could be:

| | | |
|---|---|---|
| Competent | Good motivator | Good listener |
| Confident | Inspirational | Good teacher |
| Assertive | Approachable | Inclusive |
| Fair | Supportive | Committed |
| Decisive | Caring | Dedicated |
| Conscientious | Patient | Friendly |
| Hard-working | Enthusiastic | Careful |
| Optimistic | Empathic | |

Try to use a broad combination of three/four of the above or others you may find relevant and develop each one in turn. Note that the person in question does not have to be a doctor. There are inspiring people outside Medicine too!

### Example of an ineffective answer

> *My father has been a major influence in my life. He is hard-working and supports my brothers and me through school. I hope I can become a good GP to make him proud.*

There is nothing wrong with mentioning the father and the GP ambition. But the answer lacks detail about the qualities that the father has or had.

**Example of an effective answer**

*One of the people who had a major influence on my life and whom I respected greatly was my uncle, who worked as a marketing director in a local engineering firm. He was someone who always saw life from a positive point of view, despite the problems that he faced at the time in terms of job uncertainty. I used to go with him to see clients during my school holidays and I observed him deal with them in many different ways. He was always very attentive to his clients, trying to understand what they really wanted so that he could deliver the best to them. Whenever clients had a complaint, he always treated them with respect and took a proactive attitude in resolving the problems that they had encountered.*

*At home, he was also always a good family man, very attentive to his family and never afraid of going out of his way to help out. When I was 10 years old, I lost a good friend in a car crash and my uncle was very supportive in trying to help me get over it. Sometimes he did not do much else than simply sit with me and listen to me, but I found this to be a great help.*

*Overall, he was a very caring man dedicated to both his family and his work. He also enjoyed life to the full and knew how to have a good time to relax and take a break from his worries. This is how he inspired me, and in many ways I am aspiring to develop the same balance in life that he had.*

Note how the answer deals with a few points only, which are backed up with a few personal examples. An effective answer does not have to list 20 qualities. Go for quality rather than quantity. It will help you make your point more effectively and will enable you to come across as more personal and more enthusiastic too.

# QUESTION 54

**Tell us about your best / worst teacher.**

Again this is a question about someone who inspired you (or did not), but this time they are imposing the context. It has to be a teacher. It does not matter who this teacher was; what matters is why they were good or bad. Many candidates waste their time with a single-line answer of the type "My best teacher was Mr Smith last year". Good for them, but not that interesting if there is no explanation as to why they were good.

**Example of an effective answer (best teacher)**

*My best teacher is Mr Jones, my biology teacher for the past 2 years. He is someone that I really found inspiring for many reasons. First, he has an absolute passion for his subject and this really comes across in the way he teaches. He is clear in his explanations, he makes sure that we have understood the main messages before the end of the class, he makes his lesson fun by introducing variety and experiments, and he also makes sure that everyone in the class is involved by making his sessions interactive. This creates a really good environment and has actually helped the class gel together more.*

*Also, he is very good natured and he has never hesitated in staying beyond hours to help me understand a particular aspect on which I wanted more details. Whenever I made mistakes in answering a question or in an assignment, he was never over-critical but, on the contrary, he tried to find different ways of explaining the concept so that I could grasp it more easily.*

*And finally, he is also someone who I could approach easily if there were issues that I need to discuss, even if they related to matters outside biology. He is very caring and I am sure that he has played an important role in helping me decide to become a doctor.*

**Example of an effective answer (worst teacher)**

*My worst teacher was probably my arts teacher last year. She simply could not understand why everyone could not be good at arts and she insisted on giving attention only to those who were good at it. This meant that 90% of the class were effectively neglected and saw the arts classes as a chore.*

*She also made sarcastic comments about some students' work, including mine, and it was hard to take it in good humour and ignore the humiliation that came with it. In my mind a good teacher is someone who is able to adapt to his students and should certainly be someone who encourages those who are not at the top. He should also be open-minded, especially in a discipline as subjective as arts.*

*Teaching is something that I enjoy doing myself and in fact I coach 10-year-old kids at football on Wednesdays. Unlike this arts teacher, I believe in encouraging people and I think I have been able to do this successfully so far.*

Note how the answer reversed the situation by explaining in the first instance why the teacher was bad and by using this as an opportunity to explain what makes a good teacher. Note also the personal conclusion.

# QUESTION 55

**Describe an instance where you made a life-changing decision.**

This is a question asking for an example. Therefore you should use the STAR strategy (see p.18-20) to answer this question. Outline the context, explain what you did, how you did it and why, and conclude by describing the outcome and what you learnt from the situation. This question is not just about the decision in itself. For example, if you simply said: "The life-changing decision I made was to decide to become a doctor", you will not provide any real information. As part of your answer you will need to describe the thinking process behind that decision and the risks that you were taking. This is really about how you approach a problem which does not have an obvious solution and which has important consequences. Can you see a parallel with Medicine here?

### Example of an effective answer

*About 5 years ago, my grandmother was placed into a home where she could be cared for in better conditions than at home. One evening we were called at home because she had suffered a heart attack and they had managed to resuscitate her. The doctor wanted to discuss "Do not resuscitate orders" with us because she was at risk of a relapse and was not able to make decisions. They were in favour of issuing an order and my parents and I went to the hospital to discuss things through with the doctor. This gave rise to a big debate in the family and I was split between the grief of having to let my grandmother die and the rational thought that she would probably be more at peace and suffering less if we let her die. This was particularly important to me because I was very close to her. Despite my personal grief, I told my parents that I felt that the doctors were best placed to make the decision and that she should not be resuscitated. My grandmother subsequently died and I have often wondered what would have happened if we had decided to fight the decision. However, I am contented by the fact that she had lived a full life and died with dignity.*

**What if you have not had a life-changing event?**
In this case, it will be a difficult question to answer. There is no point in making one up; it will be obvious from the lack of detail in your answer. However, you could rephrase the question by starting with "I can't say I have had a life-changing event in my life but I have certainly made some important decisions." And then go on describing one of them.

**ISC**MEDICAL
Interview Skills Consulting

# QUESTION 56

**What is your greatest achievement?**

This is a very broad question which could attract all kinds of answers. This could be an academic or a personal achievement, linked either to a single event or a lifelong achievement.

Examples include:

- Specific grades that you achieved or prizes that you won
- Ambitions that you have fulfilled through hard work or despite adverse conditions
- Projects in which you were involved, where you made a difference
- Success in anything that was competitive (the higher the competition the better).

Whatever you mention, it must be a real achievement and you must describe what makes it an achievement. For example:

- Passing your driving test is not really an achievement unless you did it when you were busy and had little time for lessons, or unless you passed it after having spent weeks in plaster.
- Getting a 98% mark for your assignments is not an achievement if everyone else got 99%. Where do your marks place you?
- Speaking four languages is not an achievement if all you can say is "Bonjour", "Buongiorno", "Una cerveza por favor", "Sauerkraut, bitte".

Finally, you must explain what you did to gain this achievement (selling a few important leadership, team playing, initiative and communication skills in the process) and explain what it means to you.

Interview Skills Consulting

**Example of an effective answer**

*One of my greatest achievements was to organise fund-raising activities in favour of a local child who needed to go to the US for a life-saving operation. I enlisted the help of two friends and we set out to organise a number of activities over the course of the year.*

*We worked hard together to plan all the events. We split up the tasks according to our strengths and preferences. I organised regular meetings with my friends so that we could touch base and deal with any problems. I also asked for advice from other people who had organised similar events before and went out in the field to find companies who would be willing to offer sponsorship in return for advertisements during the events.*

*We raised over £5,000 and the child could go to the USA for the operation. I was proud of what we had achieved as a group and of the tenacity and enterprise that I demonstrated to achieve such a great result.*

**Another example**

*I have always been a keen sportsman and have always seen sport as a means to test my ability to surpass myself. Since I was a child I have been successful in several local competitions, winning a few medals on the way.*

*Last year, I was given a chance to enter a national fencing competition. Fencing is one of my favourite sports because it is about technique and precision rather than strength and the competitive atmosphere is often more friendly than in other sports. Out of 30 people selected for the competition, I came third. I felt it was amazing to have been selected for a national event through the hard work that I had put in at a local level, but coming third gave me a real sense of achievement. I had to work hard to achieve this, including attending extra training sessions, no mean feat in view of the fact I had to revise for my exams at the same time. But all my hard work paid off and I managed to get good grades at my exams too.*

Interview Skills Consulting

# QUESTION 57

**What are you most proud of?**

This question is very similar to the previous question. In fact, you could actually give the same answer, since you will obviously be proud of any of your achievements.

However, you may also consider the question in a slightly broader sense, as you could also be proud of particular skills that you may have acquired. For example, you may be proud of the way in which you developed good communication skills or good organisation skills through a variety of means or events. You may also be proud of the fact that whenever you faced difficulties you always kept your spirits up and worked hard to find a solution to your problems. Nevertheless, if you choose this approach, you will need to back up your claims with examples and will need to discuss actual achievements, which takes us back, again, to the previous question.

### Example of an effective answer

*I am particularly proud of the organisation and time management skills that I have developed over the years. I am particularly proud of the success of the final year's sports day that I organised.*

*I was in charge of the whole programme. I enlisted the help of some friends to whom I delegated some important tasks to help me set up the sports activities, fund-raising programmes, prizes and also the guest invitations. I had discussions with everyone involved so that we could set realistic targets and prioritise the work accordingly. I also organised regular meetings so that we could share ideas and resolve any outstanding issues. Through good organisational skills, teamwork and a lot of effort, we produced a successful event that we were all proud of.*

# QUESTION 58

**How do you cope with criticism?**

As this is a question asking how you would cope with something, you should use the four 'R's framework (see p.21): Recognise the situation, Recruit information, Resolve the situation and Reflect on it.

Essentially, by asking this question, they want to test that you have an open approach and that you are keen to learn and to improve. They also want to know that you can take proactive action to resolve problems and that you are able to communicate effectively in a context where you may be placed on the defensive. This is the message that you need to communicate through your answer.

## Example of an effective answer

*It is not always very nice to be criticised but, as much as I can, I try not to take it personally. Ultimately, there will always be a reason behind a criticism, whether it is justified or not, and I think it is important to take it with an open mind as it can be an important learning exercise. I have learnt to recognise criticism, even when it is given in a disguised manner. I try to stay calm and collected and to take on board the messages that are being given to me. If possible, I try to get as much information from the other person as possible about the exact nature of the problem and some ideas about how I could improve. I might also consult some of my colleagues to see what they feel about the issue. If I feel the need to justify myself then I will put my point across in a non-judgemental manner in order to encourage a discussion. If I was at fault then I will apologise and I will use this as a learning experience and try to reflect and correct my behaviour. If this was a simple misunderstanding and I am not at fault, I will be as diplomatic and sensitive as possible. Ultimately, if someone has criticised me, it is because they perceived that there was a problem even if there might not have been one. I will ensure that such a misunderstanding never recurs.*

# QUESTION 59

**How do you cope with conflict?**

There are different levels of conflict and the answer will also vary depending on whether you are actually involved within the conflict or whether you are independent.

This is another question which should follow the four 'R's structure (see p.21) and the answer to which will involve communication skills, team playing, initiative and maybe even leadership. Although it is a theoretical question, try to include examples from your real life to make it sound more personal.

## Example of an effective answer

*As captain of the hockey team, I occasionally have to deal with conflict between team members. These occur for various reasons ranging from a disagreement over tactics that we may use in a forthcoming game or between two members who have become annoyed with each other following someone's mistake during a match. We have also had conflict between people who were fighting to be selected for the same position.*

*My approach has always been to find the best way to resolve the issue as quickly as possible while making sure that I could preserve the team spirit. The team has grown stronger as a result. My first approach is to identify where the tension lies and to discuss the issue separately with each protagonist. This usually enables me to get a lot of information about how everyone feels and avoids direct confrontation. If I feel that I need to do so, then I might also ask for advice from other team members who may have ideas to resolve the problem, though I am sometimes reluctant to involve too many people at one time.*

*I try to remain as flexible and fair as possible and I also try hard to make the two parties work on a way forward rather than attempting to impose my own point of view. I think that, ultimately, it is crucial to try to obtain a win-*

*win outcome or at least a face-saving outcome and this is what I aim to achieve through discussion and negotiation.*

*Of course, my main preoccupation is really to anticipate and prevent possible conflict so I work hard to ensure that the team members get on well together. When conflict does occur, having a close team also helps a lot in ensuring a quick resolution.*

Other conflict situations that you can discuss include having to deal with a difficult person in one of your summer jobs. For example, if you had to discuss how you dealt with a difficult customer at the service desk, you could detail how you made sure that you let them express their opinion to allow them to vent their anger and to get all the facts. You could talk about how you made sure that you remained calm and identified another colleague who had the right knowledge and skills to help you out, etc.

# QUESTION 60

**As a doctor, who would you regard as part of the team?**

This is a small trick question to test whether you have an open or obtuse view of the medical environment. Essentially, you must look at the concept of "team" in its broadest sense. And don't forget the non-medical staff!

**Immediate team**
- Other doctors working with you, senior and junior
- Nurses and healthcare assistants
- Managers (bed managers, ward managers, practice managers)
- Secretaries
- Other staff such as radiographers.

**Peripheral team**
These are people who you work with but may not be with you all the time.
- Doctors from other wards if working in hospital
- GPs if working as hospital specialist
- Hospital specialists if working as a GP
- Dieticians
- Porters (some people failed for not mentioning them!)
- Physiotherapists
- Occupational therapists
- Social workers
- Police in some cases
- Community doctors and nurses
- Teachers in some cases.

**And of course**
- Patients, who should be involved at all stages in their own care.

There is no real technique in this question, other than making sure that you mention people from all walks of life, that you do not forget patients and that, for each type of colleague, you mention what role they play in the team.

# QUESTION 61

**Why is research important?**

---

A very factual question that requires an answer with a bit more depth than the often quoted: "Because we can discover new things". One could probably write entire books about this topic but in 2 minutes you will need to come up with something practical and simple.

Research is of course important for the advancement of Medicine as it enables doctors and private institutions to derive new techniques, new technology and new drugs that all contribute to better care for patients.

Research leads to publications and the build-up of knowledge that can then be used to improve standards of care in Medicine. This process of analysing information and evidence derived from research and applying one's clinical judgement to make it relevant to individual patients' situations is called Evidence-Based Medicine. We address it in more detail in Q.107.

Research can take many forms. It can be lab-based, or patient-based, or even sometimes simply literature-based (i.e. analysing the different pieces of literature existing on a particular topic and drawing conclusions from it).

Once you have briefly explained what research is about (keeping it nice and simple), you can conclude by saying that it is something that you take an interest in (give the names of a few articles that you read recently) and that you look forward to getting involved in research projects at some stage as a doctor.

# QUESTION 62

**What research have you done?**

This question will only be asked if you have declared on your personal statement that you had an involvement in research (e.g. if you are already at postgraduate level). To provide a complete answer, you should:

- Describe the nature of your research

> *I have a basic degree in Pharmacology. In the last year of my pharmacology degree, I was involved in a project which aimed to test whether … As part of this project, we looked at … and used different methods to test … My role consisted of …*

- Detail the outcome in terms of publications and presentations

> *After 4 months of research and analysis we concluded that … We presented the results at … and also published those results in …*

- Explain what you learnt from your research personally

> **[Clinical]** *During my research, I learnt a lot about the topic and gained specific laboratory skills such as dealing with lab animals, PCR and other techniques.*
>
> **[Academic]** *After writing up and presenting the results, I am now a lot more confident in analysis, reading and critiquing other scientific papers. I have also learnt about data collection and analysis skills.*
>
> **[Generic]** *This also taught me a lot about rigour and how to organise and plan my work efficiently.*

- Define your future involvement in research

> *I found the experience really interesting for all these reasons and I would be keen to pursue some research interest once I become a doctor, and, why not, before that at medical school.*

# QUESTION 63

**What type of research would you be interested in doing?**

This question can be asked to everyone. If you have already done some research in the past, then you could use the opportunity to discuss the research that you have already done (see Q.62) and finish off by saying that you would be keen to continue exploring that field, or some other field that you identified as interesting on the way.

If, however, you have not done any research at all until now (which will be the case for many candidates), then you should concentrate on a field of Medicine that interests you, or on a topic that maybe you have read about recently. You may also want to discuss whether you are interested in lab-based research, clinical (patient-based) research, etc. Whatever you discuss, make sure it is not some obscure topic but something which is likely to have some global impact. You can discuss the obscure topics when you get to consultant level.

## Example of an effective answer

*I am still in the early part of my career and have not really had the opportunity to embark on a research project. However, from my various readings and biology subject, I am particularly interested in becoming involved in molecular or genetic science research. I think we are at a very exciting time in Medicine at the moment. Programmes such as the Human Genome Project have really opened up numerous opportunities for scientists and clinicians to get involved in finding the causes for many genetic conditions and, hopefully, their cures in the future. I really hope to be able to contribute in this field in the future.*

**Another example of an effective answer**

*I have always been interested in molecular biology. I really believe the potentials are endless. Molecular biology can help us, first of all, to understand the normal physiology. From the norm, we can then find out more about the disease processes. This can of course point us in the direction of finding a cure for cancer, genetic conditions and AIDS. Therefore, for the final year at medical school, I am hoping to be involved in a project in either physiology or pharmacology. I understand this university is very active in projects such as the molecular basis of Multiple Sclerosis and Alzheimer's Disease and I hope to be actively involved in this field in the future.*

# QUESTION 64

**If you were to set up a new medical research project, what would it be?**

As for the previous questions, you have to demonstrate some degree of knowledge in scientific subjects. It is generally better to talk about diseases that have high impact, such as HIV/AIDS, Breast Cancer, Multiple Sclerosis, etc. If you choose something too specialised you run the risk of being asked awkward questions about a topic that you know little about, which will not help you further your cause.

To create an effective answer, you will need to name your area of interest and explain why this would be a good idea. Having a broad topic helps a lot in that respect.

### Example of an effective answer

*I think one of the exciting fields in Medicine at the moment is the possible use of vaccines to cure cancer. I have recently read about the randomised control trials in treating cervical cancer. I really think that this is an exciting field in Medicine. The fact that vaccines were developed to prevent the infection of HPV virus and subsequently have the potential to cure cervical cancer is a real breakthrough. This vaccination technique has the potential to lead to cures for common cancers such as prostate and breast cancer. Of course, this may also be the answer for developing a vaccine in a devastating disease such as HIV/AIDS. This is why I would probably choose this area as a possibility for a new research project.*

ISCMEDICAL
Interview Skills Consulting

# QUESTION 65

**How do you go about researching something you know nothing about?**

This question is a generic question to test your ability to show initiative and inventiveness. There may be occasions where you will be asked to research on an unknown topic, not least if you have the opportunity to get into a medical school that uses problem-based learning as a teaching tool, but also in your professional life where you may be asked to give presentations about topics that may be new to you and require a degree of homework. Incidentally, your answer does not have to be constrained to the field of Medicine.

If you don't know something, the answer will either be in a book or journal, or in someone else's brain. To get answers you might therefore want to try the following:

- Talk to people who are experts in the field or have undertaken a similar type of research previously
- Look on the Internet and in specialist medical databases
- Consult journals and magazines. Look in books.

**Example of an effective answer**

> *I was particularly interested in Herceptin recently; I kept hearing about it but knew nothing about the drug. I started off finding out about the medication from various daily newspapers. I also asked my GP and my biology teacher about the drug and the controversies surrounding it. This gave me the idea to go to the library, where I found out about monoclonal antibodies and how they are used to tackle breast cancer cell receptor HER2. I also used the Internet to find out about the controversies surrounding the licensing of the drug and the various court cases that took place as a result. Using all these resources gave me a lot of information about the topic and talking with others allowed me to put everything in perspective. In the process I also learnt quite a lot about the process of drug licensing and breast cancer in general.*

# QUESTION 66

**What makes a good teacher?**

Teaching is an essential activity in a doctor's life. Just as you have been taught by other doctors, you will be expected to teach others too. This question is related to Q.54 but is asking for a more generic and more complete approach. A good way of formulating your ideas is as follows:

**Knowledge:** a good teacher has a thorough understanding of his subject. This enables him to be credible with his students by appearing competent. With a strong knowledge a teacher is also able to address any issues or questions that students may have.

**Communication skills:** a good teacher should be able to take advanced information and to translate it in a language that is easily understood by his audience. A bad teacher would make the same information confusing. A good teacher is also able to choose teaching methods that are appropriate to the audience and to the topic being discussed.

**Generating interest:** the best teachers will encourage students to learn by generating in his students an interest in the topic. A bad teacher will ensure that students are interested by generating a fear of failure (e.g. "if you do not know this, you will fail your exams"). In order to generate interest, a good teacher will need to be passionate himself about the topic.

**Respect:** a good teacher must be respected by his students. To achieve this, he must build credibility by being thoroughly prepared for teaching sessions, by being fair in his assessment of the students, by making himself available to discuss issues that students will raise during or after the session and, generally speaking, by ensuring that he provides the best quality to his students at all times.

Interview Skills Consulting

# QUESTION 67

**How important is teaching in the medical profession?**

There is only one answer to this question, which is that it is vitally important since this is what enables doctors to progress through their careers by acquiring new knowledge and learning new skills.

Doctors are involved in teaching in different ways. They can:

- Supervise other doctors on a day-to-day basis and provide guidance as and when necessary
- Help prepare junior doctors for exams through teaching classes and mock exams
- Organise departmental teaching sessions
- Give presentations to other doctors, both within and outside their place of work (e.g. at conferences)
- Teach in theatre through observation, demonstrations and practice. Surgical teaching can also involve the use of mannequins and videos.

Teaching is important because:

- It helps doctors and associated professionals develop new skills and build their career.
- Good teaching promotes better knowledge, better skills and therefore better patient care.
- It enables the team to spend time together away from day to day activities. This can help create bonds between individuals and therefore promotes team spirit.

# QUESTION 68

**Who should a doctor teach?**

Again, a very factual question where you need to demonstrate a breadth of understanding of what a doctor does.

Doctors should have the responsibility of teaching the following people:

- Medical students
- Junior and senior doctors from their close team
- Doctors from other specialties and GPs
- Nurses
- Paramedics
- Healthcare workers such as dieticians, physiotherapists, social workers
- Administrative staff such as secretaries and managers
- Patients on disease management and healthcare issues.

Do not forget the patients!

Interview Skills Consulting

# QUESTION 69

**When you are a doctor, would you like to get involved in teaching?**

This question is almost a trick question because whether you like it or not you will have to get involved in teaching in one way or another. Also, under the framework of clinical governance (see Q.102), there is a requirement for all doctors to be involved in teaching activities of some kind.

In answering the question, you should of course put across your enthusiasm for teaching, highlighting any experience of teaching that you have gained whether by helping others do their homework, or presenting in front of a group of people, or otherwise. In addition, it is important that you mention why you enjoy teaching (it is rewarding to see others progress through your own efforts; teaching facilitates teamwork and it also enables you to learn through your preparation).

### Example of an effective answer

*Teaching is an activity that I know I will enjoy and that I would very much like to pursue as a doctor. I have always been involved in teaching in one way or another. As a child and a teenager, I was always involved in supervising my little sister during her homework, answering her questions and explaining to her difficult concepts in different ways. More recently, I have presented a number of topics to my class, including one on green energy and one on enzymes. I really enjoyed the preparation for the presentation as well as the delivery. I had made sure that I knew my subject well and as a result the feedback was that everyone found the talk and the questions and answers session very informative. What I enjoy about it is the fact that you are able to make someone's knowledge evolve through your own work and that you do learn quite a lot from it yourself.*

# QUESTION 70

**Give an example of a situation where you held an opinion but had to change your view.**

This question is about a range of skills, including personal integrity, team playing, honesty, and willingness to learn. Since it is a question asking for an example, you will need to use the STAR approach (see p.18-20), describing first the situation and the opinion that you had formed. Secondly, you will need to outline what happened that made you change your mind, explaining in detail the thinking process that you went through and how you felt about the situation at the time. Finally, explain how the situation ended, emphasising what you learnt about it and yourself at the time.

### Example of an ineffective answer

> *Last year I hesitated about taking a gap year. After discussing the matter with my parents and a few friends I eventually took a year out and have not had any regrets since.*

The answer provides no detail about why the candidate thought a gap year may not be useful, the arguments that family and friends put forward, what made him change his mind, and what he learnt from the situation.

### Example of an effective answer

> *On my way to school, I have to cross an area of my town where a lot of homeless people sleep and it can sometimes feel a little unsafe if you are on your own. I had the preconception that homeless people were people who had little initiative and were simply happy living off other people's money. My beliefs were fuelled to some extent by anecdotal evidence on TV or in newspapers that some homeless people could earn a lot of money simply by begging. Discussing the topic with one of my friends, he mentioned that he knew someone who had held a highly paid job and had ended up homeless following a bitter divorce from his wife. His comment puzzled me and I wondered whether I had simply misunderstood their situation from the beginning. We discussed the matter further and*

*eventually decided to have a chat with some of the people that we saw every day on the pavement. There, we found an amazing mix of people, each with their own sad story but with sometimes a culture that was astonishing. Following that episode, my friend and I started working at a local shelter one day per week and carried on chatting to our new friends on occasions. This really showed me how easy it can be to be prejudiced and how we must make sure that we know all the facts before passing judgement.*

# QUESTION 71

**What is the worst mistake that you have made?**

Like any negative question, you should not regard it as an attempt to trick you into saying something horrible, but instead as an opportunity for you to explain how you react in adverse circumstances. This includes your ability to show integrity throughout your behaviour.

In order to make the answer interesting, it will need to be an event where you learnt a valuable lesson. If the worst mistake that you have made is to choose rope climbing instead of athletics at school, there won't be much to talk about. On the other hand, try to strike the right balance by not choosing an example with consequences that can be regarded as extreme. They won't forgive you for having put your neighbour's cat in the microwave for the sake of scientific experimentation.

Doctors are human and make mistakes. You need to get over it. What really matters is that, when you make a mistake, you are able to:

- Spot it and own up to it (insight, honesty)
- Take immediate steps to correct it (initiative)
- Involve the right people to advise and help out (teamwork and communication)
- Apologise accordingly (honesty, communication)
- Analyse the situation to identify what went wrong and draw lessons from it (willingness to improve)
- Apply the lessons learnt to other similar situations
- Ensure others do not make the same mistake.

If you can discuss as many of the above points as possible, your answer will be complete.

ISC MEDICAL
Interview Skills Consulting

**Example of an effective answer**

> *I would say that my worst mistake is possibly a wrong decision that I made during a Duke of Edinburgh expedition which went wrong as a result of it. I was the team member who was responsible for the equipment for directions. The mistake was to forget to charge the battery of the equipment before the event.*
>
> *When we were in the forest, the equipment failed. At first I felt that something was not quite right but I was fairly confident that we would be able to reach our destination so I did not mention it to the others straight away. As we got lost further inside the forest, reality dawned on me and I felt increasingly uncomfortable at the idea of having to face my angry team mates' reaction. I mentioned tactfully to the team leader that I may have made a mistake and that we needed to stop to discuss the situation before it became potentially more difficult to resolve. I apologised to my team mates for having forgotten to check the equipment thoroughly and explained that we had got lost as a result. I emphasised that I took full responsibility for our position and that I would work hard to put us back on track, but that I also needed their assistance to achieve this. At first, some of the team members were angry but, after a while, we all pulled together and had a fruitful discussion about what our next steps should be. Eventually, and only an hour late, we made it to our destination. The next day, this became an endless topic for jokes and, in the end, the incident had actually made us closer as a team for having shared this experience.*
>
> *I learnt quite a lot from the incident, and particularly how important it is to own up to your mistakes quickly so that they can be resolved as soon as possible. This also showed me how important it is to apologise and communicate effectively as it helps bring people on board. Finally, it gave me an opportunity to witness first hand how forgiving friends can be and that honesty is always the best policy.*

Note the use of the word "possibly" at the beginning, which helps in softening the impact of what is coming afterwards (i.e. you pretend that you do not remember well at the beginning, so it can't be that bad). It all helps!

# QUESTION 72

**How do you know what you don't know?**

Once you have recovered from the shock of the question's wording, you need to clarify in your mind what it means. Essentially, as a student, and later as a doctor, you will have gaps in your knowledge.

There will be things that you know are missing from your knowledge, in which case you will need to find ways of gaining that missing knowledge. There will also be things that you don't know and that you didn't even know existed. For these, you will need to do some digging to identify what you should have known in the first place.

## Identifying gaps in your knowledge
Essentially, there are many ways in which you identify gaps in your knowledge:

- Assessing yourself against a known list of criteria (syllabus, tick list of skills to acquire, common level of competence for people at your level).

- Getting feedback from others.

- Through experience. You see someone who does something that you can't do or knows something that you don't know but that you feel you should know.

- Taking account of complaints and comments.

- Learning from your mistakes and bad experiences.

- Reflecting on your good experiences and how you could be even better.

**ISC**MEDICAL
Interview Skills Consulting

**Remedying your weaknesses**
Once you have explained how you go about identifying what you don't know then you should explain the steps that you take to bridge the gap. This could include:

- Seeking advice and learning from colleagues
- Attending suitable courses (in-house or external)
- Applying for suitable exams
- Reading books or finding information on the Internet
- Observing others
- Working extra-time to gain more experience
- Taking the initiative to get involved in activities or projects where you will gain further experience and confidence.

# QUESTION 73

**Which question would you most want to ask if you were interviewing others to enter medical school?**

The basis for this question is really to determine what you feel you should find out about a prospective doctor. Essentially, what you will want to know is whether the candidate is capable of going through medical school and capable of becoming a good doctor. The question you would most want to ask would therefore need to be fairly broad-ranging to allow the candidate to express himself about himself. In that respect, any question you would ask would revolve around the themes of motivation, ambition, and interpersonal skills. For example:

**Tell me about yourself? What can you offer to our school? What are your main strengths? Why should we choose you? Why are you the best candidate? Why do you think you will make a good doctor? etc.** These are questions of a similar nature that enable you to detect what a person feels they have to offer and how they organise information. To an extent, these questions also enable you to see how much preparation the candidate has done on a topic that they should know more than anyone else: themselves.

**Why do you want to do Medicine? Where do you see yourself in 10 years' time? What are you seeking to achieve in your medical career?** These questions are motivation questions that also allow the candidate to express and demonstrate a variety of skills.

Of course, there are many other questions that you can ask and this book will provide you with a wide range. It almost does not matter which question you choose providing you are able to explain what you are seeking to achieve by asking it. You should also describe what type of answer the candidate would need to give to convince you that they are suitable.

**Make sure that you are able to answer your own favourite question!**

Interview Skills Consulting

**Example of an effective answer**

*The question that I would most want to ask would be a question that is not too direct and gives the candidate a good opportunity to talk about their multiple facets while giving me information about their motivation for Medicine, their interpersonal skills, their ambitions and their organisational skills. The question would therefore need to be a general background question such as "Tell me about yourself", or "Why do you think you can cope with medical school?" Through these questions I would expect the candidate to present a wide range of information in an organised and easily digestible format, which would include:*

- *A general academic background*
- *A description of his work experience, what he observed and gained personally from them*
- *An idea of why he feels that Medicine is the career that he wishes to pursue*
- *An interest in research and teaching others*
- *His listening abilities and empathy as well as his ability to work well in teams and lead them when required*
- *An ability to make decisions*
- *A hard-working temperament, an ability to work well under pressure and a recognition that having a social life and hobbies is important to help anticipate stress and deal with it.*

ISCMEDICAL
Interview Skills Consulting

# QUESTION 74

**Tell us about an interesting book that you have read or film that you have seen.**

This question is fairly common and, contrary to appearance, it is not primarily designed to detect whether you have weird or eclectic tastes. No one will mind if you prefer watching horror movies instead of *The Little House on the Prairie* or if you prefer light-hearted comedies to books on social issues. What really matters is that there is something that interests you in the first place and that you are able to discuss why you enjoyed it.

Since you are only required to speak about one book or one film, it may be a good idea to place that book or film into the context of everything else that you enjoy reading or watching.

### Book or film?
Generally speaking, it is a safer bet to discuss a book than a film because:

- The success of a film does not rest entirely on the story line but also very much on the actors that it contains. If the interviewers happen to dislike the main actor or if the storyline was weak, you may struggle to make any impact.

- Books are more neutral in their approach and people do not tend to have such strong preconceived ideas about them. In addition they represent a greater effort from your part (it takes longer to read a book than to watch a film with the same story) and this may subconsciously go in your favour.

### Which one should you choose?
The choice of a good book or film is always difficult. You should select a book or film that you have really enjoyed so that you can talk about it in a passionate way. Each type of book or film can help you raise different issues. For example:

***Biographies*** are an ideal platform to discuss social issues, how success can be reached and how to overcome hurdles, how someone may have inspired you, etc. (assuming you read Mandela's or Gandhi's biography and not Donald Duck's).

***Novels*** are a good platform to raise social issues, stories about good and bad communication, resilience, power, etc; all of which can then be discussed in a generalised fashion. Again you would need to select a novel that would place you in a positive light to start with (e.g. you might think about avoiding mentioning Barbara Cartland).

***Thrillers/Crime novels*** are a good tool to talk about the power of analysis and deduction, together with the satisfaction of following a hero through the process. Crime novels are also a good platform to reflect on teamwork, leadership and communication.

***Comedies*** can be mentioned although you would need to make sure that you can derive more out of them than a simple indescribable personal enjoyment.

Whatever you wish to choose, ensure that you do not limit yourself to quoting a title and an author. Go into some depth about what you gained from the film or the book.

### Example of an effective answer

*One of the books that I found interesting recently is The Da Vinci Code by Dan Brown. Looking beyond the controversy that the book created, I found that it was thoroughly entertaining as it had a good pace and an enjoyable plot, full of intrigue. Although I never felt that it was written in the best possible prose, I thought that Dan Brown did very well in keeping the reader's imagination despite the complexity of the scenario. One of the other aspects that I enjoyed about the book is the manner in which it interprets the history of arts and the manner in which it portrays Michelangelo's work.*

*Generally speaking, I enjoy reading all sorts of books ranging from historical novels to biographies and thrillers. I try to read two or three good books per month. I find reading very soothing and I feel that it complements well the other activities that I do, such as sport and music, to help me relax when I have been exposed to pressure and stress.*

Note how the description steers clear of the controversies surrounding the book and presents a generic critique of the content of the book from a personal perspective. Also, the answer highlights a few features of the book from your point of view but does not go into a massive amount of detail (you don't want to bore the interviewers). If they want to know more, they can ask; it will give you an opportunity to take the interview to the level of a discussion rather than an interrogation, which will help you achieve a better rapport with them. Finally, note how the answer concludes by broadening the subject onto other hobbies (no harm in reminding them!) and how they help you relieve pressure and stress.

## Another example of an effective answer

*One of the films that I particularly enjoyed watching was Tea with Mussolini, with Judy Dench, Maggie Smith and Cher. The film dealt with life in Italy during Mussolini's reign and particularly about the escape of an American Jewish woman played by Cher. It was a pleasant mix of historic reality and of comedy which made it appealing to all ages. One of the things that I enjoyed about the film was the portrayal of solidarity between human beings in very difficult situations and the fact that those who had nothing to gain from the situation went out of their way to save the American Jewish woman. I also enjoyed the frequent references to art, through Judy Dench who was playing a mad artist based in Tuscany.*

*As well as watching films that have a historic base, I also enjoy comedies, adventure films and romantic films. Another film that I have enjoyed is The English Patient, which deals with the handling of human emotions. I enjoy going to the cinema with friends as well as watching videos. As well as helping me relieve stress, it gives me a good opportunity to socialise with my friends and colleagues.*

# QUESTION 75

**Do you know what it is like to be a medical student?**

This question is not only about your idea of what the next 5 years will be like but also about how you found out about it. This would include open days, talking to students and lecturers, reading the prospectus, visiting the school's website, etc. You need to present a balanced view of medical school but ultimately you must make sure that you emphasise the work required and the skills needed more than the social aspect.

### Example of an ineffective answer

*I think the next 5 years are going to be very hard. I am very motivated and enthusiastic, so I will attend all lectures and complete essays and pass exams at the highest standards. I will excel in finals and other activities. I really think you will not be disappointed in selecting me.*

This answer is a bit basic, trying to push the right buttons without really going about it in a subtle manner. Also, it does not show a great level of awareness of medical school and why it will be hard.

### Example of an effective answer

*Nobody can really say that they know what it is like to be a medical student if they have not been through medical school themselves; however, having spoken to many people and read up on it, I feel that I have a good idea of what is awaiting me. It is no secret that medical school is hard and can sometimes be stressful. All the students that I have talked to during the open day have mentioned this as the biggest step that they have had to overcome. There are many lectures and workshops to attend, homework and personal studies to undertake, presentations to prepare and generally an awful lot of information to assimilate. On top of this we all come from an environment where we have been spoon-fed a lot and we are going into an environment where we have to think for ourselves, which requires a lot of personal skills and resilience. As a medical student, you have to know how to work in teams. You also have to know how and when to take the*

*initiative and take leadership in the projects that you are handling. You also need to keep your knowledge up to date by reading up on issues and finding your own information. Being someone who is very organised and meticulous, I am ready for all this. At the same time, I also have a number of personal interests which will enable me to deal with the pressure and stress involved. I intend to continue to pursue my sporting interests in football and rowing with my new friends at university.*

# QUESTION 76

**Why do some students who qualify as doctors give up Medicine and never practice?**

This is a question about some of the less appealing aspects of Medicine. To produce a complete answer, you will need to think about the different aspects of the profession. Using the TAGS framework (p.14) should help you with this.

### Training & Experience / Clinical
- They find Medicine too complex or the training too lengthy.
- Too much learning to be done before you can have responsibilities.
- They can't cope with being personally responsible for a patients' life or death.
- They come from an environment where they were the best and, amongst people of a similar calibre, they do not feel that they can shine.
- The exams are a burden and once you qualify there are more exams and assessments. It will take years to become a consultant.

### Academic
- They do not enjoy research or reading about it. It was fun as a 17-year-old but reading research papers at a more complex level is no longer enjoyable.
- They do not enjoy teaching others or get frustrated having to work with juniors who are not independent.

### Generic
- Teamwork is not for them; they might prefer a profession where they can be more independent.
- Medicine is stressful. As well as long hours and big responsibilities, you have to cope with sick people all the time (including children) and death.
- They do not feel particularly ambitious and they feel uncomfortable in a competitive environment.
- Their ambitions lie elsewhere (e.g. they might have been pushed into Medicine by their parents).

- It can be demoralising to deal with people who complain about every little thing or people who have high expectations.
- They can't multitask.

### Social
- Long hours or unsociable hours can make it difficult to have a stable private life.
- No regular pattern to life means that it can be difficult to plan and have regular hobbies.
- Some doctors change job often. This can disrupt family life.
- Health problems or personal problems.
- No real financial reward (no bonuses as big as in the City!). Friends who are not doctors have a better lifestyle and more money.
- Jobs are not guaranteed. What would you do if you did not succeed to gain a position that you liked?

### Delivering the answer
The question is very factual and all you need to do is develop a number of the key ideas described above. Simply list them in some kind of orderly fashion (TAGS should help you) and explain what you mean for each.

### Concluding your answer
It would be a good idea to conclude the answer by reminding the panel about a few good qualities. This could be something like:

> *As far as I am concerned, I am a tenacious person with high ambitions. I am also very determined and well organised. This, I am sure, will help me get through the difficult times that are unavoidable.*

# QUESTION 77

**Studying for Medicine is a long and stressful process. What makes you think that you can cope with it?**

This question is really about motivation and handling stress. The answer to it will therefore combine a number of elements that we have encountered in previous questions. Amongst other things, you will need to talk about:

- Your motivation for Medicine and your hard-working nature
- Your ability to handle stress and work well under pressure
- Your organisation skills and ability to multitask
- Your ability to seek help when necessary
- Your ability to work in teams and your sociability
- Your work-life balance.

Again, you will need to raise each point in turn and back them up with personal examples that show that you have demonstrated those attributes.

### Example of an effective answer

*Going into Medicine is a decision that I have reached by myself having weighed the positives and negatives of the profession and I would not go into it if I did not feel that I could cope. I have always worked very hard in everything that I have done and working in an environment that is stressful and demanding is more likely to motivate me further rather than put me off Medicine. I have good organisation and time management skills, which helps manage several tasks at the same time and ensures that I can plan my work ahead. For example, last year I was able to sail through my studies and achieve good marks and to find the time to have a Saturday job as well as my work experience and a couple of hobbies.*

*I get on well with people at all levels and, in particular, I find it easy to ask for assistance and advice when I need it. This means that, if I have a problem, I can find a way out very quickly, which saves time and worry. Finally, I have good mechanisms to deal with stress and pressure. I have*

*learnt some very good relaxation techniques which helped me through my 'A' Levels. I also like playing music and doing drama, and I am hoping to be able to continue some of these activities at medical school. I am very close to my family and to a couple of very good friends and I know that they will provide me with the moral support that I will need during the next 5 years.*

# QUESTION 78

**What do you know about problem-based learning (PBL)? How does it compare with traditional teaching methods?**

## Problem-based learning
PBL is a teaching method used in many medical schools in the UK. It is a method whereby you "learn to learn", which, for some candidates, is a big departure from the spoon-feeding that they have been receiving until now. As the name indicates, it is problem-based, i.e. you are given a problem, scenario, issue or question to resolve. That problem is multidimensional and therefore contains a range of learning points.

In order to find solutions, you tend to work with a small group of other medical students between whom various tasks will be allocated. Once everyone has done their research, the group will meet and the topic in question discussed. That discussion may lead to further problems being identified, with further research and meetings needed to finalise a solution and consolidate learning points. In order to ensure that the learning process is efficient and that time wasting is minimised, PBL groups are supervised by a facilitator/tutor who will ensure that the group keeps its sense of purpose and direction.

## How it compares with traditional methods
In most cases, the traditional method of teaching includes 2 years of preclinical studies, during which basic subjects such as biochemistry, physiology, anatomy, pharmacology and sociology are taught in a lecture format. After the 2 years, students may choose to embark on a BSc programme. Alternatively, the students may choose to embark on a 3-year clinical programme, where they are exposed to all specialties in the clinical setting. Hence the approach is much more academic. It is sometimes referred to as "system-based", i.e. you learn Medicine by system (heart, lungs, kidneys, etc.) rather than by using a problem that may deal with several systems at the same time.

**What are the advantages and disadvantages of PBL?**

## Advantages of PBL
- Provides a practical view of Medicine, as applied to concrete problems.
- Suits well those who have initiative. Promotes entrepreneurial spirit.
- Small group teaching. More involvement from each student (whereas traditional teaching may be more passive in nature).
- Relies on teamwork. You can therefore learn from others.
- Since you will have spent time researching a topic, you will be more familiar with the details than if they had been spoon-fed.
- Can be more rewarding once you achieve your desired objective.
- Promotes team spirit.
- Facilitator makes sure that you do not go off track.
- Early exposure to real-life issues and patient contact.

## Disadvantages of PBL
- Quality of the learning depends on the quality of the problem or scenarios. A badly set up PBL programme can yield little results.
- Some topics may be best taught formally.
- PBL teaching only works if, at the end of the year, you have acquired the full knowledge that you were meant to acquire. If there are gaps, you may need to complement it by attending more traditional lectures or by doing more of your own reading.
- Relies on the quality of the facilitator's input. Rigorous training is essential.
- Students who have a more academic way of learning may not feel entirely at ease.
- Your learning experience depends on the work others in the team are willing to put in. The team may be disrupted by a lazy or non-motivated student. It could also be made dysfunctional by a student who wants to go too quickly and is more interested in getting a result than in learning.

Interview Skills Consulting

# QUESTION 80

**What are the advantages and disadvantages of traditional teaching?**

### Advantages of traditional teaching
- Suits candidates who are autonomous in their learning
- Presents full information in a systematic basis about all systems and relevant syllabus items
- Easy to set up
- Ensures all candidates receive the same information
- Provides good background before students are "released" on patients. They might benefit more from that patient contact when it takes place
- Students drive their own learning experience.

### Disadvantages of traditional teaching
- Provides theoretical background with no real-life application for the first few years
- Patient contact is delayed, which may demotivate some students (who had a more practical idea of Medicine)
- Does not suit people who learn in a less structured manner
- Sitting in on endless lectures can be boring
- Students may be intimidated in a large theatre and may not have the courage to participate and ask questions
- The pace of learning is regulated by a big group and, if you are not above the average, you may be at a disadvantage. Conversely, if you are towards the top, you might find it frustrating to have to comply with the average speed.

ISCMEDICAL
Interview Skills Consulting

# QUESTION 81

**What do you know about our course, why does it suit you and why does it interest you?**

The answer will depend on the type of teaching that the school provides, whether it is PBL, traditional or mixed. Before the interview, make sure that you have read their syllabus, looked at their website and, if possible, talked to students at the school.

### Example of an effective answer for a PBL school

*From what I have read in the prospectus and on your website, I can see that XXX medical school adopts new teaching methods such as PBL. I have learnt a lot about PBL after talking to a few medical students and also reading about the subject and I find that it is a method that suits the way that I like to learn. I find that sitting in big lecture theatres can sometimes be counterproductive as you simply have to assimilate information. I like the fact that PBL provides a practical approach to Medicine, which is really what Medicine is about, as opposed to simply reading books, which can be quite dry. I have always enjoyed finding out information by myself and in that sense the PBL approach, with its supervised small group structure, is ideal. In fact, it is similar to the approach that I took when I revised for my 'A' Levels, when I organised a small study group with a couple of my friends so that we could learn together and utilise our time more effectively. I like the idea of learning from each other in a small team; this is less intimidating and promotes team spirit. I am focused, enthusiastic and organised and I think these qualities will enable me to make a good contribution to my team in a PBL environment.*

Interview Skills Consulting

**Example of an effective answer (traditional teaching)**

*From what I have read in the prospectus and on the website, I understand that XXX medical school adopts the traditional methods of learning and that, in the first few years, students attend lectures on pre-clinical subjects such as biochemistry, anatomy and physiology. This is the method that I have always been taught with and which I have found successful in the past. I always find attending lessons or lectures the first step of learning as it gives me the background of the subject, and I can then build on it by reading books. I am a motivated and focused person who studies well independently.*

*I am sometimes a little bit frustrated with truncated learning methods such as PBL, where one has the opportunity to learn only a segment of a vast subject, although it can sometimes have advantages in terms of giving a practical view on things. Overall, I feel that the teaching that the school offers, together with the level of support available through workshops and personal tutors, is a good and efficient system, and I am confident that it will enable me to exploit my full potential.*

# QUESTION 82

**This course requires a great deal of independent study. Will you manage?**

In order to demonstrate that you can study independently, the best thing that you can do is to not speak hypothetically but to bring forward all your experience and your ability to organise yourself, plan your work and use all resources available to help you achieve your goals.

Be careful though; by talking about your independence, there is a small danger that you end up sounding selfish and like a loner. Although you want to demonstrate that you can study independently at university, you still have to show that you are flexible. The education system in Medicine is evolving all the time; it is important to have a flexible attitude towards your own education.

**Example of an effective answer**

> *For my GCSEs and in my sixth form, I was very independent in the way that I organised my studies. Obviously, I attended all lessons to gain a good understanding of each topic and I did all the homework required. I also took the initiative to gain information from different books about the topics that we were studying and by visiting related websites to broaden my understanding. Being able to study the same issues in different ways was very useful in giving me a thorough understanding of the topics.*
>
> *I am a goal-oriented, organised and enthusiastic person and I study well on my own. I also find it interesting and relaxing to study in small groups. On occasions, when a topic was more difficult, I organised discussions with my friends so that we could think about the issue together.*
>
> *Having already built up the culture of independent study, I feel that I can take this with me to my university education and be equally successful.*

# QUESTION 83

**60% of medical school applicants are female. Why do you think that is?**

No one really knows the real reason, and there are probably several factors that come into play. You will therefore be judged on your ability to display a range of possible reasons and on the clarity of your reasoning.

- **Statistics:** there are more girls than boys alive at the age of 17 anyway for several reasons including the fact that more girls than boys are born and that boys experience a higher mortality than girls during their teenage years due to risk taking.

- **Academic success:** girls tend to perform better than boys at exams, achieving better grades. They may also feel that they can resist the pressures of medical school better than boys.

- **Government campaigns:** for a long time, Medicine was a male-dominated profession and the government campaigned hard to encourage girls to take up the profession. This may have led to an increase in applications through the influence of school teachers.

- **Work-Life balance:** Medicine has changed dramatically. A general awareness of the stress levels experienced by doctors together with the introduction of the European Working Time Directive has helped reduce working hours. In addition, numerous posts have been created for flexible trainees and workers. This makes it easier for women who want to have a family to pursue a career at the same time. The most dramatic effect has been for GPs.

- **Type of work:** women may feel more at ease in building a good rapport with patients. Also, boys may be more inclined to take up jobs that pay more, such as law and finance.

# QUESTION 84

**What are the extended roles of nurses in healthcare?**

The issue of "extended roles of nurses" has become increasingly topical and is causing many controversies. We will deal with these in the next question. Generally speaking, you must be very careful to consider nurses respectfully as there may be one on the panel and, in any case, it is always good to demonstrate a little bit of respect and team spirit towards people with whom you will be working. During your medical career, nurses will greatly contribute towards your education and your ability to care for your patients effectively.

**Background**
The introduction of the European Working Time Directive has led to a decrease in the number of working hours for doctors. The overall impact is that more doctors are needed to care for patients; this has encouraged the profession and the government to take a number of steps.

One of these steps has been to recognise that some of the tasks traditionally performed by doctors could actually be done by other people if these people were adequately trained. Similarly, a number of patients could be seen by other health professionals instead of doctors. As a result, some nurses have been able to take on an extended role.

**How have nurses' roles been extended?**
The main areas nurses are involved in are:

- **Clinical nurse practitioners in specialist fields.** These are nurses who have a lot of experience in one specialty and can take on some of the duties traditionally performed by doctors in that specialty. This could involve running specialist clinics, following up on patients previously seen by a doctor, and even doing minor operations or procedures. These nurses can take histories and examine patients, carry out investigations, and prescribe drugs (within limits set down by protocols and signed off by consultants). Nurses can also run walk-in centres where they can make

decisions about acute patient care. There are several grades, running up to "nurse consultant".

- **Nurse managers.** These are nurses who have taken on a managerial role; for example, recently, we have seen the reintroduction of matrons on wards. In the community, there are nurses who are responsible for managing other nurses over an entire region.

- **Research nurses.** A small number of nurses are involved in research activities.

See the next question for the advantages and disadvantages of the increasing role of nurses.

# QUESTION 85

**What are the advantages and disadvantages of the increasing role of nurses?**

Your answer to this question should be diplomatic. This is a controversial issue on which many doctors hold very strong views. At the interview, your job is not to get into this controversy but to debate the advantages and disadvantages. Also, don't forget that nurses may be on the panel. Be careful not to upset them!

### Advantages
- It may free up doctors' time, which enables doctors to concentrate on more complex patients or procedures. In turn, this reduces waiting lists and therefore increases patient satisfaction.

- It can provide better continuity of care for patients. Doctors change posts often throughout their training whereas nurses do not move on as frequently.

- Nurses may be able to spend more time with patients. This also increases patient satisfaction and may help identify other issues that could not be identified in a short consultation time (e.g. psychosocial issues).

- It acts as a motivator for nurses, who can now have careers well beyond the basic nursing level. This encourages retention of staff, motivation and good morale.

- It may be more cost effective. However, some studies have shown that in fact the savings are not noticeable or that nurses may actually prove more expensive. Although most nurses (not all!) do get paid less than doctors, they may see patients for a longer period of time and, if they cannot deal with a patient, they will still refer them to the doctor (when it may have been more cost effective for the patient to see the doctor in the first place).

**Disadvantages**

- Nurses are taken away from frontline nursing care (though admittedly only a small number of nurses are affected by this).

- Nurses take charge of simpler patients and simple procedures, which were traditionally dealt with by junior doctors. This will therefore reduce the opportunities for junior doctors to encounter these patients and procedures, which will impact on their training.

- Nurses with extended roles work on a protocol basis. Their input is therefore limited to the boundaries of the protocol. In addition, since the nurses' training is not as comprehensive as the doctors', they may not be able to recognise at all times when a patient should be handled outside the protocol.

- There is an issue of patients' confidence. Patients may not want to be treated by nurses and may request that a qualified doctor deals with them instead.

To finish on a positive note, it would be good to explain how ultimately it is all about finding the right balance so that doctors and nurses can share duties but in a way that works best for patients (who should be everyone's first priority).

# QUESTION 86

**Does the bulk of medical treatment occur in the community or in hospital?**

The short answer is: in the community.

Your reasoning should include:
- Many people self-medicate. You do this when you buy any drug without prescription at your local pharmacy or supermarket.

- GPs are the obligatory first port of call and many people do not go on to see a specialist following a GP consultation.

- Recently, GPs have started to develop special interests (diabetes, dermatology, ophthalmology, minor surgery, etc.) and actually provide basic specialist care in clinics at their practice. This reduces further the burden on hospital doctors.

- A large number of patients have chronic diseases (asthma, diabetes, arthritis, etc.). Once the patient has been seen by a specialist, the care is often transferred to the GP, who will monitor and manage the treatment. Treatment may then be either self-administered or provided by community nurses.

- There are specialist doctors such as community paediatricians or community psychiatrists who provide treatment in the community.

- Hospital specialists are encouraged to run "outreach" clinics, i.e. beyond the hospital site.

Overall, hospital treatment actually covers a small proportion of medical treatment. The government is currently pushing to substantially increase the amount of care being provided in the community and this trend can therefore only grow.

**How do politics influence healthcare decisions?**

There is an ongoing debate about whether the NHS would be better run by clinicians or by politicians. An argument in favour of clinicians is that they know best what patients need and the impact that decisions could have on the ground. An argument in favour of politicians is that the NHS is a public institution funded by taxpayers and that it is therefore only right that policy should be directed by people who have been elected by those who fund it.

Currently, politics have a major impact on the delivery of healthcare. Examples would include:

1. **Working hours:** the European Working Time Directive has substantially reduced the number of hours that a doctor can work (by limiting the working time of anyone who is employed to 48 hours per week). This has led to a need for more doctors, a need for better and more focused training and a need for a change in the role of other workers such as nurses, as well as a reorganisation of shift patterns. Further reforms may need to be implemented if European legislation imposes a degree of uniformity across all health systems around the EU.

2. **Funding:** the level of care that the NHS can provide is dictated by the budget that the government makes available. That budget comes from National Insurance contributions, which must be limited if the elected politicians do not want to incur the wrath of the electorate. Thus, for a politician, it is a trade-off between well-funded quality healthcare and not losing votes because of high taxes.

3. **Rationing:** because budgets are never enough to provide the full care that patients would expect, choices have to be made about how scarce resources should be allocated. Restrictions can be implemented in many ways; for example by not allowing some categories of people to have access to certain drugs or surgery, or by not allowing some drugs or

treatments on the NHS at all (e.g. most drugs used for cosmetic purposes). These are political decisions.

4.  **Targeted investments:** by making fundamental policy decisions and major investments at a high level, with huge impact on the ground; most recently, the introduction of the Choose & Book system to allow GPs to book patients directly into hospital clinics, the introduction of a centralised information storage system for patient records or the change to the training structure of junior doctors.

5.  **Public health:** by funding major campaigns for issues of major importance and helping the NHS pass on messages to the general public (e.g. the fight against sexually transmitted diseases, MMR vaccination, etc.) aimed at changing public perception.

6.  **Regulation:** politics can also intervene indirectly; for example through the regulation of the pharmaceutical industry, which is a major source of funds for clinical research. There is a fine line between making sure that drugs are purchased at a reasonable price from companies so that best possible use can be made of taxpayers' money, while ensuring that pharmaceuticals retain the means to fund appropriate research.

# QUESTION 88

**Do you think it is right to allow private healthcare to run alongside the NHS?**

You should ensure that you set out the pros and cons of private healthcare before you give your own opinion. At the interview, make sure that you do not engage in political lobbying against the unfairness of a private sector reserved for the rich of this world. It may be unfair but there are two sides to the coin and you must demonstrate that you can show depth of thought, an open mind and the ability to present convincing arguments in a clear manner.

### Arguments in favour of private healthcare

1.  Private healthcare takes patients away from the NHS waiting lists. This means that NHS users can actually be treated more quickly as a result.

2.  Those who use private healthcare facilities actually pay twice. They pay their standard National Insurance contributions and also have to pay for their healthcare privately on top of that. For the NHS, it means that the money can be redirected to other patients instead. Incidentally, at the last general election, the Conservatives were proposing that patients who used private healthcare should have part of their care paid for by the NHS. The idea was that they should benefit from part of the saving that the NHS made on them. The idea did not catch on at the time.

3.  Some private healthcare is actually subcontracted back to the NHS (for example a private hospital may not be able to afford an MRI scanner and might send its patients to have it done at the local NHS hospital in exchange for payment). Similarly, some hospitals have private wards, which are rented to their doctors in the context of their private work.

4.  Some doctors with higher ambitions want to supplement their income through private work. An impossibility to do private work could lead to doctors leaving Medicine, or leaving the country, or even taking on other

jobs. All this would reduce their availability to the NHS (so-called 'brain-drain').

5. The NHS cannot cope with all the demands placed upon it because of budgetary constraints. Introducing a private sector into the equation creates a market economy which should drive efficiency and ultimately create better results (Note that the trend is now to create a market economy within the health system, precisely for this reason – in particular, GPs will be able to refer patients to the NHS and the private sector alike, within set constraints).

6. If there were no private healthcare sector in the UK, many people might go abroad to receive treatment. Any subsequent complications of substandard treatment would still have to be followed up by the NHS when patients return to the UK. One could therefore argue that you might as well treat patients where you can control the standard of care rather than having to deal with the consequences of their treatment abroad. If too many people went abroad, they might also refuse to pay their National Insurance contributions, which would have serious consequences for society and the NHS.

7. There is a fundamental issue of personal liberty and individual choice. Should a rich person be denied access to important care simply on the basis that a poorer person could not afford it and on the basis of equity?

**Arguments against private healthcare**
1. Private healthcare primarily benefits the wealthier part of the population or people who are employed by some of the bigger companies. This leads to inequality by selecting against the poorest (who also tend to be the neediest). "The haves and the have-nots."

2. Some private institutions subcontract services back to the NHS. For example, a private hospital might send its patients to the local NHS hospital for an MRI scan, with those patients effectively buying priority slots and jumping queues. Also, there are so-called "private wards" in NHS hospitals, reserved for private patients of the NHS doctors working at that hospital. NHS doctors and nurses may still be called to these patients, e.g. in an emergency, which would take them away from their work. This inevitably diverts NHS time and resources away.

3. Because private healthcare is financially driven, there is an issue with the motivation of the doctor, which may not necessarily be altruistic. Also, with a financial incentive, doctors may be more inclined to follow the patient's wishes rather than their best clinical judgement (i.e. have a commercial relationship). This motivation may also mean that patients are booked for investigations that may not be required (in a bid to extract money from insurance companies). Such investigations may even be detrimental to health (e.g. too much exposure to X-rays).

4. Time spent by doctors treating private patients would be better spent treating NHS patients. (In practice, this argument is a bit weak as such doctors would do their private work in their own time.)

5. Private healthcare does not provide full coverage. If a patient is in a private setting and requires intensive care urgently, this patient may be worse off as he may need to be transported to a better equipped establishment such as a local NHS hospital. The patient may suffer from this delay in implementing more dependent care.

**Discussion**

Once you have set out a range of pros and cons, you need to give your own opinion. This should be fairly balanced (some people on the panel may have a private practice while some others may be firmly against it). In fact, you may want to conclude that the arguments on both sides are so powerful that it is difficult to see how a definite answer could be given without upsetting half of the population.

# QUESTION 89

**How should healthcare be funded?**

First of all, you must get out of your mind the fact that there is a right or a wrong answer to this. This question is an ongoing question in politics and, if they have been fighting over it for dozens of years in Parliament, you won't find the answer in 2 minutes at an interview.

What this question is really asking you is whether you can have a small debate between the various options, which takes us back primarily to the previous question: "Do you think it is right to allow private healthcare to run alongside the NHS?" However, it may be an idea to have some basic knowledge of what is going on around the world too. Here are a few broad examples:

**Scandinavia:** healthcare is funded solely by taxpayers. As a result, taxation is high and private healthcare is not very prominent.

**USA:** the majority of healthcare provision is through the private sector and only the poor are treated by the State. Everyone else must have insurance cover to fund their own healthcare.

**France:** Mixed system. Taxation is high to finance a public system used by everyone. Individual practitioners charge whatever they wish for each consultation or treatment. A set tariff is reimbursed to the patient by the State. The difference between the actual fee and the reimbursed tariff is picked up by a private insurance company if the patient has taken out excess insurance.

Ultimately, every system has its advantages and its flaws. Every system is constantly criticised either for being too expensive, too unfair, too inefficient or too open to abuse. In addition, local culture plays an important part in deciding what different societies find acceptable. For example, a US-style system would be difficult to introduce in Europe where social protection is high on the agenda.

Interview Skills Consulting

# QUESTION 90

**What do you think about the way doctors are perceived in the media?**

There is a tendency for candidates to view the media's perception of doctors as negative. In a sense, a degree of negativity is inevitable since happy events do not make exciting news unless they are truly outstanding, while the slightest negative anecdote can make front page news. The ongoing occurrence of various scandals (Shipman, Northwick Park research trials, etc.) does not help their cause either.

You must first present the different points of view before discussing your opinion. And don't forget that the word "media" includes a wide range of media and not just tabloid newspapers.

**Positive portrayal of doctors in the media:**
- Heroic events such as the role of doctors and paramedics during the aftermath of the 7 July 2005 bombings.
- Pioneering operations such as the separation of conjoint twins.
- Important discoveries such as a possible vaccine for cervical cancer. (Although such discoveries are not always made by doctors, but often by research scientists, they are often associated with clinicians in the public's mind.)
- Glorifying and glamorising doctors through well-known TV series, showing amazing feats of deduction, clinical skills and procedures in a dramatised fashion, presenting doctors as god-like characters.
- Fly-on-the-wall documentaries that show real-life doctors doing day-to-day caring, where the viewers can easily relate to the patients.

**Negative portrayal of doctors in the media:**
- Dr Shipman killing numerous patients.
- Major scandals such The Bristol Heart Hospital Scandal, organ retention scandal at Alder Hey Hospital (Liverpool), clinical research going wrong at Northwick Park Hospital, etc.
- Controversial topics such as MMR and autism.
- Doctors involved in botched operations and generally any GMC investigation related in the media.
- Financial gains made by doctors (private practice, GP salaries).

**What do you think about the portrayal of doctors?**
In your discussion about the portrayal of doctors, you will need to discuss whether the portrayal is correct and fair. Arguments that you may wish to develop include:

- The media are using information to generate sales or advertising. Therefore the tendency is to present newsworthy items, which are often at the two extremes of the spectrum (either very positive or very negative). This may give people the wrong impression about doctors. Very positive news may raise expectations beyond reason. Very negative news may decrease public confidence.

- The media play an important role in highlighting the flaws of the system and exposing faulty practices. This ensures that the system does not cover up any wrongdoing and that doctors stick to a behaviour characterised by personal integrity.

- The media play an important role in debating important health issues and in questioning political decisions. For example, the controversy about the MMR vaccine was fuelled by the media in search of the truth. This forced all parties to reveal their evidence, and increased transparency. This quest for transparency keeps doctors alert and ensures that they remain accurate in the messages that they convey to the public.

# QUESTION 91

**What does the phrase "inequalities in healthcare" mean to you?**

Inequalities in healthcare occur when individuals or groups are not treated in the same manner as others in similar situations. There are several ways in which inequalities in healthcare manifest themselves, which we have set out below. In your answer, you should address a handful of these points (and others that you may have derived for yourself). Do not just list them, but expand on them a little to show an understanding of the issues.

### Socio-economic inequalities

Parts of the population are less educated than others and consequently have a poorer understanding of their own health needs and poor awareness of the availability of appropriate services. This has several consequences:

- Common health prevention messages may not find their way to the individuals concerned (avoiding unwanted pregnancies, smoking cessation, healthy eating, living and lifestyle). For this reason, the government is enhancing health promotion targeting through the appropriate media.

- Available services may not be used to their optimum by people in such vulnerable groups. The government is promoting a drive to increase the level of services being provided in a community setting, which should address part of that problem.

Similar arguments and solutions exist for other minority groups based on ethnicity, language barriers and immigration status.

### Geographical distribution of healthcare resources

This is commonly referred to as "postcode lottery". It refers to the fact that individuals are receiving different levels of care depending on the region where they live. For example:

- There is a geographic concentration of resources and skills. People living in urban areas have easier access to healthcare facilities (including GPs) than people living in cities.

- Primary Care Trusts can make independent decisions about the provision of treatment based on their available budgets. This can mean that treatments available in one Trust may not be made available in another Trust.

**Public healthcare vs. private healthcare**
See Q.88 for comprehensive arguments.

# QUESTION 92

**What are the arguments for and against people paying for their own healthcare?**

Be careful with this question. Its wording suggests that it is not about public vs. private sectors (see Q.88) but about what the consequences would be of moving from the current insurance-based system in the UK to a system whereby patients would pay for their healthcare as and when they need it (as if they were going shopping). If in doubt, ask the interviewers to clarify what they mean.

### Arguments for paying for your own healthcare
- Currently, you pay National Insurance contributions whether you need the NHS or not. Under this other system you would only pay for what you need. This would be a distinct advantage if your health is good.

- It would prevent time-wasting patient visits (e.g. patients going to the GP for a simple cold) as patients would only go if they really needed to.

- It would introduce competition at doctors' level, which would lead to a "fight" for your custom and therefore increased standards of care.

- It may encourage people to have healthier lifestyles in order to minimise the need to use healthcare facilities.

### Arguments against paying for your own healthcare
- It would place the poorest at a clear disadvantage. Not only are they the neediest group, they are also those who could afford healthcare the least.

- Knowing that they have to pay, some patients may put off going to see a doctor or may not go at all. This may cause problems if medical attention is urgently required.

Interview Skills Consulting

- This may encourage situations whereby doctors refuse to treat patients until payment has been made, even in cases of emergency (there have been cases in the US where doctors refused to admit patients until someone could produce a credit card).

- With a choice between several possible treatments or procedures, patients may choose the cheapest available as opposed to one with the best outcome.

- Patients with chronic illnesses would face spiralling costs, at a time when they may also be out of work.

- It would create a relationship between the doctor and the patient that is based on money. This may affect the doctor's integrity as he may be more inclined to follow the patient's wishes rather than what he feels is best for the patient.

- Unscrupulous doctors could take advantage of the process by organising more investigations than required or referring patients to their friends.

- Some patients may turn to cheaper alternatives such as some forms of alternative medicines, which may not be adequate or even safe for their condition.

- It may encourage a black market in health practices, which would be unregulated and dangerous for patients (see, for example, the practice of backstreet abortions before abortion was legalised).

# QUESTION 93

**How does Medicine now compare with 100 years ago?**

## Knowledge and Medical Advancement

- 100 years ago, there was less scientific knowledge. Doctors did not understand fully the mechanics and chemistry of the human body; they mainly treated symptoms in the best way they could but did not have the tools to get a full picture of the origins of a particular condition.

- Technology has led to a number of inventions (X-rays, MRI scanning, CT scanning, ultrasounds, etc.) that have enabled doctors to produce more accurate diagnoses. Medical knowledge has expanded massively since WWII along with the levels of communication (travel, telecommunications, computers, Internet.). This has enabled scientists and doctors to share information more readily and has greatly enhanced medical research. This in turn has resulted in the development of diagnosis and treatments.

## Specialisation

- 100 years ago, doctors were mostly General Practitioners. There was not enough knowledge to have specialist doctors in many fields.

- Nowadays, there are over 60 specialties, some of which are branching out further.

## Attitude towards patients

- 100 years ago, Medicine was fairly paternalistic. It also adopted a "doctor knows best" approach (the doctor was the boss and patients did what they were told).

- Nowadays, Medicine attracts a much more varied population (more women, doctors from various ethnic backgrounds, etc.). The emphasis is on patient-centred care and doctors have essentially become patient health managers. Their role is to propose. Except for a few scenarios, the final decision always rests with the patient.

**Free care and formalised frameworks for regulation and probity**

- 100 years ago, the NHS did not exist (created 1948) and most of the care was provided on a private basis, i.e. essentially reserved for the rich. Nowadays, care is provided more or less free of charge to everyone.

- The Royal Colleges and other institutions such as the GMC evolved to take on a regulatory role and to become the guardians of high clinical standards. Since the 1990s, this has been marked by the introduction of the clinical governance framework (see Q.102).

**Nature of the work, role of the doctor**

- 100 years ago, the emphasis was on treating symptoms. Because doctors had little understanding of diseases, there was little emphasis on prevention.

- Nowadays, and particularly since the 1980s, there is much more emphasis on prevention to deal with the more common diseases (lung cancer, cardiac diseases, skin cancer, etc.). The arrival of the Internet has also facilitated the dissemination of information and therefore helped raise the level of awareness of the population.

- The doctor now has a wider role. He does not only treat patients but also gets involved in regular teaching activities. He is also required to audit his own practice and may get involved in management issues (risk management, staff management, etc.).

**Revolutionary changes to the nature of diseases to be treated**

- A number of major discoveries have changed the nature of the beast doctors were fighting. Vaccination has enabled humans to control a large number of common diseases and antibiotics have also radically altered the management of common infections. Coupled with a strong hygiene policy and medical advancement, this has raised the life expectancy of the population considerably. This does not come without consequences (more cancers, more geriatric diseases, etc.).

- For the most part, the UK has an affluent ageing population, which has led to the evolution of diseases "of excess" such as coronary heart disease.

- New diseases have also emerged (such as HIV/AIDS) to complicate the picture further.

**Multi-disciplinary approach to patient care**

- 100 years ago, most doctors practised in isolation. Nowadays, the emphasis is on teamwork and a multidisciplinary approach. This involves doctors with doctors from other specialties at all grades. It also involves working with specialists from other disciplines and associated professionals such as specialist nurses, physiotherapists, occupational therapists, dieticians and social workers.

Note that the above applied principally to the UK and other developed countries. In the developing world, the picture is different. New technologies are slowly finding their way there, but infectious diseases and malnutrition remain the main preoccupation in an environment where resources are limited.

# QUESTION 94

**What are alternative medicines / complementary therapies?**
**What is your opinion on them?**

**What they are?**
These terms apply to therapies that are different to conventional medicine, i.e. the medicine taught at medical schools in the UK. They tend to be given by non-medical practitioners, although some doctors now integrate some of these therapies within their practice. They can come in many forms, including:

- Homeopathy
- Acupuncture
- Aromatherapy
- Reflexology

- Hypnosis
- Herbalism
- Chinese Medicine
- Crystals

The terms "alternative" and "complementary" apply to all these types of therapy but are distinguished by the way in which they are used.

Alternative Medicine = therapy taken <u>instead of</u> conventional treatment.
Complementary therapy = therapy taken <u>alongside</u> conventional treatment.

At an interview, you would be wise to make it clear that you understand the distinction and address both of these contexts despite what the question might be, as those terms are often wrongly used interchangeably.

**Arguments for:**
- Some therapies involve a high level of contact between the therapist and the patient. The time spent treating the patient is often considerably longer than a conventional doctor's consultation and may have a beneficial effect on the patient.

- Many therapies do not involve taking substances into the system and therefore there is a low level of side effects experienced by the patient.

- Some therapies involve a spiritual component which, along with the greater therapist-patient relationship, may fulfil the needs of patients who require a more holistic approach to their care.

- When conventional medicine is failing a patient or where options have run out, alternative therapies can offer further hope.

- Although they may not necessarily treat the underlying medical condition, they may still have a role in treating side effects of conventional treatments or complications of the underlying condition.

**Arguments against:**
- The evidence base backing these therapies is not as substantial as compared to the evidence available for conventional medicine. The evidence is mostly based on anecdotes or small controlled series, not all of which have been shown to be reproducible. This is weak compared to the stringent standards imposed on research for conventional medicine.

- Conventional Medicine rests on scientific principles of pathophysiology whereas the mechanism of action of alternative therapies is often poorly understood.

- Some complementary therapies involve taking substances that may be toxic (such as liver toxicity of some Chinese Medicine treatments) or that may interact with conventional treatments being taken simultaneously.

- Currently, alternative therapies are poorly regulated, if at all. This has allowed charlatans to abuse the trust of some of their patients.

- In most cases, an alternative therapist will not be a trained conventional doctor and, therefore, will not be in a position to advise the patient with the full picture in mind. This may lead to patients making ill-informed and sometimes harmful decisions.

# QUESTION 95

**Do you think the NHS should provide alternative therapies?**

Alternative therapies are a sensitive topic and doctors can have very extreme views on this matter. Those views are often linked to personal pride, personal experience and anecdotes, or ignorance of the facts.

At an interview, you will not be judged on your personal views but on the manner in which you bring together your arguments to reach a conclusion. All in all, it helps to keep an open mind, particularly when there are so many unknowns about the topic and when some doctors are starting to practise alternative therapy alongside their conventional practice.

### How to answer the question
If you say yes, they will throw at you all the negative aspects of alternative Medicine identified in the answer to Q.94. If you say no, they will do the same with the positive aspects.

The only sensible answer to this question is: "it depends on whether the NHS can get around all the negative aspects". You should therefore list those negative aspects (see Q.94) and explain what would be needed to get around these. This would include:

- More research (i.e. widening the evidence base)
- Better knowledge of mechanism (also widening the evidence base)
- Understanding of harmful effects and compatibility with current treatments
- Improved regulation
- Adequate training
- Ensuring that alternative practitioners also have a conventional medical background.

# QUESTION 96

**Should the NHS deal with patients who have self-inflicted diseases?**

Many candidates have a narrow understanding of this question and spend 2 minutes talking about suicide and other forms of self-harm. These are not self-inflicted <u>diseases</u>.

Another misinterpretation is to discuss how the NHS currently deals with self-infliction. This question is not about what the current status is. It is asking for a debate about whether it should deal with such patients.

**What are self-inflicted diseases?**
Some common conditions include:
- Skin cancer following prolonged exposure to sun-rays
- Obesity following bad dietary habits
- Lung cancer due to smoking
- Liver cirrhosis following excessive drinking
- HIV following conscious high risk-taking behaviour
- Hepatitis C following injected drug use
- Heart disease and hypertension following an unhealthy lifestyle.

**In favour of the NHS dealing with self-inflicted diseases**
- The large majority of diseases are self-inflicted to some extent, even though the link may not be obvious. Indeed, bar a small number of genetically inherited diseases, most are linked in one way or another to our lifestyle. Excluding self-inflicted conditions would restrict a health system to treating only a minority of conditions.

- It follows from the above that most of us will need to see a doctor for an issue which will bear some relation to our lifestyle. Public perception would be greatly damaged if we could not get help for some of the most common diseases.

- Assuming that we may want to exclude some self-inflicted diseases from NHS care, it would be difficult to determine the extent to which a disease is self-inflicted and therefore whether it should be treated or not. (Consider, for example, the case of a woman who had unprotected sex with her long-term husband because she trusted him, but where the husband acquired HIV through a one-night stand and refused to notify his wife. Would you say that the wife's HIV was self-inflicted? How would you know that she is not lying simply to get treatment?)

- On public health grounds, it is necessary to treat any transmissible diseases (such as sexually transmitted diseases), to control them and to prevent onward transmission.

- Some self-infliction (such as excessive drinking or smoking) may reveal underlying issues (e.g. psychiatric conditions or psychological ill-being) that may need to be identified and treated. Not allowing patients to visit a doctor for a self-inflicted illness may prevent the treatment of those underlying causes.

- We are in a free society where individual choice is of crucial importance. The NHS should complement this society choice and not work against it.

**Against**
- Patients with self-inflicted diseases often relapse. They may feel that they have got away with it before and return to their high risk behaviours. Treating them might therefore be only a temporary measure for a problem which may recur later on, e.g. ongoing sexually risky behaviour, alcoholism relapse following liver transplant.

- Allowing treatment of self-inflicted diseases may remove individual responsibility for one's own health. For example, people will not consider some behaviour as high risk in the first place because they know that they will receive treatment if they need to. In some cases (such as drug-related conditions), treating patients may actually be seen as encouraging illegal activities.

- In a system where resources are scarce, it is important to prioritise how budgets need to be allocated. Public perception of the health service may

ISCMEDICAL
Interview Skills Consulting

be worsened if they see people who are less deserving in their eyes receive treatment when they themselves are struggling to be treated. This is an argument that the media used a lot in relation to the use of lottery funds. Much fuss was made about the fact that some funds were allocated to charities dealing with transsexuals and refugees, amongst others.

**Important conclusion to raise**

Ultimately, it is down to society to decide how it wants to use its own health system. Based on the arguments above, it would be very difficult to separate with certainty self-inflicted from non-self-inflicted diseases and therefore such an exclusion system would not be fair or practical.

ISCMEDICAL
Interview Skills Consulting

# QUESTION 97

**Should the NHS fund non-essential surgery?**

The best approach for questions such as these is to see whether you can start answering by defining some of the key terms. When you look at the question, you should be asking yourself what "non-essential" means. By discussing this term, you will get ideas that you can develop during your answer.

### What does non-essential mean?
Most people relate the concept of non-essential to cosmetic surgery. Although cosmetic surgery probably constitutes the bulk of it, there are other interventions that would qualify too. The concept of "non-essential" is ambiguous in itself as well as subjective. What may be regarded as non-essential by someone may be essential for someone else. For example, take a moment to think about the following cases:

- If a good-looking woman wants to have cosmetic surgery on her nose because she thinks that it is too big and is depressed as a result, does it constitute non-essential surgery? What if this would cure her depression?

- If a woman has breasts so large that she gets backache as a result, would breast reduction be essential surgery?

- What about a man with very thick glasses requiring laser surgery because he cannot stand the weight of his glasses any longer and his eyes are too dry to wear contact lenses?

- What about a 40-year-old man who requests a vasectomy because he already has four children and does not want to use condoms? What if he later wants a reversal of his vasectomy? Should this be funded by the NHS too?

### Arguments in favour of funding non-essential surgery

- Although some procedures may look like non-essential, the problem may affect the patients deeply from a psychological point of view. Carrying out a surgical procedure may prove more effective than letting the psychological problem progress further, with a potential risk of developing into a depression that may prove more expensive to resolve later.

- Not funding non-essential surgery pushes people to self-fund the surgery, which may lead to significant debts for the patient.

- Not funding may push people to choose to have surgery in other less regulated environments. This could have consequences on the NHS if patients then need help from the NHS to deal with complications.

### Arguments against funding non-essential surgery

- Requests for some non-essential treatments such as cosmetic surgery may only be the result of a deeper primary problem such as lack of self-esteem or depression, which may be treated better through psychological or psychiatric intervention. Treating the underlying problem may also be more suitable because cosmetic surgery is unlikely to resolve the psychological problem and the patient will slide down a slippery slope, requiring more and more surgery.

- Knowing that treatment for non-essential surgery is available free of charge, people may find new problems to which they never paid attention before (e.g. a woman who had no problems with her breasts but now feels that she may as well have them enlarged).

- Whereas non-essential surgery results from a request driven by the individual's own initiative, the need for essential surgery is driven by external events (e.g. a disease, an accident, etc.). As a result, the need for essential surgery can be reasonably anticipated from one year to the next, but allowing non-essential surgery to be funded by the NHS would open floodgates. This would lead to a gridlock situation and/or a need for additional funding. This in turn would lead to an increase in taxes, which would be shared by all taxpayers. Everyone would pay for other people's non-essential surgery, which would be unfair for those who do not require it.

ISCMEDICAL
Interview Skills Consulting

# QUESTION 98

**In what ways can doctors promote good health?**

Doctors can promote good health by:

- Setting a good example to patients, for example by eating healthily, keeping fit and not smoking

- During consultations, encouraging patients to have a healthy lifestyle (safe sex, no smoking, low fat diet, exercising, etc.)

- Displaying posters in their surgery and distributing leaflets to patients

- Promoting support groups (smoking cessation, Alcoholics Anonymous)

- Recommending the services of a dietician.

However, health promotion goes well beyond this and also includes disease prevention and preventing the worsening of any existing illness a patient may have ("secondary prevention"). This includes:

- Screening programmes for target populations (e.g. breast cancers, cervical cancers, etc.)

- Immunisation campaigns and services

- Family planning/sexual health clinics, well-women's/men's clinics and other specialist clinics (diabetes, etc).

# QUESTION 99

**Should doctors show a good example to patients?**

### Arguments in favour of doctors showing a good example
- Doctors need credibility in order to be trusted by their patients. A patient may find it difficult to take seriously a recommendation to stop smoking and eat healthily if he sees his doctor smoking while eating a burger.

### Arguments against doctors showing a good example
- This is an issue of individual choice. The health messages given by doctors are commonly accepted facts; it is then down to each individual to treat that advice in the way they want.

- Defining "good example" is not easy. A pattern of behaviour may be a good example for someone and a bad example for someone else. For example, a GP drinking 15 units of alcohol per week would be a good example for most people, but not for an ex-alcoholic. In addition, people's bodies react differently to others. Some people may have a metabolism that can cope with a certain amount of unhealthy food, while others are more sensitive.

- Following every single health message to the letter with a view to showing a good example may make the doctor's life hell. Which type of food has no sugar, no salt, no fat, and can still taste interesting?

What matters is that everyone should do everything in moderation. Unfortunately, it does not matter if you eat burgers in moderation. The day a patient sees you eating one, he will assume that it is part of your normal diet. This is a dilemma that will never be resolved until patients are able to take personal responsibility for their own health.

# QUESTION 100

**What is holistic medicine?**

This term is used extensively nowadays. In an era when patients are placed at the centre of the care, doctors must find ways of addressing their needs from various angles.

Holistic Medicine means that you are treating the patient as a whole, i.e. not only the physical aspect but taking into account social, psychological and spiritual issues. Examples of holistic Medicine include the following:

- A patient has a rash. An easy option would be to give him an ointment to apply to rid the patient of that rash. A holistic approach would be to determine whether this rash may have a psychological origin or be due to a stressful lifestyle. On top of providing treatment for the rash, the doctor would assist the patient in overcoming those other issues. He would also study how the rash and the treatment affect the patient's life, work and self-esteem, and would ensure that any negative effects are minimised.

- A patient has been diagnosed with a chronic illness such as Multiple Sclerosis. As well as helping the patient to cope with the physical aspects of the illness, the doctor would consider the psychological impact of the illness on the patient and on the family. He would also consider the implications of the illness on the patient's social life, including financial, and any modifications that may need to be made to help the patient to cope effectively. A condition with long-term deterioration may have a significant impact on an individual.

# QUESTION 101

**Would you say that Medicine is an art or a science?**

Before you can answer this question, it is crucial to have a good understanding of what these two terms mean.

There are many possible definitions for "science", but essentially it is the systematic acquisition of knowledge that is verifiable and a process for evaluating empirical knowledge. Art, on the other hand, is the product of creativity or imagination.

It would be too easy to think of Medicine as a science simply based on the fact that it is all about accumulating a vast amount of facts about a topic based on observation and experimentation. The application of that knowledge is not as straightforward as it seems and, in many ways, makes Medicine closer to an art than a science. For example:

- Communicating with patients in order to gain a proper history can be a challenge. In many cases, there will be protocols to follow (which would make the process scientific) but patients do not always respond in accordance to theory. Extracting that information may require some ingenuity and creativity, making it an art.

- In general, anything to do with communication is an art as you need to adapt to the person or group that you are addressing. Breaking bad news to a patient is an art that not many doctors master, in the same way that being an effective teacher is an art. In particular, neither can be easily reproduced as patients and students are all different.

- Medicine also involves leading and managing teams that will help you provide the best care for your patients. Although there are management theories that you may apply, such a role relates more to a form of art where you have to use your imagination to resolve complex situations

such as conflict or demotivated colleagues. The intervention of human feelings in the equation makes all the difference.

- There are some more obvious relationships between art and Medicine; for example a surgeon's ability to close a wound without leaving a scar, or the obvious sculpting skills of a plastic surgeon.

Nothing is ever as simple as it looks. It is fair to say that Medicine combines aspects of both art and science. Your answer should reflect this.

# QUESTION 102

**What do you know about clinical governance?**

Generally speaking, the word governance refers to the implementation of a framework that ensures the good working order of an institution and helps monitoring the long-term strategy and policy of that institution.

Clinical governance essentially ensures that the quality of care provided by doctors is maintained at a high standard and is constantly improved. It includes several pillars:

**Clinical Effectiveness and Research**
Making sure that the treatments offered to people do what they are supposed to do. This means keeping up to date by accessing good quality information and using interventions that have been proven to be effective (Evidence-Based Medicine – see Q.107). It also involves supporting and implementing the National Service Frameworks (NSF) and being aware of local priorities for healthcare.

**Risk Management**
Risk Management involves having robust systems in place to understand, monitor and minimise the risks to which patients and staff are exposed as well as learning from mistakes whenever they occur. When things go wrong in the delivery of care, doctors and other clinical staff should feel comfortable to admit it and be able to learn and share what they have learnt. This includes reporting any significant adverse events via critical incidents forms, looking closely at complaints, etc. Once risks are identified, they are assessed for their likelihood of occurrence and the impact they could have if an incident occurred. Processes are then implemented to reduce the occurrence of such risks and to minimise their impact. The level of implementation often depends on the budget available and the seriousness of the risk.

ISCMEDICAL
Interview Skills Consulting

**Education and Training**
Education and training covers the support available to enable staff to be competent in doing their jobs and to develop their skills so that they are up to date. Professional development needs to continue through lifelong learning. For doctors, this involves attending courses, on-the-job training, etc. Continuous professional development plays an important part in education and training, as do appraisals, which are meant to identify and discuss weaknesses, and opportunities for personal development.

**Patient and Public Involvement**
This means listening to what the public thinks of the services provided, and learning from their experiences. It may mean changing the way you work in order to be responsive to patients' needs and involving service users when planning new services, above all putting the patient at the heart of what you do. The National Patient Safety Agency (npsa.nhs.uk), Patient Advice and Liaison Services (www.pals.nhs.uk) and the use of complaint procedures contribute to this process.

This also includes the concept of openness, which relates to the need for the NHS to be upfront with the public in relation to its own problems. As part of openness, the NHS publicises complaints procedures to patients, deals with problem doctors openly and encourages doctors to admit their own mistakes as part of a blame-free culture.

**Clinical Audit**
See Q.103 for full details.

**Using Information**
The NHS holds an enormous amount of information about patients and needs to be able to access it efficiently and make the best possible use of it; for example audits that monitor quality, measure progress and enable future planning. This means learning how to use computers in readiness for moving to the Electronic Patient Record and understanding how the Data Protection Act relates to your work. This also includes having systems in place to protect confidentiality.

**Staffing and Staff Management**
Staffing and staff management includes recruitment, management and development of staff. It also includes implementing effective methods of working and good working conditions, i.e. with equal opportunities, free of bullying and harassment.

**Answering the question**
Note that you would not be expected to know clinical governance inside out. This is a concept that you will have plenty of time to become familiar with once you qualify. However, you should have a good understanding of its role in Medicine and at least be able to present its essential components.

All pillars are important but some deserve more time some others. In 2 minutes you simply do not have time to discuss all 7 pillars in any great depth. Our recommendation would be to define and discuss briefly at least the following:

- Clinical effectiveness
- Clinical audit
- Risk management
- Education and training
- Patient and public involvement

but to mention the last two in passing. This will not only save time but will also help you concentrate on the more meaty topics and those that play a stronger role in the day-to-day work of doctors.

# QUESTION 103

**What do you know about the audit process?**

Audits are a systematic examination of current practice to assess how well an institution or a practitioner is performing against set standards. Essentially, it is a method for reflecting on, reviewing and improving practice.

**How does an audit work?**
The audit process is often referred to as the "audit cycle", essentially because it is a continuous loop. The process is as follows:

1. Choose a topic for the audit, i.e. a practice to be investigated.
2. Define a standard that you would like to achieve.
3. Collect relevant data.
4. Compare results of analysis against standard.
5. Identify changes that need to be made in order to reach standard.
6. Implement changes and give time for those changes to be fully operational.
7. Re-audit (complete the loop) several months later to measure the impact of the changes.

**Why are audits important?**

- The main purpose of an audit is to identify weaknesses in your practice and increase the quality of service provided to users.

- Audits also help to identify inefficiencies and ultimately may lead to a better use of resources.

- Audits are also used to provide information about quality of care to outside agencies, for the production of league tables, etc.

- Audits provide opportunities for training and education.

# QUESTION 104

**What do you know about the European Working Time Directive?**

The European Working Time Directive will take full effect in Medicine in 2009. Essentially, it limits the number of hours that an employed doctor can work to 48 hours per week. It also restricts the amount of time that can be worked by doctors to a total of 13 hours in any 24-hour period.

**Positive consequences**
- Doctors are more rested and less stressed; this has a positive effect on the care of patients.
- Junior doctors have more time to study and concentrate on non-clinical matters (such as getting involved in research activities, often done in their own time).

**Negative consequences**
- Patients are cared for by more doctors and continuity of care is therefore diminished. Good care relies on better communication between all doctors more than before. There is a need for clear handovers between shifts and accurate record keeping in order to avoid misunderstandings.
- Junior doctors spend less overall time with patients and therefore training opportunities are reduced.

**Other impacts**
The NHS also now needs more staff to care for patients. This has led to:
- An increase in the number of places at medical schools in the UK
- An increase in the role of nurses (see Q.84 and Q.85)
- A restructuring of hospitals at night (see question Q.105)
- A restructuring of the training of junior doctors (Modernising Medical Careers – see question Q.106).

Whether these are positive or negative developments is the subject of much controversy. See the next few questions for details.

**What is "Hospital at Night"?**

This refers to a change in the way hospitals are organised at night-time. As a result of the implementation of the European Working Time Directive limiting the number of hours that doctors can work (see Q.104), it became necessary to ensure that hospitals worked more efficiently during the night in order to free up resources that would be better utilised during the day.

Previously, junior doctors worked in isolation within their own specialty during the night. This had the advantage of ensuring that specialist help was available for each discipline but one of the main problems was that, while some doctors were being kept busy, others may not have been so busy at times. It was felt that care could be provided more efficiently if idle doctors could be redeployed to assist those who were stretched. Also, it was felt that there was no real need to have so many doctors on-site during the night – there are over 60 specialties after all.

The "Hospital at Night" model follows the following approach:

- A significant proportion of the non-urgent work is moved from night-time to day-time (e.g. non-emergency patients who can wait will wait).

- A multidisciplinary approach whereby the team consists of fewer junior doctors who would each handle several specialties (as opposed to simply their own). Senior help is available remotely, with senior doctors being called in if necessary.

- Some duties traditionally reserved for doctors being taken over by other staff (e.g. nurses), who are also part of the night team.

- Better coordination of clerking (documenting a hospital admission) to avoid duplication.

# QUESTION 106

**What is "Modernising Medical Careers" or "MMC"?**

MMC refers to a change in the way junior doctors are being trained to become consultants. Under the old so-called "Calman" system, doctors trained as follows:

Notes:
- PRHO = Pre-Registration House Officer
- SHO = Senior House Officer
- SpR = Specialist Registrar
- The above 10-year timeframe is an average training timetable. In practice, the training timeline differed for each specialty and some doctors may also take longer to progress depending on their success at the Royal College examinations and at selective interviews. For example, SHO often varied between 2 and 4 years, while the SpR period often varied between 4 and 7 years.

**Features of the old "Calman" system**
- Under the Calman system, there was no systematic teaching for SHOs. Doctors were trained by preparing for relevant exams and on the job. Any formal teaching provided at the hospital would need to be organised by ambitious trainees or altruistic consultants. In addition, there was no formal form of assessment other than Royal College examinations at SHO or early SpR level.

- There was a bottleneck at the end of SHO training once doctors had gathered the necessary conditions to enter Specialist Training. For those who could not get into an SpR training post, this would sometimes mean

remaining at SHO level for some time with few real chances of entering their chosen career.

## Drivers for change

- It was felt that doctors should specialise earlier. This would allow the provision for specialty targeted knowledge early on in their career rather than spending time at SHO level learning skills they may not require later on.

- Many doctors were disillusioned at the thought of having spent years preparing to enter the specialty of their choice, only to find that they could not get an SpR training post.

- A reform of the training structure needed to take place in order to ensure that trainees acquired all the skills required in a systematic manner, rather than on an ad-hoc basis.

- The training of doctors should become shorter, i.e. producing consultant specialists sooner.

## The new training system

The new system is often referred to as the "MMC system" or the "Foundation system". Its main features are:

- It starts with 2 years of foundation training aiming to provide a broad based training for all medicine and surgery. Those 2 years consist of a rotation between a number of specialties (typically 6 x 4-months). The second year has an emphasis on training for acute conditions.

- At the end of the 2 foundation years, individuals generally embark on a general medical or general surgical programme for 2 years before making a choice about the specialty they wish to pursue. A competitive entry process will then take place to select the best candidates for each specialty. Successful candidates will enter specialist training posts. Unsuccessful candidates will be allocated "career grade posts", although they will benefit from training to some extent.

- The training of doctors is now competency-based, i.e. a syllabus has been drawn up, establishing the skills and competencies that each doctor must acquire. Targeted teaching and experience is provided, complemented by various types of assessments to make sure that doctors have achieved the desired levels.

- Those applying for General Practice will be able to enter GP Vocational Training Schemes after the second foundation year (whereas under the Calman system they could do so straight after the PRHO year).

The new training structure thus looks as follows:

| FY1 | FY2 | BMT/BST | HSpT | Subspec. | Consultant |
|-----|-----|---------|------|----------|------------|
| 1 YR | 1 YR | 2 YRS | 3 YRS | 3 YRS | |

Notes:
- Again the above is a typical representation but may vary between different specialties.
- BMT = Basic Medical Training
- BST = Basic Surgical Training
- HSpT = Higher Specialist Training
- Subspec. = Years of subspecialisation. In some specialties, this may also be used for research purposes.

Discussion
- You will notice that, overall, the actual training time is not shorter than under the old system (still approximately 10 years). This is because, despite the original intention to reduce the number of years of training, the reduction in working hours imposed by the European Working Time Directive has meant that training time was already being slashed by over 30% and that therefore it would be impractical to reduce the number of years as well. Reducing both the years and the hours would have meant an overall reduction in training hours of 50%, which could seriously compromise the quality of care doctors could provide once fully qualified. Consequently, the decision was made to add further years to the training, which could be used for further subspecialisation once the core training has been completed. These added years may also be used for research purposes.

- Some specialties are more competitive than others and are therefore likely to attract large numbers of applicants. Only a few doctors would be selected for training posts. Others would then need to work in a non-career grade post or in a training post for another specialty. This may lead to many doctors becoming disillusioned.

- One of the reasons for introducing MMC was to remove the bottleneck that occurred at SpR entry point. The new system now has two bottlenecks: one for entry into Basic Training and one for entry into Higher Specialist Training since selection will still be made, to some extent, on Royal College exam results and based on selective interviews.

- Essentially, the new system has evolved to become very close to the old system, with different names being used and shorter training time due to the introduction of the European Working Time Directive. The main advantage is that the change has forced every specialty to rethink how doctors were being trained and has forced the introduction of a much-needed training structure. It has also formalised assessment procedures.

- Many doctors are concerned about the quality of care that the doctors trained under the new system will give. Medicine and surgery are based not only on skills learnt through books and practice, but also on clinical judgement. This clinical judgement is the result of hours of experience. With working time being cut down to 48 hours per week (from an average of probably 65 hours previously), there will be fewer opportunities for junior doctors to learn the "art" of Medicine.

Interview Skills Consulting

# QUESTION 107

What do you know about "Evidence-Based Practice" or "Evidence-Based Medicine"?

### What is Evidence-Based Medicine?

Evidence-based Medicine (EBM) has been defined as "the conscientious, explicit, and judicious use of current best evidence in making decisions about the care of individual patients. The practice of evidence-based Medicine means integrating individual clinical expertise with the best available external clinical evidence from systematic research."(David Sackett et al. "Evidence-Based Medicine: What It Is and What It Isn't" *BMJ* 312, no.7023 (1996).

In 2000, David Sackett revised his definition as follows: "integration of best research evidence with clinical expertise and patient values" David Sackett et al. *Evidence-Based Medicine: How to Practice and Teach EBM* (New York: Churchill Livingstone, 2000), 1.

Generally speaking, you should be weary of using ready-made definitions as they simply demonstrate your ability to regurgitate ready-made answers and do not highlight any personal understanding of the issues at stake. The above definition also uses words that are unfamiliar to most people and which are best avoided (for example few people know that "judicious" means "based on sound judgement").

Try to build your own practical definition, showing that you have a good understanding of what EBM entails. EBM is essentially the analysis of best available research evidence combined with your own clinical expertise and judgement to determine how it can best be applied to a specific case, taking into account patient values.

Interview Skills Consulting

## How evidence-based Medicine works in practice

The whole point of evidence-based practice is to ensure that you do not rest on your laurels by practising the Medicine that you once learnt in your textbooks (or by using anecdotal knowledge handed down from professor to professor), but that you resolve clinical problems by using the highest quality research, controlled and analysed by stringent scientific methods, i.e. evidence. In many situations, the analysis work will have been done for you and guidelines will have been set out by institutions such as NICE (National Institute for Health and Clinical Excellence), particularly when common conditions are concerned. However, for more unusual clinical cases, you may have to do the work yourself. There are several steps involved in evidence-based Medicine:

1. A clinical problem arises out of the care of a patient.
2. Construct a well-defined clinical question from the case.
3. Conduct a search on studies carried out on the condition or problem in question by using the most appropriate resources. This would usually involve querying online databases of research publications.
4. Appraise that evidence for its validity (i.e. methodology and sturdiness of conclusions reached) and applicability (i.e. usefulness in clinical practice).
5. Combine the best evidence that you have found with clinical practice and patient preferences; then apply it to your practice.
6. Evaluate your performance with the patient.

## The meaning of "best available research evidence"

In order to use a given course of action to manage a patient, doctors need to find evidence that the proposed management is the best available. Other clinicians or researchers will have carried out research at varying levels and will have produced papers explaining the results of their findings. Depending on the type of research undertaken, the evidence will be more or less strong.

For example, if someone has simply reported on a single case that they met in an isolated country, this will be a very low level of evidence because you would have to manage your own patient based on what happened with a single other patient. However, if you find a randomised control trial based on thousands of patients similar to yours then the evidence will be stronger. If you have found a paper that analysed the results of several randomised control trials based on thousands of patients (so called meta-analysis), then your evidence will be extremely robust.

ISCMEDICAL
Interview Skills Consulting

# QUESTION 108

**What do you know about Practice-Based Commissioning (PBC)?**

### Practice-Based Commissioning
Practice-Based Commissioning (PBC) is a concept that applies mostly to General Practice. With the recent changes made to the GP contract in 2004, GPs have been granted more autonomy and greater budgets. PBC contains two major ingredients:

**1 – GPs must purchase services from service providers out of their own funds.** For example, if a GP wants to refer a patient to a diabetes clinic, he will need to pay a standard fee for the service out of his own funds. Similarly, the GP will need to purchase any investigation that he requires for a particular patient (X-ray, MRI scan, etc). The "referral fee" is fixed by the NHS for each service required and is calculated as an average of the cost of such service over the country (with a few complex adjustments).

**2 – Patients can choose where they want the service to be provided (within limits).** The Primary Care Trust will select the best service providers for each particular service. The GP will then give patients the choice between a number of these selected providers.

### Advantages
- Because GPs must fund the service out of their own funds, they must make sure that they only purchase services that are necessary. This is a good way of making sure that NHS funds are utilised judiciously.

- Because the fee is the same wherever the GP sends the patient, the service providers (such as local NHS hospitals, private businesses, GPs with special interests, etc.) will be competing on the ground of quality of service. In essence, the GP will make sure that the patient gets the best value for money. This will encourage competition and should lead to better quality of care.

- Patients can be assured that only the best providers have been pre-selected for them and can then make a choice based on their own preferences.

- GPs have a greater say in the types of services that should be available in their local area. This should ensure that the services provided match the demands of the population that they serve.

**Disadvantages**
- If GPs have to pay for each service out of their personal budget, they may not be inclined to refer some patients when it may be necessary to do so. There is a need for a tight control to avoid a negative impact on patient care for patients in "grey area" situations.

- Introducing a market-type economy within the NHS could have dangerous consequences. Although the most inefficient service providers may become more efficient in order to compete, some may be forced to close down altogether. This would then place an extra burden on other providers and may lead to a reduction in the quality of care being provided.

- Although patients are offered the choice, in practice many of them do not really know how to make that choice. The GP may then decide for them, and may impose a choice that works in their favour (for example by referring to their friends or even to another business that they own). Tight controls must be in place to prevent this.

- The tariffs are set for each procedure at an average level and do not take account of the complexity of the patient. This means that service providers may make a loss or a profit depending on the patient they deal with. Some providers who handle mostly complex patients may find it difficult to survive unless the tariffs are revised to take account of that complexity. In time, this may lead to some service providers refusing to treat certain patients because the tariff imposed by the NHS does not cover the true cost of the care provided.

- Because service providers receive a fee from the GP every time a patient is being referred, they are reluctant to refer patients to another doctor

within the same hospital without going back to the GP. The GP can then refer the patient again and the hospital will get a referral fee twice. This is good for the hospital as they will get two fees, not so good for the GP's pocket, and inconvenient for the patient.

ISCMEDICAL
Interview Skills Consulting

# QUESTION 109

**What do you know about "Payment By Results" (PBR)?**

### Payment by results (PBR)
PBR is effectively the other side of the coin from PBC (See Q.108). It refers to the fact that service providers such as hospitals are being paid for each service that they provide, in a context where patients can choose where they want the service to be provided. Therefore, in order to attract referral (and hence money), they must ensure that they provide a competitive service in terms of quality (i.e. deliver results). The advantages and disadvantages are very similar to those of PBC, but you must raise them from the perspective of the service provider.

### Advantages
- This introduces an element of competition and therefore increases the quality of care being provided.

- Providers of care are rewarded for what they do rather than for what they announced they would do. Each patient and procedure has a price tag. This system introduces greater transparency and is fairer.

- It forces providers to become more efficient and have tighter budget controls if they want to provide the service within the tariff imposed by the NHS.

- It forces providers to respond to the needs of their patients. If they don't, then patients will simply choose to go elsewhere. Consequently, the services will simply not be financially viable and will need to be closed.

**Disadvantages**

- The tariff received does not take account of the complexity of the patient, but only of the type of procedure/service required. Therefore a hospital receiving a complex patient may spend more money on the patient than they actually receive for the service. There is a danger that service providers may become choosy. There is also a danger that some providers may go out of business if they treat too many loss-making patients.

- It may drive some much-needed service providers out of business if they are finding it hard to compete due to internal inefficiencies.

- Having an efficient service is one thing, but introducing a strong business element into healthcare may lead to a decrease in the human aspect of Medicine in a bid to save time and resources.

# QUESTION 110

**What are the issues affecting the NHS currently?**

Addressing this question should not be too difficult if you read the press regularly and take an interest in what is going on in the NHS. There are two types of issues that you may address:

**Long-standing issues**
These are issues that have been around for some time and which characterise a big system such as the NHS. These include funding issues, inefficiency issues, bed shortages, waiting lists, postcode lottery, etc. You should bear in mind that these issues are mentioned by many candidates, though few are able to discuss them beyond the obvious. In reality, although you should of course mention all these issues, it would be difficult to address them without linking them to solutions being implemented, which are set out below. Make sure you read the press before your interview so that you can be fully aware of the relevant facts.

**New issues**
These originate in recent decisions, policies or events such as court cases or scandals, and can be used easily to demonstrate the efforts that you have made to keep up to date. This includes new developments such as
 - European Working Time Directive (See Q.104)
 - MMC and the difficulties that this poses (see Q.106)
 - The increasing role of nurses and adverse reactions (see Q.84 and 85)
 - The Hospital at Night policy and its consequences (see Q.105)
 - Practice-Based Commissioning (see Q. 108)
 - Payment by Results (see Q.109).

It also includes current issues linked to mediatised events such as:
 - Shipman case and its implications on how doctors operate and are monitored (see Q.111)

- Sir Roy Meadows case in relation to expert witnessing at trials requiring medical opinion
- Rationing of scarce resources and policy decisions made by trusts to restrict access to such resources to whole categories of patients (e.g. Herceptin, knee operations for obese patients, etc).

You should ensure that you keep fully up to date with all major (and recent!) developments. Looking at websites such as www.bbc.co.uk/health would certainly be of great help, as interviewers tend to ask questions about issues that originated weeks before the interview.

If you are asked to discuss recent issues in the NHS, you should ensure that you discuss a general message to accompany your example. For example, discussing the factual details of the Herceptin cases will not really highlight the issues at stake unless you accompany your answer with a discussion on the problem of scarce resources.

In order to be able to engage in a discussion about a topic and present an interesting picture to the interviewers, you will not only need to be well informed by reading about the topics in question, you will also need to show an ability to debate and understand the issues from different perspectives. This will come of course from your own ability to analyse the facts and draw appropriate arguments. But you will also considerably benefit from sitting down with your friends and family debating current events and politics. Many candidates fail because they are missing a lateral thinking and debating ability. This can only be gained through practice.

# QUESTION 111

**What do you know about Shipman?**

## The facts

Harold Shipman was practising as a GP in the Manchester area and was convicted for the murder of 15 patients and forging a will, although it is alleged that he actually murdered hundreds of his patients, mostly by injecting opiates (morphine, etc.) into their body.

Shipman had started to experience blackouts 4 years after graduating from medical school and, although it was first thought to be due to epilepsy, it transpired that he had in fact an opiate addiction. He was convicted and fined £600 for this. He was also barred from taking up any job which would give him access to controlled drugs. At this point the GMC did not take any steps to strike him off the Medical Register.

In 1977 he took up a post as a GP in Clyde and, although regarded as arrogant by his colleagues, he was well regarded by his patients. In 1992 he left his practice to set up on his own, taking with him a long list of patients. In 1997 staff at a funeral parlour started to become suspicious at the high level of deaths from elderly people who did not seem to be particularly ill prior to their death. Their death had either been certified by Shipman or followed a recent visit by Shipman. A rival GP surgery also became suspicious. As a result, the police were notified but were unable to reach any conclusions.

Nothing more happened until the daughter of one of the victims became concerned at the fact that her mother had left her possessions to her GP and launched an enquiry about the possible forgery of the will. This resulted in Shipman being charged and convicted for 15 murders and forgery; the other murders were not investigated thoroughly as Shipman had already been jailed for life anyway and many of the alleged victims had been cremated, which made any enquiry difficult.

In 2001 Dame Janet Smith conducted an enquiry into the murders and concluded that 215 deaths could be attributed to Shipman, 45 were most likely murdered by Shipman (but this was only a strong suspicion) and 38 cases could not be proven due to insufficient evidence.

## Consequences of the Shipman case

The Shipman case led to a number of changes directly or indirectly. In particular:

- **A move away from single-handed GP practices.** As Shipman was working on his own, there were few opportunities for colleagues to check on what he was doing. As a result, he was able to murder many people without questions being asked.

- **Tighter regulations on the use of controlled drugs.** Not only was Shipman able to get hold of controlled drugs despite an earlier conviction, he was also able to get hold of large quantities to murder hundreds of patients.

- **Tighter regulation of death certification.** Shipman managed to get many patients cremated, which required two signatures (one by him and one by another doctor). There was failure on the part of these other doctors to recognise the situation. There are now plans to report all deaths to a coroner. This would introduce an additional degree of scrutiny, though it may overburden coroners.

- **Review of the revalidation process**, which ensures that doctors have the necessary skills to practise. It was recognised that there had been a failure on the part of the GMC to deal with Shipman when it could have made a difference. Obviously, hindsight is always easy to invoke, but the GMC was criticised at the time for acting too much in the interest of doctors and not enough in the interest of patients. Ultimately, it must also be recognised that no amount of bureaucracy will ever prevent a murderer from operating, though it may make it easier to stop one in his tracks at an early stage (rather than wait for 200 murders).

# QUESTION 112

**How long does it take to become a consultant?**

This is a question to which you either know the answer or you don't. The question is made harder by the fact that the system has recently changed.

Before the introduction of MMC (Modernising Medical Careers – see Q.106), which changed the structure of the training of junior doctors, it would take at least 7 years to become a consultant, though the average was probably around 10 years (made up of 1 year at PRHO level, 3 years at SHO level and 6 years at Specialist Registrar (SpR) level). Obviously, this varied for each specialty, with surgical specialties taking on average longer than medical specialties.

With the introduction of MMC, training was restructured and the syllabus was condensed in order to ensure that doctors who specialise only train on what is necessary. The average is therefore likely to get closer to 8 years, although it is recognised that most doctors who get to that level may subsequently undertake further training, for example in a subspecialty, bringing the total number of years close to 10 years.

Note that these figures are averages, as some people with convoluted careers may take much longer. They also assume that consultant posts are available straight away so that there is no unemployment period to take into account.

Note also that, although the number of years is effectively 10, both under the old and the new system, the introduction of the European Working Time Directive (see Q.104) has reduced the amount of hours worked each week to 48 hours, hence the actual overall amount of training hours has considerably reduced.

Interview Skills Consulting

# QUESTION 113

**How long does it take to train as a GP?**

The answer is 5 years after medical school (it used to be 4 years before the introduction of MMC).

Under the new system, candidates for GP training must have undertaken 2 years of Foundation Programme, followed by a dedicated 3-year GP Vocational Training Scheme (or GP VTS). During these 3 years, they will spend 2 years in a hospital environment as a trainee and 1 year at a GP Practice, with the grade of GP Registrar.

# QUESTION 114

**Tell us about the four ethical principles of Medicine?**

This is a question which you should be able to answer without hesitation. There are only four principles, they follow common sense and they are key to providing a good answer to many of the ethical dilemmas or scenarios that you may face at an interview and during your medical career. The four principles are as follows:

### Autonomy
Patients are entitled to their opinion and to making decisions for themselves. In particular, patients have the right to choose the treatment that they feel is best for them and also have the right to refuse to be treated. A key factor for this principle to apply is that the patient must be in a position to understand and process the information at his disposal to make an informed decision. This is referred to as "patient competence" (see Q.116).

Please note that the principle of Autonomy refers to the right that the patient has to accept or to refuse a treatment or procedure that is offered by a doctor. It does not mean that the patient can demand from doctors the treatment that they want.

### Beneficence
The word comes from the Latin "bene" = "good" and "facere" = "to do". Doctors must "do good" and act in the best interests of their patients and/or society as a whole.

### Non-maleficence
From the Latin "male" = "bad, harmful", this term means that a doctor should act in such a way that he does not harm his patients, whether it is actively or by omission.

**Justice (sometimes also called "equity")**

Put simply, this is about fairness across the population. Patients who are in the same position should be considered in the same way (i.e. you can only discriminate on the basis of different clinical needs). Benefits, risks and costs should also be spread fairly. This includes taking into account that some resources such as money, time, organs, etc. are in short supply.

**Right to confidentiality – the fifth element**

Confidentiality is not strictly speaking an ethical principle, but it is linked to several of them. For example, confidentiality can be part of patient autonomy and the right of the patient to control the information that pertains to their own health. Confidentiality can also be linked to non-maleficence in that you may harm the patient by revealing information about them.

Ethical dilemmas originate from the fact that there is a clash between two or more of the above principles. For example, consider the daily decisions that a physician in ITU has to make for a patient who is in great pain and needs large doses of morphine. Giving the patient an increasing dose of morphine helps relieve his pain and is therefore consistent with the principle of beneficence as it is doing good to the patient. However, an increased dose of morphine may also bring the patient closer to his death, thus harming him. Here, the principle of beneficence clashes with the principle of non-maleficence and the physician will therefore need to strike the right balance to act in the best interest of the patient.

# QUESTION 115

**What does the term "informed consent" mean to you?**

Informed consent means that the patient has consented to a procedure or treatment, having been given and having considered all the facts that were necessary for them to make a decision in their own best interest.

**How consent works**

Before a patient can give their consent for a particular procedure, the doctor must explain a number of facts, including:

- Options for treatment or management of the condition (whether this is through surgical or medical management). This includes the option not to give treatment.

- The aim of the planned procedure or treatment, including any consequences, common or serious side effects.

- Details of the planned procedure or treatment, its benefits, chances of success, as well as common or serious risks and side effects, and how these might be managed.

- Consequences of providing the treatment versus consequences of not providing the treatment.

- Details of any secondary interventions that may be required while undertaking the first one (e.g. blood transfusion if heavy blood loss during surgery) and for which the patient should provide consent beforehand as they will be unable to do so should it be required in an emergency.

- Details of who will be performing the procedure and whether doctors in training will be involved (particularly important for surgical interventions).

Interview Skills Consulting

- A reminder that the patient can change their mind at any time and that they can seek a second opinion.

- Any costs that the patient may incur (mostly relevant for private work).

Following on from this, the patient should be given any appropriate written information such as leaflets explaining the procedure, its risks and benefits. The patient should also be given enough time to reflect so that they do not feel pressured into making a decision.

Only competent patients can give consent. For more details on competence, including seeking consent from children, see the next question.

ISCMEDICAL
Interview Skills Consulting

# QUESTION 116

**Only competent patients can give consent. What is meant by "competent"?**

Consent can only be taken from patients who are deemed to be "competent", i.e. who understand the information and are capable of making a rational decision by themselves. Competency is a legal judgement.

Doctors also frequently talk about "capacity to consent" or "mental capacity". This is a medical judgement. Capacity is formally assessed by doctors and nurses who must be sure that a patient is able to understand a management course, to comprehend the risks and benefits and to retain that information long enough to make balanced choices. As with competency, capacity is situation and time specific, i.e. a patient may have capacity to decide on a breakfast menu but not on an option for a knee amputation.

The two terms have a similar meaning but in different contexts (legal and medical) and you will find that, for that reason, there is a tendency for people to use them interchangeably. However, it may be useful to understand the distinction between the two, if only to answer a picky interviewer's question on the matter. For our purpose, we will use the word "competent".

**Adults**
Most adults are competent. If an adult is not competent, for example because they are confused or have a serious mental disorder, then no other party can give consent on their behalf. There are two possible outcomes:

1.  The patient has issued an advance directive (also called "living will") at an earlier date. This stated how they would wish to be treated if at some point they were no longer able to make decisions for themselves. Doctors would then need to abide by the patient's decision, even if such a decision was not necessarily in their best interest.

2.  The patient has not indicated any particular wishes, in which case the decision will rest with doctors to act in the best interest of the patient. However, doctors should involve relatives in order to ascertain what the patient would have wanted in view of their personal views and beliefs.

**Children aged 16 or 17**

Children aged 16 or 17 are presumed to be competent (except of course in cases of certain mental disorders or other obvious reasons).

**Children below the age of 16**
**(Gillick competence / Fraser guidelines)**

Children under the age of 16 can be deemed competent to give consent providing they are shown to be mature enough to understand the information given to them about the procedure and its consequences. However, the doctor has a duty to discuss with the child the possible involvement of the parents or legal guardian in the discussions. Note that if the child refuses to involve the parents then the doctor will have to respect their decision, as this would otherwise constitute a breach of confidentiality (see Q.117 for further details on confidentiality). A doctor will only be able to involve the parents against the will of the child if the child is deemed not to be competent (in which case parental involvement is mandatory) or if the child is in danger (in which case you would involve social services or the police).

These principles are called "Gillick competence" or, more commonly now, "Fraser guidelines" after the name of a complainant and judge respectively in a famous court case. Please note the following:

▪   The competence of a child is assessed in relation to the procedure concerned. For example, a 5-year-old boy will most certainly be competent for the application of an antiseptic on a small cut, but will not be competent to give consent for the removal of one of his testicles.

▪   Although a child can give consent for a procedure or treatment if competent, in England and Wales they cannot refuse consent for a procedure or treatment that is deemed in their best interest. For example,

if a doctor established that a boy with a form of cancer needed a surgical intervention, the boy would not be allowed to refuse. The decision would need to be made by his parents. However, this causes several problems since, in order to force the treatment onto a child, the parents would need to get the child to hospital in the first place!

- If both the parents refused to give consent on behalf of their child for a life-saving procedure, you would need to act in the best interest of the child. If possible, you should get a court order to impose the treatment. If time is of the essence, you may be in a position where you can impose treatment provided you can justify that decision later in court if needed.

Important note: As mentioned above, children cannot refuse consent for a procedure or treatment. This applies in England and Wales. However, in Scotland, children are allowed to refuse consent.

# QUESTION 117

What do you understand by the expression "patient confidentiality" and when can it be breached?

### What is the duty of confidentiality?

Except for very specific circumstances addressed below, all doctors should protect the confidentiality of their patients at all costs. Breaching the confidentiality of a patient could have serious consequences for the patient (for example divulging an illness to a family member) and his trust in the medical profession. It could also prevent the patient from divulging crucial information about his health in future. Ultimately, it would constitute a serious professional fault from the doctor's part and, in extreme circumstances, could lead to the end of his career as a doctor.

### When can you breach confidentiality?

### 1 – Implied consent has been given by the patient

For example, a patient will understand that you need to provide information about them to other members of your team in order to care for them (for example nurses, or a hospital consultant if you are referring). However, if a patient explicitly mentions that they do not wish you to share information with a colleague, you must comply with their request and work around it if possible.

Other forms of implied consent include a patient who visits your surgery with a family member and openly discusses their situation with you. However, you must be careful when it comes to disclosing important information. For example, a patient may have brought her husband along but, if you feel that you have to break bad news or deal with a sensitive issue, you will need to check with the patient first.

## 2 – Information required by a court/judge

For example, if the police need access to medical records in the course of an investigation (insurance fraud, etc.). This requires a court order.

## 3 – In the public interest and to protect the patient or others

This includes:

- Where the interest to society or others of disclosing the information without the patient's consent outweighs the benefit to the patient of keeping the information confidential.
- Notification to the authorities of notifiable diseases (e.g. meningitis, tuberculosis, mumps, measles, etc. – see www.hpa.org.uk for full list). Note that HIV and AIDS are <u>not</u> notifiable.
- Suspected cases of child abuse or of neglect, physical or emotional abuse, where the patient cannot give consent to disclosure.
- Informing the DVLA if a patient's condition may affect his driving (e.g. diabetes in lorry drivers, epilepsy, etc.).
- When the information can help with the fight against terrorism or in identifying a driver who committed a road traffic offence (though the disclosure should be limited to the strictly necessary data, i.e. often address details and not clinical information).

# QUESTION 118

**Would you be happy to let a Jehovah's Witness die because he refused a blood transfusion?**

There are several aspects to consider:

**Patient's autonomy.** Jehovah's Witnesses do not accept the use of blood products from another person even if such a decision may lead to death. In accordance with the principle of autonomy, any patient is entitled to make their own decision, even if this defies the doctor's idea of their best interest. Therefore, if the patient is competent, or if they have made a "living will" refusing a transfusion, then you will have to respect their decision.

**Beneficence.** As a doctor, you still have a duty of beneficence, even if it is sometimes overridden by the patient's autonomy. Without exercising undue pressure, you must make sure that they have made their decision with full knowledge of all the facts and that they understand the consequences of not accepting the transfusion. There are also other aspects that you may want to consider. For example, is transfusion the only option? Are there other people that the patient can talk to before making a final decision (for example a liaison group for Jehovah's Witnesses)? Once you have done everything you can for the patient, you can only accept their final verdict. It does not mean that you will be happy to let them die. In a sense, you may take it as a personal failure, but you should be content with the thought that you have tried your absolute best.

**Competence/Capacity.** Just because someone makes a decision that you feel is irrational (e.g. accepting to die by refusing treatment), it does not mean that they are not competent to make that decision. If you felt that someone was making an irrational decision because they may not be competent, you would need to seek advice from colleagues and possibly a psychiatrist about the way forward. If the patient were deemed to be non-competent, you would still need to take account of their beliefs and what they would have decided if they had been competent. You may need help from the relatives for that.

# QUESTION 119

**What would you do if a known Jehovah's Witness arrived in A&E unconscious, bleeding profusely and needing an urgent blood transfusion?**

The first thing you would do is stop the bleeding. Unless the patient had previously indicated that they would not want to be treated in case of an emergency, nothing would prevent you from doing it because the patient is unconscious and cannot give consent (hence you would need to act in their best interest).

The issue of the transfusion is a bit more delicate. First of all, you should not jump to conclusions. The patient may be a Jehovah's Witness but they may not follow their religion in an orthodox manner. Thus you cannot assume that the patient would be against a transfusion unless they had made a specific request not to be transfused. Such a request could be either documented in your notes if the patient had been in hospital previously, or they may even carry a card with them. If you have any doubts, your first port of call would be to see if you have quick access to a relative. They may be present or easily reachable. They may assist you in deciding what the patient would have wanted, had they been able to make an informed decision. Note that, although the relatives can assist you in the decision, the final decision rests with you.

If you have no information about what the patient would have wanted, or if time is of the essence (the question says the patient needs an urgent transfusion), you will need to act in what you believe to be the best interest of the patient. To play it safe, you may wish to investigate any alternative to blood transfusion. Alternatively, you may simply decide to go ahead with the transfusion. In doing so, you may be taking the risk that the patient may later disagree with your approach and take legal action but provided you can justify your decision, you have nothing to fear. For this reason, you may want to involve seniors and other members of your team at an early stage, including perhaps the hospital's legal team to cover all sides.

# QUESTION 120

**A mother comes to A&E with a child who is bleeding profusely and refuses to allow you to administer a blood transfusion to the child. Why do you think this may be and what would you do?**

Make sure you do not fall into the trap. Everyone has heard about Jehovah's Witnesses refusing blood transfusion and this is an easy link to make. You should open your mind to other possibilities. Aside from religious beliefs, it is also possible that the mother is simply worried about the procedure itself. This could be because of the thought of having someone else's blood into her own child or because she fears a risk of infection (e.g. HIV, Hepatitis or other infection). Once you have addressed the bleeding, you will need to address with the mother the reasons why she is unwilling to give consent for the transfusion. Depending on the reasons, you would act in different ways.

If the child is deemed to be competent (see Q.116), then you can accept consent from the child himself. Although you would need to manage the communication process with the mother (who may be angry at your decision), you would be entitled to disregard her opinion. Once the (competent) child has given his consent, you would simply proceed with the necessary treatment.

For the remainder of this question, we will assume that the child is not competent, in which case consent for the procedure would need to be obtained from the mother herself.

If the mother is simply worried about the act of the transfusion, the risk of infection or other practical issues, then it is more a matter of reassuring her with a suitable level of listening skills and empathy, as well as explaining to her how blood is screened and how safe the blood would be for the child. You may want to involve other people in the discussion such as a senior colleague (some patients react better to consultants than to junior doctors), a nurse or anyone the patient would trust. With sufficient explanation the mother may then change her views and concur with your line of treatment.

If the mother still refuses treatment, either by principle alone or because of an underlying religious belief, then the decision to treat would have to be taken in line with what you believe to be in the best interest of the child. If you do treat (going against parental decision), the approach would be different depending on whether this is an emergency or not. If it is an emergency (i.e. you need to give blood straight away), you would need to be sure that, should criminal proceedings be taken against you at a later date, you are confident that you can defend your actions as being taken in the best interest of the patient. If the treatment does not need to be administered immediately, then there is the possibility to discuss the situation further with your multidisciplinary team and, in rare circumstances, to apply for a court order which would allow you to proceed with the treatment.

In any case, you will always need to ensure that you involve senior or specially trained colleagues in the discussions as much as you can, as well as the hospital's legal team if there is time for this and if there is any risk of the matter leading to litigation.

# QUESTION 121

**Do you think it is right for patients to make the choice as to what is in their own best interest?**

### Arguments in favour of giving patients the choice
- Patients are responsible for their own body. If they can make decisions about their lifestyle, they should also be able to make decisions about the healthcare that supports it. They are also more likely to go through with the treatment if they have been involved in the decision process.

- Having to explain different options to a patient encourages doctors to take a more thorough approach rather than rushing into their own preferred option. By questioning doctors, patients act as a counterweight and ensure the provision of safer care.

- Several approaches may be suitable, each with different impacts on the patient's lifestyle. The patient should be able to choose what suits him best.

- The patient and the doctor share the responsibility for the outcome should anything go wrong.

### Arguments against giving patients the choice
- The patient may not have the background knowledge to make the best decision for themselves.

- The patient may be unduly influenced by other parties such as relatives.

- Patients may make decisions based on external information (anecdotes from friends, information from the Internet) which may not be accurate or appropriate for their situation.

# QUESTION 122

You have one liver available for transplant and must choose one of two possible patients on the transplant list. One is an ex-alcoholic mother with two young children and the other one is a 13-year-old child with a congenital (from birth) liver defect. They both have equal clinical needs. How would you go about choosing who gets the liver?

This is a very common question which comes in different forms. You sometimes also see the issue of smokers and lung transplants. You must remember that there is no clear-cut answer to such a question. There are only issues to raise. Also note that the question is not actually "Who would you give the liver to?" but "How would you go about choosing?" The panel are far more interested in your thought process than in whether you can zoom in on a particular answer.

**Prejudice and assumptions**
There are a number of traps that candidates fall into because they adopt an approach that is too simplistic. Look at the following statements made by candidates to justify their choice and try to derive why they may not be entirely suitable:

- The 13-year-old girl is younger than the mother and therefore will live longer and has more to offer to society.

- The mother is an alcoholic and therefore her problem is self-inflicted. That makes the young girl more deserving.

- Most alcoholics relapse. Therefore the liver will be wasted on the mother. She will just start drinking again.

- If the mother dies, the two children will be orphaned and will not cope on their own. This would be unfair to them and therefore the mother needs to be given the liver.

Interview Skills Consulting

The common thread between all these statements is that they are making some kind of assumption. Although there may be some truth behind those assumptions and therefore they cannot be completely discounted, it is dangerous to take such a simplistic approach. You should recognise that the information available in the question is simply not sufficient to make any kind of decision. In your answer, you should highlight specific additional information that would help you justify these assumptions. The following considerations should give you a framework of how to think through this.

### Ethical considerations – how to approach the question

When dealing with ethical situations, you must take a step back and identify the main issues that the question raises. Do not stick to headline or bold statements as for every bold statement that you make there will be a counter-argument. Instead, you must adopt a structured approach that demonstrates that you can think logically.

In this scenario, we are considering giving a scarce resource to competing patients with equal clinical need. One of the main factors that you will consider is the patients' ability to survive that treatment in the short term as well as in the long term. There are many characteristics of each individual case which go beyond the physical, i.e. their psychosocial, background which you can allude to. But again beware of simple speculations and harsh judgements. Factors to consider are as follows:

### *Biological factors*

These are factors that will influence survival of the procedure but also successful grafting and decreased likelihood of rejection.

- **Matching**. An obvious criterion to consider is whether the liver available is a suitable match for the patient both from a tissue type and a size point of view. Although this may sound simple, you should mention this at the start so that you can concentrate on the less obvious matters during your answer.

- **Age**. Although age is not a discriminatory factor on the sole basis of a number (principle of Justice), you will look differently at a situation where a patient who is old is concerned. For example, an older person may be less able to survive surgery or its complications, and therefore may be considered less suitable compared to a younger and fitter person. Having

said that, an older person may also be considered fitter than a younger one. This will be dictated by individual circumstances. Doctors often talk about someone's physiological or biological age, rather than the number of years they have actually lived.

- **Co-morbidity**. One of the patients may have other diseases that substantially affect their life expectancy, such as some form of terminal cancer with little time to live. In addition, co-morbidities may affect their ability to deal with the long-term medications (immunosuppressants) that they will be required to take after surgery.

- **Risk of recurrence of the underlying disease**. There are diseases that are not cured by removal and simple replacement of an organ. For example, a congenital metabolic defect which leads to the accumulation of a toxin that damages the liver will not be eradicated simply by replacing the liver. Transplant will merely postpone the death of the patient until the new liver becomes damaged too.

In the case of alcoholism, this is a condition which, if it continues, will also affect the new liver and to some extent it falls into the above category. However, it is avoidable, unlike congenital conditions, and therefore may also fall into the next category. See below.

### Psychosocial factors
These are factors or issues driven by the individual's surrounding lifestyle, environment and psychological state, but which may ultimately lead to biological reasons for a less successful outcome following transplantation.

A healthy lifestyle will contribute to the individual's overall health and any decision may therefore be influenced by the lifestyle that the patient may follow after transplantation. But please be aware that this should be an objective consideration rather than a prejudiced assumption. For example:

- **Lack of commitment to maintain a lifestyle appropriate to maximise chances of success.** In the case of an alcoholic, this would mean assessing the probability that this particular patient may relapse. However, although it may be true that the majority of alcoholics relapse, her position will need to be assessed individually. Even if she presented a risk of relapse (for example because it was established that she did not

have a very strong will, or if she indicated that she would probably drink again), it would not necessarily mean that you would have to give up on her. On the contrary, she would require supplementary care of a psychological or psychiatric nature.

- **Failure to adhere to post-operative long-term immunotherapy and follow-up.** Not taking the required medication would lead to a rejection of the liver, therefore rendering the whole process useless.

**Impact on society**
The principle of Justice allows for the fact that doctors may choose the good of society above the good of the individual patient. Essentially, you would be looking at the loss to society resulting from the death of that patient. It may be very obvious that the two patients have very different number of quality years to live (e.g. a 2-month-old baby versus a 100-year-old man) but, in most cases, it will not be so clear-cut. However, talking through these issues will help you score valuable points. Some of the issues you could consider include:

- Two children would be orphaned, with adverse consequences on their life. They would also need to be supported by the State.
- It would not be fair for the young girl to be refused treatment because the other patient had children (after all she never had the chance to have children herself. Also you would not want to encourage people to have children in order to get better care for themselves).
- Although two children would be without a mother, it has happened to many people before, who then went on to lead successful lives.
- If the young girl were not to receive the transplant, her parents would suffer equally. Those parents may be old and may require her support in years to come.

Overall, as you can see, there are many contradictions that come into the debate and that you will never be able to resolve without further information. The final decision is made not by an individual clinician but as a result of deliberations by a specialist panel of multidisciplinary staff. Your role is to balance the arguments and demonstrate an open mind.

# QUESTION 123

**Should alcoholics and smokers receive equal treatment to those who don't drink and don't smoke?**

This question deals primarily with the issue of self-infliction. The arguments for this are contained in our answer to Q.96.

The question of whether alcoholics and smokers should be treated equally also brings into play the scarcity of resources available to the health system. In an ideal world where resources are abundant, the question would simply not arise as there would be enough to deal with everyone. In fact, it could even be argued that alcoholics and smokers need more help than others in many respects. In particular, it is worth recognising that addiction is a psychological/psychiatric condition in itself which would benefit from extra help from the health system and from you as a doctor.

# QUESTION 124

**What would you do if an obese patient demanded an immediate total hip replacement which will fail in 6 months?**

There are several issues to consider here.

### 1 – Justice (clinical need)
The patient has a clinical need that is the same as other people (who may not be obese) and therefore he is equally entitled to the hip replacement as anyone else. One could also effectively argue that this should be a basic human right for the patient.

### 2 – Justice (interest of society)
On the other hand, if there is a near certainty that the obesity will make the hip replacement fail, one has to wonder what purpose the hip replacement will serve other than simply relieving the patient for only 6 months to the detriment of other people on whom the money may be spent more efficiently. In other words, there is a risk that the treatment will not really benefit the patient in the long term, and may also go against the interest of society as a whole by diverting resources unnecessarily.

### 3 – Impact on the patient of going ahead
The patient may actually be worse off in the long run if you went ahead with the operation straight away. The failure may have a psychological impact. In addition, the operation itself presents possible risks of failure, including severe or even fatal complications. In other words, an immediate operation may actually harm the patient, whereas postponing the operation may be more beneficial. This would allow the doctor to fulfil both the beneficence and non-maleficence ethical principles.

### 4 – Can you do something to resolve the obesity problem before proceeding with the hip replacement?
The main issue here is that the obesity will render the hip replacement useless within a short period of time. If you can work on the obesity and

reduce it, then the patient may be able to benefit from a hip replacement but at a later stage. This would involve different steps, including:

- Discussing the nature of the problem with the patient and ensuring that they understand the consequences of the obesity. You will need to work with the patient to achieve a satisfactory outcome.

- Enlisting the help of other professionals such as a dietician and a physiotherapist to guide the patient towards a healthier lifestyle and overcome the pain.

- Ensuring appropriate pain relief for the patient while he is working on the obesity problem.

Providing treatment immediately is not necessarily in the best interest of patients and you must weigh up the different arguments. In this question, you have a perfect opportunity to discuss the various ethical principles and to explain how taking a holistic approach to the care of the patient can actually produce good successful results.

**5 – What if the patient insists that he wants the treatment?**
Although the patient has a right to autonomy, i.e. to make his own decision, such decisions can only be taken amongst a choice offered to him by the Trust and the doctor. If the Trust has made the decision not to fund hip replacements for any obese patients, then there is little that the patient can do about it and he will need to challenge the Trust's decision in court (as happened in the case of Herceptin). Alternatively, the patient may seek treatment by another Trust that is more willing.

If there are no restrictions imposed by the Trust, the doctor will need to balance the arguments and decide whether the benefits of having the hip replacement outweigh the risks. If the risks outweigh the benefits, the doctor could refuse to proceed with the hip replacement. The patient would be entitled to a second opinion from another doctor.

**Conclusion:** The best approach may therefore be to consider reducing the obesity problem so that the operation can go ahead with fewer risks and a more successful long-term outcome.

# QUESTION 125

**A young woman presents with rheumatoid arthritis. She has tried all the conventional treatments but is still having problems. Unless her symptoms improve, she will have to give up work in the near future. There is a new but very expensive treatment available. Treatment for a single patient costs as much as conventional treatment for ten patients. The drug is not effective in all patients and in some cases gives rise to a worsening of the symptoms. What do you do?**

This question gives many clues about the issues to be addressed. Your role will be to highlight those issues and explain the extent to which they present a dilemma.

### 1 – Beneficence vs. non-maleficence
First, you would need to determine if the treatment would actually benefit or harm the patient based on the patient's history, and your examination and knowledge of the patient. On one hand the drug may go against the patient's best interest by worsening the symptoms, but on the other hand it may improve the symptoms too.

If the balance of probabilities were such that, in your opinion, the patient would be harmed by the new drug then you may consider not prescribing the new drug, even if the patient was asking for it (otherwise you would be going against the non-maleficence principle). If, however, you felt that there was a decent chance that the patient may benefit from the new drug, you would need to discuss the facts with her so that she becomes fully equipped to make a decision as to whether she is prepared to take the risk or not (principle of autonomy). Your role will then consist of providing as much information as possible to help her make that fully informed decision and you would need to ensure that she is not being coerced at any stage.

## 2 – Impact on society (Justice)

The problem becomes more complex if you introduce the issue of cost and scarce resources in the equation, i.e. if giving the new drug to the patient may actually make others worse off. In your decision-making process, you would need to consider the benefits to the patient versus the benefits to society as a whole. Giving the patient the drug will take valuable resources away from ten other patients, but on the other hand those patients may never materialise. In addition, the impact on society is itself ambiguous. Giving her the drug could have the following impacts:

- **Society will be worse off** because it may open floodgates and many other patients will request the same treatment (in some cases, through court cases). This could prove very expensive indeed, well beyond the ten patients mentioned above. Overall, it may actually divert a vast amount of funds towards a treatment that may or may not work, when those funds may be better utilised in other ways.

- **Society will not benefit.** If the patient does not take the drug then she will need to stop working. Consequently, she will contribute less to society, she is likely to be placed on benefits, she will stop paying taxes and the cost to society may actually be greater than if she were to be placed on the treatment in the first place. She may also have dependants who would be worse off as a result of her decreased level of activity.

The case will need to be judged on its own merits and on personal circumstances at the time. Because of possible financial implications, a decision is likely to involve communications with managers at Trust level to determine whether the treatment may be given.

Such situations are very complex to explain because there isn't a simple algorithm that you can follow. All you can do is look at the situation from different angles and make a decision based on the balance of the arguments presented. At an interview, the interviewers will use these ambiguities to confuse you. It is inevitable that you will end up presenting contradictory arguments, but you should always remember that this is due to the nature of the ethical dilemma rather than your own inaptitude. You must retain your confidence and use the confusion to your advantage by highlighting how this demonstrates the complexity of the problem.

Interview Skills Consulting

# QUESTION 126

**You are the Health Secretary and you have a budget of £10m available to you every year. With that budget, you will be able to make a treatment or procedure available on the NHS. You have been given the choice between only two options: a treatment that will considerably alleviate the pain of arthritis sufferers and a surgical procedure designed to repair a hole in the heart of neonates. Both treatments/procedures have exactly the same overall annual cost. What would you do?**

Since, for the purpose of this question, you are the Health Secretary and not a doctor, you do not have to stick firmly to the established ethical principles, although using them as a guide will be useful in helping you establish an answer to the question. Obviously, dealing with this issue at a macro level, your main concern will be to obtain the best value for money from the point of view of society as a whole.

### 1 – Benefit to the individual
One issue that you need to consider is the effect that each treatment is likely to have on the individuals that will receive it.

- Arthritis sufferers will experience a better quality of life. They may be able to regain a degree of physical ability that they had long lost. There may also be other treatments available, even if they are slightly less effective.

- For the neonates, it is simply a case of life or death. If they do not get the treatment on the NHS, they will need to obtain it privately at great cost, which is likely to be prohibitive.

From the point of view of the individual, it could therefore be argued that the neonates will clearly benefit most as it will enable them to live, while arthritis sufferers will simply benefit from an enhanced quality of life.

**2 – Benefit to society**
There are many ways in which society will be affected by the decision:

- How many people are affected? If there was a large discrepancy between the number of people affected by the treatment every year (e.g. if the £10m budget can provide treatment for only two neonates versus 1 million arthritis sufferers) then you would need to give careful consideration to the question.

- How much will those affected contribute to society? For example, the neonates will go on to lead normal lives that would be taken away from them if they did not get the treatment. On the other hand, those with arthritis (who may be young as well as old) could take up better jobs and increase their contribution to society. Those who had to stop work because of the arthritis may be able to start work and a lead a "normal life" again. The answer to this would depend on the effectiveness of the drug, and the occupations of those involved as well as their average age.

- How much aftercare will be needed for the neonates? Does the £10m cater for the whole of their care or simply the initial procedure? The answer may influence the overall cost and therefore the outcome.

Ultimately, there is no answer to this question. It is purely a matter of deciding which arguments you feel are stronger than the others.

Also not to be forgotten: the question is asking you to place yourself in the skin of a politician and any decision may also depend on which alternative is the biggest vote winner. Do you play the sympathy card by choosing in favour of the neonates or do you seek to please arthritis sufferers, most of whom are of voting age? There is no need to be cynical at the interview, though you might want to introduce an air of realism by demonstrating an understanding of the fact that clinical and political decisions are not always based on the same principles.

# QUESTION 127

**A 14-year-old girl presents to you asking for a termination of pregnancy. What are the issues?**

This question deals with many important concepts.

## 1 – Can the girl actually have an abortion?

The first thing to do would be to confirm the pregnancy and determine how old the foetus was as, over 24 weeks, abortion is not an option. You must also take into account her competence. See Q.116 for full details. If the child is Fraser competent then she will be able to consent to the abortion without the need to involve her parents. If she is not Fraser competent, then you must involve her parents. You will be assessing her competence by discussing, amongst other things, the circumstances of the pregnancy with her, her understanding of contraception, of the consequences of abortion, etc. – in other words, her general maturity in relation to the circumstances.

## 2 – Confidentiality

The issue of confidentiality arises if the girl is competent and refused to involve her parents. Although the issue of the abortion itself is fairly straightforward, there are other issues to consider. For example, has she been abused or raped? How old is the boyfriend? If you feel that the child is at risk then you may need to breach confidentiality (see Q.117) and notify the parents, or social services, or even the police in some cases. Because of the sensitive nature of the situation, you will need to remain very vigilant about the manner in which you handle the situation. Generally speaking, if you feel that a third party should be involved (for example if you want to involve social services because she was raped), you should discuss the issue with the patient first. It is always better to come to an agreement rather than impose your own decision onto the patient (which should be your last resort). As well as saving you from breaching confidentiality, it involves the patient in the decision process and facilitates a more successful outcome.

## 3 – Holistic approach

Any girl having a child or an abortion at the age of 14 will need to be followed up in many ways. There will be:

- Physical considerations: physical impact of the abortion itself, treating any conditions linked to her sexual activity (sexually transmitted infections – STIs).
- Psychological considerations such as mental well-being prior to pregnancy, consequences of the pregnancy and of the abortion on the girl, etc.
- Social consequences including impact on her relationship with her family, with the father of the child, housing issues (e.g. if she decides keep the child after all or if her family is rejecting her).

## 4 – Education

There is a need to discuss prevention with the patient, particularly in terms of contraception and prevention of STIs.

## 5 – Trust

You will only be able to achieve an optimal result if you work with the patient and you do not take a paternalistic approach. Teenagers can be volatile in their emotions and gaining the girl's trust will be crucial to the outcome. You will therefore need to ensure that you communicate with her at the right level, that you take a non-threatening attitude and that you reassure her that you are there to help her. This could be particularly difficult in situations where you have to involve third parties and breach confidentiality. But this is where Medicine becomes an art!

## Important note for anti-abortion candidates

Doctors are allowed to refuse to deal with patients who request abortions or contraception if it means going against their own faith or personal principles. However, this does not exempt them from their duty of care towards the patient and, in such circumstances, they would need to refer the patient to another doctor who can deal with them in accordance with their wishes. If you belong to this category, there is no harm in mentioning it at the interview, although you would need to be very careful not to miss the point of the question which is really to see whether you can think laterally about the issues involved. You should therefore aim to present the issues in a general sense rather than focusing too long on your own beliefs.

ISCMEDICAL
Interview Skills Consulting

# QUESTION 128

**An elderly lady refuses to take her medication for heart failure following a recent heart attack. Not taking the medication exposes her to serious risks, including possible death. She presents to your surgery with her husband who wants you to talk some sense into her. What are the issues?**

### Confidentiality

The question mentions that the husband is present. You will therefore need to ensure that the lady is happy with her husband sitting in on the conversation so that you do not run the risk of breaching confidentiality by revealing information that she may wish to keep from her husband.

### Beneficence vs. Autonomy

By refusing to take her medication, the lady is exposing herself to a serious risk. On one hand you need to respect her right to autonomy, i.e. the right she has to make decisions for herself. However, you also have a duty of care towards the patient and must act in her best interest. Since you cannot force her to take the medication, you must at least make sure that she has all the elements to make the most sensible decision for herself. You will achieve this by educating her about her condition, the role of the medication, the consequences of taking and not taking it, etc. This must be done in a neutral manner so that you are not seen to be coercing her into her decision.

Autonomy also means that you have to respect the patient's decision once you have tried your best. If the patient ultimately wants to die, then you will need to make sure that you accompany them as best as you can in their journey towards death.

### Holistic approach

You must look beyond the obvious. Just because someone exercises their right of autonomy does not mean that you have to give up on them without

trying your best. Everything has an explanation, even if you cannot understand it. There must be a reason behind her refusal to take the medication. Maybe it has unwanted side effects, maybe she is depressed, or maybe she actually wants to die.

There may also be social aspects such as not liking living at her current care home or with one of her relatives. Such a decision must have deeper rooted reasons that you must try to discover if you want to care for the patient in the best possible way.

By addressing the underlying issues, you may actually resolve her problem of non-compliance with treatment.

**Competence**
In some cases, the elderly lady may not be competent. You will then need to consider what she would have wanted to do if she had been competent (see Q.116). The relatives may help in that regard.

However, you also need to consider competence in the context of the situation. Even if you felt that she would have wanted to take the tablets, you would find it hard to enforce it upon her without committing assault if she bluntly refused. Therefore, ultimately you will need to use your communication skills to arrive at the desired result.

Interview Skills Consulting

# QUESTION 129

**What would you do if a patient came to you asking for advice about a non-conventional treatment that they had found on the Internet?**

Many candidates answer this question with "I would not want to prescribe any treatment that is not conventional". Although they are perfectly right, this does not actually address the question. The question does not ask whether you would prescribe the patient but simply states that the patient is asking for your advice. In particular, you might consider that the patient may go ahead and purchase the treatment regardless of what you think of it.

Obviously, you will not seek to recommend that he goes ahead with the new treatment, but simply mentioning this at the interview will not take you very far. There are multiple facets to this question that you must address and debate. The simplest approach is to take a thematic approach whereby you address each issue in turn, rather than a chronological approach replicating the possible consultation with the patient.

### Your duty
Although the patient will make up his own mind about whether to purchase the treatment in question, you still have a duty of beneficence and non-maleficence towards the patient. The patient will have his reasons for wanting to purchase the treatment and you would need to identify what these may be. Also, you would want to make sure that the patient has all the elements in hand to make his decision. Your role in this process is therefore important. If you simply turned the patient away and patronised him, he may make the wrong decision through ignorance.

### Gathering information
There are two areas where you need information: on the treatment and on the patient's reasons and hopes.

The treatment:
- What claims are being made about the treatment?
- What does it contain?
- How is it regulated? (For example, it may be non-conventional in the UK but conventional somewhere else. Any information helps).
- Ask the patient to provide you with the address of the internet site.

The patient:
- Why does the patient feel the need for this treatment?
- What problems is the current treatment causing?
- Is he intending to replace his current treatment by the new one or to take the new treatment in addition to his current one?

Once you have gathered some crucial information you will have a clearer idea about what to do.

### Investigating the treatment
You may be able to find out more information about the treatment in different ways. For example, you could:
- Ask the patient to bring you one of the pills so that you can have it analysed in a lab.
- Ask some of your colleagues and pharmacists whether they have heard of the treatment.
- Contact the sellers and obtain further information.

### Informing the patient
Once you have done your research, in order to act in the best interest of the patient, there are a number of messages that you will need to give him. These include:
- Addressing the concerns that the patient has expressed about his current treatment.

- A warning against information found on the Internet and any claims made thereon.

- An explanation of what the product in question is and of the impact that the ingredients are likely to have on the patient.

- A warning that the product has not followed the same rigorous testing as a conventional drug would and is not approved in the UK.

- An explanation of the consequences of giving up any current conventional treatment or of taking the internet treatment in addition to any current conventional treatment (the two may interfere).

**Holistic approach**
The patient's needs should be fully assessed through your discussion. As well as handling the physical aspect by reviewing his current treatment if necessary, you should also address the psychological issues that the patient is facing. It may be the case that the patient's wish to move towards a non-conventional treatment is linked to the fact that they are depressed because their current conventional treatment is showing poor results. Addressing the psychological aspect may put the patient back on track. There may also be social issues. For example, the conventional treatment may stop them from enjoying their favourite hobby, or may reduce their mobility around the house. This would all need to be discussed and you may need to involve other colleagues (such as occupational therapists, physiotherapists, etc.).

**Patient autonomy**
Ultimately, it will be the patient's decision to carry on or terminate their current treatment. However, you must make sure that you are giving them all the information that they need to make an informed choice. While you can be assertive in presenting some of these facts, you should not be coercive.

# QUESTION 130

**What would you do if a patient offered you a £50 voucher as a gift at Christmas?**

Before we start looking at the question, bear in mind that it does not really matter what religion you are; the question mentions Christmas as a pretext for a debate on integrity, not for a religious debate. Any answer of the type "I would refuse it because I am not a Christian" or "My religion does not allow me to accept gifts" would simply not be enough.

**What are the issues?**
There are two aspects to consider:

**1 – Professional judgement.** As a doctor, you must care for all patients without prejudice, i.e. you cannot be influenced by other factors, and certainly not bribes. The question now is: does the £50 voucher received represent a bribe or not? Is it likely to influence your judgement? What if it were £500? Where is the limit?

**2 – Doctor/Patient relationship.** What if the present comes from an old lady whom you have been treating for many years and who is obviously not trying to bribe you? What would be the impact on the doctor-patient relationship of refusing the gift?

To bring a successful resolution to the problem, you will need to exercise your professional judgement without endangering your relationship with the patient.

**Discussion**
Essentially, the main problem associated with accepting the gift is whether you will be influenced by it. If the gift were a box of chocolates, one could barely argue that you would treat a patient better as a result of that gift. But if it were £500, then you may be influenced, even if subconsciously. Or, even

worse, the patient could use this as a weapon later on when they do need you. Many Trusts have adopted policies to deal with this. Policies vary, but generally are as follows:

**Policy 1: Accept nothing.** If you really cannot refuse it because you fear that it would endanger the doctor-patient relationship (e.g. an old granny's box of chocolates), there are a number of options open to you which would enable you not to benefit directly from the gift:

- Share with staff or other patients (if it can be shared: chocolates for example)
- Give to charity (particularly if it is cash) or place the money in the practice's fund to be used to improve services (e.g. artwork, repaint the waiting room, etc.)

**Policy 2: Accept if small gift in kind** (e.g. flowers, small pen, chocolates) but do not accept cash. If the value of the item is over a certain amount (say £10) then discuss with practice manager. The advantage of such policy is that you can accept small gifts and therefore avoid damaging the doctor-patient relationship for most situations. If the gift is too great, discussing with the manager ensures that others are aware of the situation and that you are not abusing the situation.

**Policy 3: Tiered approach.** Below a small amount (say £10), accept. Between that amount and a medium amount (say £10 to £30), discuss with practice manager. Above the medium amount (£30), refuse.


### How to handle it
Your first step would be to familiarise yourself with the procedures in your practice or hospital so that you know how to handle the matter. If there is no policy, you will need to look at the level of the gift and the intent behind the gift. For example, there will be no real harm in accepting a small bouquet of flowers from a long-term patient, but it may look odd to accept an expensive case of wine from a relatively new patient.

Generally speaking, if you have any doubt about what to do, there is no harm in raising the issue with a manager or a senior colleague. They will appreciate your openness and integrity.

You must also ensure that you communicate adequately with the patient, particularly if you are going to refuse the gift. It should be explained clearly and politely that you appreciate their gift but that it could be seen as clouding your judgement.

### Typical probing questions

Once you have answered the question about the £50, interviewers tend to like asking about all sorts of gifts. Regular appearances include:

- **What if you receive a cauliflower?** (Yes it was a real question!) Unless this is a rare breed that you do not yet have in your collection, you are unlikely to be influenced by such a gift. There are therefore virtually no risks of possible influence here. (You may wonder about the patient's mental state though!)

- **What if the gift is only £2 in cash?** The gift is small so the risk is minimal, but the fact that it is cash means that you should really avoid keeping it. Give it to charity or to the practice's funds.

- **What if the patient gives you a bottle of wine every year?** You need to see how this fits with the relationship that you have with the patient. If you manage their chronic condition all year round, then the gift is merely a thank you present with no real other intent. If, however, you only see the patient once every 5 years for a fungus, you would wonder about the reasons behind the gift. Discussing the situation with a senior colleague would help you sort it out promptly and professionally.

Candidates are usually scared of such questions because interviewers can ask them in many different formats. However, if you always go back to first principles, you have little chance of getting it wrong. Always explain the principles behind your reasoning.

# QUESTION 131

**Do you think it is right for doctors to have conferences, training sessions and study material sponsored by pharmaceutical companies or other corporate sponsors?**

Again, this is a question about integrity, though, unlike the previous question, the doctor-patient relationship does not come into play. Instead you need to balance professional integrity against the need for education, which may not be provided if such sponsorship did not exist.

### Advantages of allowing corporate sponsorship
- Education budgets are small and many doctors must pay for their education out of their own pocket. This acts as a deterrent and enabling corporate sponsorship allows doctors to develop faster.

- Greater awareness by doctors of courses available through circulars sent by corporate sponsors.

- Allows good introduction to new products from pharmaceutical companies.

- Allows greater relationship building with the industry.


### Disadvantages of allowing corporate sponsorship
- Sponsors might only support speakers who are biased in their favour (risk of corruption, however small).

- Doctors may feel obliged to prescribe certain drugs rather than others as a result.

Interview Skills Consulting

**Discussion**

Although there is a risk of bias associated with such sponsorship (and the risk must be real, otherwise the companies would not provide funding!), ultimately you must balance this against the need for education. It is simply a matter of being conscious of the risks involved and of making sure that you are not unduly influenced.

Obviously, this will also depend on the nature of the gift. For example, a cheque for £150 to attend a conference based in London would not cause a real problem. But what about an all-expenses paid one-week trip to Barbados for a conference sponsored by a major pharmaceutical? The answer would very much depend on the nature of the work you will be doing there. It is also generally accepted that the gift should be limited to the doctor himself and that no sponsorship should be allowed for travelling spouses (as it would obviously serve no educational purpose!).

# QUESTION 132

**What is your opinion about euthanasia and assisted suicide?**

### Definitions to clarify semantics

#### *Euthanasia*
Euthanasia is where a second party terminates someone's life as an act of mercy. It is sometimes termed "mercy killing". Euthanasia is currently illegal in the UK.

#### *Assisted suicide*
Many people include the concept of assisted suicide under the generic term "euthanasia". Assisted suicide is effectively a situation where the individual takes action to commit suicide with the help of a second party without whom the act would not have been possible. Assisting suicide is also currently illegal in the UK.

As mentioned earlier in the book, whenever you are asked for your opinion you should always ensure that you first present the main arguments on both sides. Your opinion matters less than your ability to explain the manner in which you think about the topic. You may include the following arguments in your discussion:

### Arguments in favour of euthanasia and assisted suicide
- Patients should be allowed to choose what is best for them.
- Patients can avoid a lengthy and unnecessary suffering period.
- Patients can die with dignity at a time of their choosing.
- It would free up beds and other NHS resources utilised for these patients.

## Arguments against euthanasia and assisted suicide

- It goes against some religious principles. It may lead to doctors or relatives playing God.
- Even if someone has expressed the wish to receive euthanasia when they are in distress, they may change their mind later at a time when they may no longer be able to express their change of position.
- There have been cases where people, who were in situations where everyone thought they were a lost cause, actually recovered.
- It would be very difficult to verbalise specific criteria for allowing or disallowing euthanasia/assisted suicide.
- If the case is not clear-cut or well documented, relatives may face murder charges (e.g. following a complaint by other relatives).
- Relatives may abuse the situation by allowing convenient euthanasia on a patient to suit their own needs.
- Relatives may pressure a patient into a situation they do not actually wish.

Note that there were discussions about whether doctor-controlled euthanasia should be provided in the UK, although the focus has now shifted towards the possibility of introducing a form of doctor-assisted suicide, whereby a doctor would provide the means for a patient to commit suicide (or to allow someone else to do it for them if they are not fit to do it themselves).

## The Swiss connection

There are institutions abroad (e.g. Switzerland) where patients can go to receive euthanasia. Following an assessment, patients are injected with a lethal cocktail of drugs, which relaxes them and enables them to die peacefully. Obviously, such a possibility is only open to people who can actually travel there. The decision would need to be taken entirely by the patient and could certainly not be made on the recommendation of a UK doctor (otherwise they would be in breach of the non-maleficence principle). There have been several high profile cases of this nature and the police are taking a keen interest in the relatives who travel with the patient. The main argument is that, by accompanying a relative to a so-called "death clinic" (or even by booking a plane ticket for them), they are effectively assisting a suicide, which is illegal. In practice though, such police investigations never lead to a conviction, particularly if it can be proven that the patient travelled there of their own free will and the relatives did not play an active role. This is perhaps a sign that society is slowly adapting.

# QUESTION 133

**A patient comes to see you and requests an HIV test. What do you do?**

There are several reasons why someone may have an HIV test. This may be a wish of their own, as in this case, or as part of other comprehensive medical investigations. The situation in which the test has been requested will obviously affect the patient's expectations of the result. In turn, this will have an impact on the way in which a positive or negative result is delivered as well and will dictate the manner in which the patient is handled prior to the test.

In general, HIV tests may be undertaken for people in the community (e.g. by GPs), admitted unwell to a hospital ward or (as in the majority of cases) in a Genito-Urinary clinic.

Before a test is taken, an assessment should be made of the patient to identify whether they are likely to be at a particularly high risk of having contracted HIV (e.g. intravenous drug user, homosexual, partner known to have HIV, etc.). Whatever the risk, the physician should always cover certain principles with the patient before the test is made. If the patient is deemed to be high risk, lengthier counselling should ideally take place, which would involve other aspects such as investigating how they might react to a positive result.

## Basic issues to cover with the patient
- Why do they want the test?
- What risk do they think that they have been exposed to and when?
- Sexual history.

A patient may not have had any significant risk of HIV but may have symptoms they believe to be due to HIV. It is important to listen to the patient, rationalise and reassure them if their risk is negligible (e.g. kissing an unknown partner in a night club).

Regarding sexual history, if the patient feels that they have been exposed to a significant risk, the physician may wish to offer a full sexual screen for other infections such as Chlamydia and Syphilis.

### Distressed patient
If the patient is quite distressed you may wish to probe further as to whether any recent sexual activity was non-consensual (i.e. rape). If this were the case, you would obviously handle the patient with great care and involve other specialist professionals.

### Timing of test
The timing of the test is very important. There is a three-month period of time from exposure to HIV to the individual production of antibodies (seroconversion). It is the detection of these antibodies in a blood sample that signifies a positive test. Therefore any blood test taken within three months of an exposure may be HIV-negative.

### Education and Support
It is also important to explain to the patient what HIV is and its difference from AIDS, as well as briefly indicating that it is no longer a certainly terminal condition and, with adherence to medications, HIV has now become a medical chronic condition with a good long-term medical prognosis.

With those with significant risks, you should also explore what social support networks they would have and how they would cope if they were to receive a positive diagnosis. If their lifestyle puts them at high risk of HIV acquisition, you should take the opportunity to encourage risk reduction measures (e.g. safe sex) as well as continued engagement with sexual health check-ups.

### Handling the question
In your answer, you should ensure that you concentrate on the general approach to the patient (and not jump straight into giving the patient a test without any prior discussion or consideration of all factors surrounding their request). Throughout the consultation, you should make sure that you adequately prepare the patient if they are high risk. If they are low risk, your emphasis should be on reassuring the patient. At some point in your answer, you should also mention to the patient that any discussions and outcomes would remain confidential.

ISCMEDICAL
Interview Skills Consulting

# QUESTION 134

**You are a physician looking after a patient who was diagnosed with HIV a few months ago. You have encouraged him to disclose his diagnosis to his wife, which he has refused to do. What do you do?**

Beware of questions asking what you would do, since, in most cases, you cannot decide much without further information. Instead, you should concentrate your efforts on raising the issues at stake and the parameters that you would use to make decisions.

This question really is: "Should you disclose the diagnosis to his wife or not?" Ultimately, your worry will be that he is exposing his wife to the risk of HIV (e.g. through unprotected sex) or that she is already positive and is missing out on treatment.

### Confidentiality and ethical dilemma
As a doctor, you have a duty of confidentiality towards your patient. This would prevent you from disclosing any information about the patient's status, including to his own GP. However, there are situations where you may be allowed to breach confidentiality; this may be possible if the patient posed a great risk to others for example. (See Q.117.)

If the wife is also one of your patients, this will complicate matters, since you will have an immediate dilemma between your duty of confidentiality towards the patient and your duty of beneficence towards his wife.

### Is the wife at risk?
You should not make assumptions about the situation. Although the patient is married, he may not be having sex with his wife, and, if he is, he may be using condoms. One of your first tasks will therefore be to discuss with the patient his personal circumstances to ascertain his wife's level of exposure. On the other hand, even if he is using condoms, condoms can split and she would therefore benefit from disclosure as, should a split happen, she would require counselling and, possibly, emergency therapy to prevent HIV

280

acquisition (PEP – Post Exposure Prophylaxis). This is all assuming that she is HIV-negative, since, if she were to be HIV-positive already, disclosure may encourage her to undergo HIV testing and allow her to benefit from medical care.

## Can you make the patient change his mind?

As an empathic doctor, you will of course understand why the patient may be worried about disclosing his HIV status to his wife. Before placing the patient in a difficult position by divulging his condition to his wife, you would therefore need to have an in-depth discussion with him about his reluctance and the reasons behind it. Through counselling, possibly involving other support staff, you may be able to reassure him and guide him through the disclosure process. If ultimately he refuses outright, breaching confidentiality may be your only option.

## Should you breach confidentiality?

If, given the circumstances and the information provided by the patient, you strongly suspect that his wife is at risk, then you may be entitled to breach confidentiality. Such decision would often be taken as a team and you would therefore need to confer with colleagues before going ahead. Ultimately, you will need to be confident that you can suitably justify your position in court, should you need to do so.

Before you breach confidentiality, you should encourage the patient to divulge the information to his wife by himself. In essence, you would set up a verbal contract with the patient whereby he should discuss the situation with his wife within an agreed timeframe, failing which you would undertake to divulge the information yourself. The timeframe involved would very much depend on the urgency of the situation and the risks involved.

ISCMEDICAL
Interview Skills Consulting

# QUESTION 135

**What is your opinion on vivisection?**

Vivisection commonly refers to animal testing (though it literally means "cutting alive" and could apply to any living entity, including human beings). It is estimated that up to 100 million animals are used each year for research purposes, with countries having developed more or less stringent codes of conduct to regulate their use. The UK is thought to have one of the most stringent codes.

Animals are used for different purposes, including:
- Studies into development
- Studies into comportment
- Studies into evolution
- Research aiming to determine new cures and treatments
- Toxicology studies
- Cosmetics development.

## Arguments in favour of animal testing
- We need to understand physiology and pathology using basic cellular studies. This can only be carried out on animals.

- We must ensure that new treatments are safe for humans. Testing on animals is essential to ensure a safe transition. Ultimately, there will always be a first human being who will take the drug in question. Not testing on animals beforehand would make that human being the first guinea pig. This would lead to even greater ethical considerations.

- Animal suffering is minimised and most do not feel anything.

- There are not many alternatives (e.g. there is only so much that a computer can simulate). Sometimes it is necessary to test in a live environment.

**Arguments against animal testing**

- This is depriving an animal from its normal life and is cruel. There is no reason to consider that an animal's life is less valuable than a human life.

- The animals are defenceless and cannot consent.

- It may not always lead to results that can be used (for example parsley is a poison for parrots, morphine anaesthetises humans but excites cats, and arsenic is harmless to sheep). Recent trials at Northwick Park hospital went drastically wrong for the first few human volunteers despite the fact that tests had been carried out on animals at 500 times the dose.

- A number of tests are unnecessarily repeated. For example, if two pharmaceuticals are researching similar drugs, they will both do tests. This element of duplication might make sense from a commercial secrecy point of view, but it means that twice as many animals as necessary are being used for testing. Introducing mechanisms whereby information can be shared more efficiently would remove some of the unnecessary testing.

- There are alternatives that can be used in some cases e.g. computer modelling or cell cultures.

**Current and proposed legislation**

Note that the European Commission has proposed a ban on testing finished cosmetic products in 2006, with a further proposed ban on cosmetic ingredient testing in 2009. However, such bans may be delayed for a long time if no viable alternatives to testing are found. As far as the UK is concerned, a voluntary agreement was implemented in 1998 whereby the government would no longer issue licences to test cosmetic products or ingredients on animals. Despite all these agreements or bans, there is nothing stopping companies performing animal testing abroad in countries where this is accepted. Without a wider-ranging ban, the problem is likely to continue.

Interview Skills Consulting

# QUESTION 136

**What are the arguments for and against the sale of tobacco?**

### Arguments for:
- People should have the right to choose what is good for them. It is their choice to take a health risk.

- Tobacco sales generate revenue through heavy taxation. This revenue can be used for the benefit of society as a whole.

- Banning the sale of tobacco would lead to the development of a black market and would make the consequences uncontrollable. People with tobacco-linked illness would not dare seek medical assistance for fear of being prosecuted, which could have an overall negative effect on society.

- Tobacco farmers (often in poor countries) rely heavily on those sales to survive. Banning tobacco would have a devastating effect on parts of the world economy.

- Some people argue that tobacco is a drug, but then so is alcohol or hamburgers to some people (with equally devastating effects). So why not allow the sale of tobacco?

### Arguments against:
- Tobacco leads to serious respiratory diseases. This drains NHS resources and effectively wipes out the benefit of the additional revenue gained through taxation.

- Not only is the smoker exposed, other people are exposed to secondary smoking. They do not have the same choice that smokers have. This includes babies, who may develop an addiction themselves through passive exposure and start smoking later on in life.

- Addiction to cigarettes might lead to addiction to stronger drugs later on in life.

- Cigarette ends sometimes litter the streets, creating an unhygienic and dirty environment (see some famous capitals in Europe for reference).

## Discussion

Ultimately, there is no denying that the sale of tobacco is crucial in bringing additional revenue into the economy, though heavy taxes also act as a regulator. A total ban would be impossible to impose without putting in place a police state; hence governments need to find a way to control the situation with a happy medium.

Smoking is a form of self-harm and to that extent it could be argued that it is the individual's responsibility to regulate his own consumption. Governments and other organisations are working hard at reconciling the various conflicting interests and actions are being taken on different counts:

***Informed choice:*** individuals may smoke at will but efforts are being made to ensure that they are aware of the consequences of smoking (campaigns on lung cancer, unsavoury messages on packets, etc.).

***Prevention:*** other than the dissemination of information about smoking, the government has tackled the issue of passive smoking by introducing a partial ban on smoking in places where food is being served. Several countries have introduced bans on smoking in public places.

# QUESTION 137

**Do you think it is right for parents to conceive a second child to cure a disease in their first child?**

### Why would anyone want to do that?

There are conditions which can only be cured through the introduction of cells or organs that constitute a perfect match and for which the only realistic chance is to find a suitable relative. If no such relative is available, it is tempting to "create" one that would match.

### Arguments for:

- The unique but powerful advantage is that the life of the first child may be saved by the second child.

### Arguments against:

- There is no guarantee that the new child will be a suitable donor for the first child. Should this be the case, it will not only have devastating consequences for the first child but, in addition, the second child may develop a guilt complex later on in life (although it could be argued that this could easily be handled through appropriate psychotherapy if and when this occurs).

- The second child may be born with the same condition as the first child. This would have a devastating effect on the whole family.

- The primary purpose behind having the second child is effectively to produce "spare parts". This could distance the siblings and may make the second child feel that he was not born out of love but out of necessity.

- This is a slippery slope leading to possible issues of genetic selection (for example if the second child must fulfil specific criteria in order to constitute an appropriate donor).

# QUESTION 138

**How do you solve the problem of transplant organ shortage?**

There are only two approaches that you can take to solving the problem of transplant organ shortages:

**1 – Remove the need for transplants** of living organs by increasing research to find alternative solutions to using real organs (e.g. grow organs on demand, use animal organs or find alternative cures for diseases).

**2 – Increase the number of organs being donated.** This is probably the most realistic and quickest-to-implement option. The question is: how do you go about it?

**Possible solutions to increase donations**
For many reasons (religious, psychological, etc.), many people feel very uncomfortable donating organs to others, even if these organs are removed after their death. The problem is even more acute when it comes to donating organs while alive. Mostly, so far, the principle has been that organs could only be taken with the consent of the donor or the family in some cases. This relies heavily on people's altruism, which is in short supply, and on potential donors carrying cards on their person.

Other than encouraging people to carry donor cards, several other suggestions have been made and sometimes implemented around the world:

**Imposing that everyone should be a donor**
Although this would inevitably resolve the issue, it poses serious ethical dilemmas. Essentially, if patients can invoke their autonomy when they are alive, why should they not be allowed to decide what happens to them when they are dead? For some people, this also raises religious issues which cannot be discounted.

**Financial incentives**

Paying for organs is currently illegal in the UK because it is open to abuse and would lead to the establishment of the traffic in organs which could have devastating effects on parts of the population. Individuals would seek to obtain organs from poorer countries to sell them at a profit back in the UK; poorer individuals in the UK would also offer their organs for sale simply to make ends meet. The main problem is the direct payment of money against an organ, which could create a market with a totally different set of values (e.g. some people would profit from other people's misery). However, other less direct solutions were tried or proposed around the world, including:

- Giving discounts on driving licences for those who wish to become an organ donor ($9 discount in Georgia, USA)

- Establishing a market for options on organs. Under this principle, a potential donor would sell the right to his organs for a small amount of money. Once the donor dies, then his estate/family would receive a larger sum of money if the organs are actually used. The advantage of this solution is that the organ is not actually purchased from the donor immediately and the future donor only gets a small sum of money. Therefore it eliminates the risk of organ trafficking and the risk of poorer people selling body parts for immediate cash (since the amount will not be substantial enough in relation to the sacrifice). Another advantage is that it is the donor who actually makes the decision. Since it is the family that will benefit, it could almost be viewed as some kind of life insurance plan.

**Reciprocity plans**

These plans are already in place in the US (see www.lifesharers.com for an example) and are sometimes called no-give-no-take plans. Essentially, they are members' clubs which you join if you have organs that you want to donate. In exchange, you are entitled to receive organs from members of the club too. The system works on a point system to determine who is entitled to what benefit. In principle, such plans look like a good idea and get around the issue of financial incentive by encouraging altruism. However, they select against people who are in poor health or who have no/few organs that may be fit for transplant.

Ultimately, the most realistic and immediate manner in which to increase donations will be to find ways of de-stigmatising death and encouraging people to get over the psychological barrier of donating organs to others. This is very much a communications exercise for the government and the NHS to undertake in order to change mentalities.

Interview Skills Consulting

# QUESTION 139

**Do you think that the government is right to impose that the NHS should only allow the MMR vaccine rather than three individual vaccines?**

The controversy stems from the fact that a study based on a small number of children has shown that there may be a link between the MMR vaccine (Mumps, Measles, Rubella) and autism. This was not helped by the fact that Tony Blair refused to answer the question as to whether his new-born son had received the MMR vaccine. There have also been a few isolated cases of people who claimed that their child became autistic following MMR vaccination, although any link would be hard to prove. The NHS is now offering the MMR vaccine only and anyone who wishes to receive the three separate vaccines instead needs to go private.

In your discussion you should consider the following facts:

- The studies showing a link to autism are based on small numbers of patients and therefore do not represent any kind of compelling evidence. Since the original study conducted on 12 patients in 1998, there have been many other studies indicating that there was no link between the MMR vaccination and autism.

- The combined vaccine is safer and more effective as children are not put at risk of catching the diseases while they are waiting for full immunisation.

- The role of the NHS is to offer what is believed to be the best solution to a particular health issue taking into account cost considerations. In this case, patients are actually offered a choice in that they can still get the three vaccines separately albeit on a private basis. This is a good compromise to ensure that patients can exercise their choice, while ensuring that the nation provides the solution of choice free of charge.

- On the negative side, the controversy surrounding MMR has put off a number of parents from vaccinating their children altogether (the single vaccines are only available privately and MMR has a "potential" risk). This has led to the re-emergence of conditions which were virtually eradicated with vaccination such as measles and mumps. An effort is therefore necessary to educate patients appropriately.

There is evidence that confidence in the MMR vaccine is returning. Uptake fell to 80% in 1998 when the first study was released. It increased to 84% in 2005/2006 (95% is needed for herd immunity).

In 2004, the editor of *The Lancet* (who published the original study) announced that he regretted having published the controversial paper because he felt that the researchers had a "fatal conflict on interest", although no details were made available about what that conflict might have been. This claim has obviously been denied by the researchers in question.

# QUESTION 140

**You are a junior doctor and, just before the morning ward round, you notice that your consultant smells of alcohol. What do you do?**

This question is becoming increasingly frequent as it enables interviewers to test your flexibility in dealing with a difficult and sensitive issue, your empathy, your team playing abilities and also your integrity. To answer this question successfully, you must consider a number of issues:

**Patient safety**
As a doctor, patient safety will always be your first priority (except where your own safety is compromised in which case it will come first).

Because your consultant is drunk, you will need to ensure that he is not dealing with patients (dangerous enough for a medic, even more dangerous for a surgeon) and that he leaves the ward. Since you are a junior, it is easier said than done, but in reality you will have other people around you to help; for example a senior nurse, another trainee doctor or even another consultant. This will need to be handled discreetly and sensitively so as not to alert patients and not to embarrass the consultant in question in front of others.

Also in the interest of patient safety, you will need to ensure that the patients that the consultant has already seen, or for whom he has made decisions, are reviewed by someone else. Once the consultant has been removed from the clinical area, you will need to ensure that patient care is appropriately covered and that the team can cope with the absence of the consultant. You will need to involve other doctors and managers to ensure appropriate cover.

As an aside you will also need to look after your colleague's safety by ensuring that he is okay and by booking a taxi to send him home so that he does not take the gamble of driving back, or by organising a room where he can sleep it off.

**Reporting the matter**

Whatever the reasons behind the consultant's behaviour, the fact that he turned up at work drunk (when most people would have called in sick) shows a serious lack of judgement that could have a devastating impact on patients. It will therefore be a matter for someone of higher authority to deal with.

You would benefit greatly by reading the GMC's *Good Medical Practice Guide* which can be accessed online via www.gmc-uk.org as it contains information that could prove valuable at an interview. If you read sections 43 to 45 of the guide, you will see that if you believe that a doctor is placing patients at risk you have a duty to share your concerns with someone in authority. There will most likely be guidelines within your Trust, in which case you should follow them, but if there are not then you should adopt the most logical route. In either case, your next step will most likely be to discuss the situation with another consultant or the clinical director (i.e. the head of your department) and let them handle the situation.

**Supporting the team and your colleague**

The team will inevitably suffer the consequences of the situation. For example, the consultant may be asked to take some time off, to go on lighter duties, etc. and you will need to make sure that you have a flexible attitude that enables the team to function well despite the problem. Whenever possible, you should also offer your personal support to your colleague in your own way.

**Communicating**

Throughout the situation, you will need to demonstrate sensitivity and care not to disrupt the team more than necessary. You should be understanding towards the consultant rather than critical and understand that there may be real issues and personal drama behind the situation. This means that you should also aim to minimise his embarrassment by not spreading gossip and only discussing the matter with relevant people.

**What if it is the first time?**

There is no proof that this is a first incident. It may have happened in previous jobs (look at Shipman!). It may be happening in private and you might simply have witnessed the first incident at work, but it still remains that without your intervention patients may have suffered. The approach is therefore the same, first time or not.

**What if he had a "good" reason to be drunk?**
**What if he pleads with you not to say anything?**
There may be several reasons for someone to turn up drunk at work. The consultant may have a personal problem (his wife left him, his mother died, etc.) or maybe he simply drunk too much at a party. If there are mitigating circumstances, then they will be taken into account by the senior person who handles the matter. But you should not attempt to cover up something as serious as this on the basis that you feel sorry for the consultant. If there is a problem, you can be understanding and empathic but it is not really up to you to resolve it. It is an issue that he will need to deal with personally with the help of the department; hence why a senior colleague should be involved.

If the consultant has a real alcohol problem, you will not do him any favours by covering up for him. In fact, if something happened later which could have been prevented if you had said something earlier, then you would find yourself in front of the GMC for negligence/breach of duty.

**What if, despite reporting the matter, nothing happens and he does it again?**
First, do not jump to conclusions. Although it may not seem like it, your seniors are probably handling the matter but they can't always keep an eye on the consultant. If the problem recurs, talk to them again and see what they say. If at any stage you feel uncomfortable with the situation, you can always choose to escalate the situation but you must do so carefully. Before escalating further (for example to the medical director or the chief executive), you may find a way to seek advice from other colleagues or even from special helplines for doctors which many institutions run. Your final resort will be the relevant Royal College and the GMC.

**What if he is your best friend?**
Whether he is your best friend or not does not change anything to the gravity of the situation. The only difference it will make is in the communication skills that you will use. If the consultant is your best friend you may be more inclined to spend a longer period of time talking to him about the consequences of his actions at the beginning. But your friend will also need to accept responsibility and understand the position in which you find yourself.

Interview Skills Consulting

**A word of warning – the tone of delivery**
Written words do not convey emotions in the same way that a verbal answer would. The above will give you a good framework to build an effective answer but you will need to complement this with an appropriate tone of voice that translates your understanding of the difficult situation that the consultant is facing and the personal drama behind the alcoholism. This is where you can show how empathic you really are!

Interview Skills Consulting

# QUESTION 141

**What would you do if you caught a colleague looking at child pornography on a computer at work?**

The situation here is different from the scenario of the drunk consultant in two respects:

- The situation does not present an immediate danger to patients through his actions, although it would be a valid argument to say that the doctor presents a danger to children in general anyway.

- His activities are illegal.

**The approach**
Your approach will consist of the following steps:
- Take note of the date and time when you have seen the colleague use the computer. This will be needed for the hospital to prove the case against the colleague if needed.

- Discuss the situation with a colleague that you trust if you need support and report the matter to a senior colleague. They, in turn, should notify management and the police once they are satisfied that there are reasonable grounds to do so.

- Support the team. Reporting the colleague will certainly lead to some form of disciplinary action and probable dismissal. The team will need to pull together to cope with the change.

- If you feel that action is slow (for example the incident recurs despite repeated complaints) then you should follow up, and escalate further if nothing is being done.

- And remember, if you do not know what to do or are worried about the consequences on you, you can seek advice from relevant helplines.

**What if the pornography is adult pornography?**
If the pornography is not child pornography then the matter is entirely different as it would not be illegal. Although he may be breaching hospital policy (which is a matter for the hospital to sort out), your main concern would really be whether his actions are actually compromising patient safety.

Your first step would probably be to have a chat with your colleague. He would need to realise that he is endangering his reputation and his career if he got caught. If you don't know him then you will need to make a decision as to whether you need to report him or not.

Issues to consider would include:

▪   Is there a policy in place in the Trust and, particularly, would you be in trouble if you did not report the matter?

▪   Is the doctor in question actually compromising patient care? After all, although looking at pornography and abusing NHS resources may not be acceptable in the workplace, he is not committing an illegal act. If, however, the doctor were compromising the care of his patients at any time or acting against the interest of the team (for example by spending too much time on the computer), then you would have strong grounds to report the matter to a senior colleague.

Ultimately, it will be left to your judgement depending on the nature of the situation.

# QUESTION 142

**What would you do if a colleague asked you to prescribe them some antidepressants?**

This question is interesting and misinterpreted by many candidates. Too often, candidates rush into answering that they would not prescribe for a colleague because it is illegal. Not only is this not entirely correct, it also fails to address the multiple facets of the question. The question is not just asking about prescription but specifically mentions antidepressants. Ask yourself why he may be requesting these drugs and you will open up a whole new line of thoughts.

### Prescribing for friends and family
Strictly speaking it is not illegal for doctors to prescribe for friends and family, although of course such practice is not best practice. There are several reasons for this:

- It is open to abuse.
- There is no centralised approach to the care of the person being prescribed in the way that there would be if that person went to their GP instead.

Note that only a few doctors are allowed to prescribe controlled drugs such as antidepressants. This includes GPs and psychiatrists. Therefore even if you were tempted to write a prescription, you would not be able to.

### Your colleague's need
You would need to establish why your colleague needs the antidepressants and why he is not going to his GP to obtain a prescription. Reasons might include:

- He may not have the time to go to his GP, in which case what you should really do is to ensure that he finds the time to do so; for example by

swapping shifts or by encouraging him to discuss the matter with a senior colleague.

- He may be retailing the drugs to addicts, in which case he would not be honest with you and you certainly would not want to be part of it.

- He may be depressed but wants to keep it outside the normal system because he is worried that it may affect his job. In this case, you would need to reassure him about the confidentiality of the GP service and encourage him to seek proper help. You would also want to explain to him that it is better to address the problem at an early stage than let it develop into an even bigger problem.

Whatever the situation, he really needs to see a GP and maybe seek specialist help, but you are not the best person to address the issue. He will need to be properly assessed and prescribed by relevant specialists rather than prescribed in 2 minutes in the corridor by you without any appropriate background.

### Fitness to practise and patient safety
There is a possibility that his depression is affecting his ability to function normally at work and you will need to address this with him too. In particular, rather than report this straight away to senior colleagues, you may want to encourage your colleague to see a senior colleague himself and discuss the matter with them so that they can derive ways of helping him out.

If you feel that your colleague presents a danger to patients and does not want to address the situation then you may have no option but to discuss the matter yourself with senior colleagues.

### Supporting your colleague and the team
If your colleague is going through a difficult time, you should show support. This could be either at a personal level by offering your time to discuss his problems or by helping the team and him to deal with any consequences (e.g. being flexible and taking on more work for a while, etc.). Empathy and teamwork are two important skills to demonstrate.

**"ISC**MEDICAL
Interview Skills Consulting

# QUESTION 143

**What would you do if one of your fellow junior doctors was not pulling his weight in the team?**

### Patient safety
Your first priority will be to ensure that patient safety is not compromised. If you feel that your colleague's behaviour is placing patients in danger in any way then you should report it straight away to someone in a senior position, such as a consultant, the clinical director (head of department) or even a senior nurse. They will handle the matter from then on.

If patient safety is not compromised (e.g. someone is simply a bit slow, is reluctant to get involved more than they should or show flexibility) then there are several aspects to consider.

### Understanding the reasons
There may be several reasons behind your colleague's behaviour. For example:
- He may have personal problems.
- He may have problems understanding specific issues or procedures.
- He may have had poor training in the past.
- He may be depressed or stressed.
- He may be lazy or feel superior.

Whatever the reason, you will not be able to resolve the problem if you do not get to the bottom of it. If you feel confident that you can approach the colleague by yourself, then have an informal chat with them so that you can address the problem. You might be able to encourage them to discuss their problems with a senior colleague who may be best placed to help them. For example, if they need some time off to deal with a family issue or if they require more training, then there would be some value in discussing the problem with an understanding consultant.

If you feel that you cannot approach the colleague easily then you can discuss your feelings with colleagues that you trust and see whether they want to be involved. Someone else may feel that they can approach the colleague.

If you feel that dealing with the problem is not something that you can handle at your level then you should raise the matter with a senior colleague who will be best placed to handle it.

**Supporting the colleague and the team**
It is likely that some form of action will be taken to resolve the matter. For example, the colleague may be given some time off, may be allocated different duties for a time while he gains further training, may be placed on lighter duties, etc. depending on the nature of the problem. This will have an inevitable impact on the team and you will need to ensure that you make yourself available to deal with the changes. This will require you to show some flexibility.

At the same time, your colleague may require some personal support (particularly if the underperformance is due to personal problems or stress). You should be there if he needs your help.

Interview Skills Consulting

# QUESTION 144

**Do you think that sending a man to the moon was money well spent?**

This question is disarming at first because it does not seem terribly relevant to Medicine. However, it is quite explicitly about how to allocate money from a national budget (sounds familiar?).

Many candidates rush into answering the question by saying that the trip to the moon did not achieve much and that the money could have been better spent on the health service. Although this is a good argument in itself, it is a little simplistic for this type of interview and there are many more aspects to consider. For example:

- When you go shopping for food or for clothes, do you always buy the cheapest items in order to give the money that you saved to your favourite charity or to the NHS?

- Do you refrain from offering presents to friends and family because that money is really a luxury and could be better utilised for the good of society?

In most cases, the answer would be, of course, "no". So, along the same line, why should a government spend all its money on the health service? We spend money on putting flowers on roundabouts. Is this a luxury or a need? One could argue that it has an important psychological impact on the population.

This question is all about what society is seeking to achieve and how the right balance can be maintained between the "useful" and the "luxuries".

**ISC**MEDICAL
Interview Skills Consulting

Here are a few arguments that should help you in your discussion:

- Space exploration is an important element in building a future for the human race. It has to start somewhere and the technology developed to place a man on the moon has been a very successful start.

- The successful moon missions have considerably boosted the morale of the nations involved. It can easily be argued that the general well-being of a population and a healthy degree of patriotism are important factors too and that a nation should be able to afford such luxuries.

- Space exploration may lead to scientific discoveries that could actually help the advancement of Medicine. This may not be immediately apparent but the rewards may be reaped at a later stage.

- The space race encouraged competition between nations and ensured a fast track technological advancement. However, it could also be argued that such a level of competition at times proved to be unhealthy, particularly during the cold war.

- Of course, it could be argued that the money could be better spent on more worthy causes, such as a better health system. On the other hand, it could be argued that, rather than investing money into the health system, one should aim to make it more efficient with its current budget. Injecting more money into healthcare does not necessarily lead to better results. It might even lead to greater inefficiencies and complacency.

- Resources could have been used to tackle poverty. There is no arguing with this, though it raises the same question about the efficiency of current funding and whether throwing more money at it would actually achieve better results.

- If we take the stance that every luxury should be sacrificed in favour of a state-of-the-art health system, people would be well looked after but would be miserable and depressed!

## Interview Skills Consulting

# QUESTION 145

**Ten years ago, most doctors wore white coats. Now, few of them do. Why is that?**

There are two issues to consider for this question.

**Infection control**
Essentially, white coats were originally designed as clothes protectors and to minimise the risk of infections as they are easy to wash often (unlike suits that have to be dry-cleaned). It was also a good way for doctors to differentiate themselves (perhaps an ego trip, but also useful in emergencies).

**Doctor-patient relationship**
In an era where the patient is at the centre of the care, the relationship between patient and doctors has taken an increased importance and in many cases it was felt that the white coat created an artificial barrier to that relationship. In an effort to get closer to their patients and to appear more professional, many doctors have dropped the white coat in favour of the more traditional suit and tie (except some GPs, who, in a further effort to get even closer to their patients, do not always bother with the tie).

Although wearing a suit has a definite advantage in terms of bringing doctors and patients closer, it also has a number of disadvantages.

- First of all, not all patients like to see their doctor in a suit. For many (particularly the elderly), the white coat symbolised a scientific authority and offered reassurance.

- Secondly, a suit is not easy to clean on a daily basis. With doctors wearing stethoscopes around their neck all day and with their tie brushing on various patients throughout the day, a suit poses an infection risk (hence recent debates about whether doctors should wear ties or not).

# QUESTION 146

**Why do you think that life expectancy in the north of England is 5 years less than in the south according to statistics?**

This sounds like a question that could be asked at an actuarial exam. It scares many candidates but if you spend 2 minutes looking at the question the answer is fairly easy.

The danger is to rush into a simplistic answer of the type: "That is because there are less healthcare facilities in the north". Although it may be true because there are more rural areas than in the south, surely it cannot account for such a big difference in life expectancy!

Here is one way of analysing the question:

**Q: What are the biggest killers in the UK?**
A: Lung cancer and heart disease.

**Q: What are the main causes of lung cancer and heart disease?**
A: Smoking and bad diet.

**Q: Who is more likely to smoke and have an unhealthy diet?**
A: People on lower incomes.

**Q: Why would there be more people on lower incomes in the north?**
A: Because it is more industrial and unemployment is higher than in the more affluent south.

Obviously, this approach is very general but it does help raise some important issues which you can use to start building an answer.

As well as smoking and diet, there are other factors that may play a role, although most likely at a lower level. Here are some arguments that you can develop:

- Statistics are often calculated over periods of several years. In particular, in order to measure the life expectancy at birth, you would need to wait until everyone from a particular year of birth has died. Therefore, the figure of 5 years is likely to include many people who were born a long time ago when living conditions were different. The 5 years quoted in the questions may not be representative of the life expectancy of a baby who is being born now. For new-born babies, the difference in life expectancy taking account of changes in lifestyles over the years may well be lower than 5 years.

- The north of England has traditionally been industrial and many inhabitants are on lower incomes than in the south. For many, this has led to a culture of excessive smoking and unhealthy diet, which itself has led to lung cancer and heart disease. This has undoubtedly been compounded by stress in many instances, due to having to raise families in difficult circumstances including threats of redundancy and unemployment. People in the south tend to be more affluent (more service-based industries) and tend to have healthier lifestyles both in terms of smoking and diet.

- Lower income is also associated with lesser awareness of health issues. People in the north on average may therefore be less receptive to health messages than in the south. Lower awareness and understanding of health issues may also mean a lower level of compliance with medication once it has been prescribed.

- Climate may have an impact on psychological well-being. The highest rates of suicide in the world are in Lithuania, Russia, Belarus, Latvia, etc. There are strong suspicions that climate plays an important role. This may also affect people living in the north of England, with possibly more depression and suicidal tendencies (note: this is purely speculative!).

- Access to healthcare may be greater in the south than in the north, as there are more rural areas in the north and services in the south are more concentrated.

- People in the south are more affluent and therefore have better access to stress-relieving activities and luxuries including holidays, gym membership, etc.

Be very careful not to generalise too much though, as you might appear bigoted. Bear in mind that we are just talking in terms of statistics here and not individual by individual. We are not saying that everyone in the north smokes, eats badly, is unemployed or on low income and is uneducated. We are talking about trends and averages covering parts of the population. If you compare individual to individual, you might even find that, for example, a lawyer in the north has a higher life expectancy than in the south because he will have a better quality of life.

# QUESTION 147

**Why do you think it is that we cannot give a guarantee that a medical treatment or surgical procedure will be successful?**

### What does successful mean?

First of all you would need to ask yourself how you define success for a surgical procedure or a medical treatment. For example, someone who needs a hip replacement may walk very well thereafter. But what if a degree of pain subsists or they limp slightly? Someone who undertakes a medical treatment may well have their original condition treated but what if the medication taken has given rise to severe side effects or, worse, to another condition? Success is not always a black–and-white concept.

In addition, you need to ask yourself whether success means success for the patient or for the doctor. A doctor will define success according to his experience and his original intentions for giving the treatment or undertaking the procedure. A patient may consider other parameters too, in accordance with their own expectation prior to treatment/procedure. For example:

- A patient may view success in relation to how much of their original lifestyle they have been able to recommence, or in relation to the degree of autonomy that they have.

- A laser eye operation which only corrects part of the patient's eyesight may be viewed as a medical success because the operation achieved a result well within the norm. But, to a patient who may have hoped for a total correction and an end to wearing spectacles, this may appear as a failure.

- A surgical operation that leaves a visible scar may be viewed as a success because it achieved its original aim, but the patient may view the remaining scar as a sign of failure or at least a lesser success.

**Patient-linked factors**
The success of a surgical operation or a medical treatment depends on many patient-related factors. In particular:

- The patient may not have revealed all the relevant information during the history taking process, therefore leading doctors to make a decision on incomplete information. This would result in the proposed treatment not being entirely suitable.

- The physical well-being of the patient at the time of the treatment or procedure is important. This could include physical characteristics or any pre-existing conditions which may interfere with the success of the treatment. For example, obesity may make a surgical procedure more complex, thereby rendering the process more risky; a smoker may have fragile skin, which enhances the risk of scarring after surgery.

- On the medical side, the proposed treatment may not have the desired result on the patient. For example, this may be because the patient is simply not responding to the treatment, because the patient has built resistance over time or because the treatment interferes with another current treatment.

- The patient may not adhere to the medical treatment or post-operative medication. This could be for many reasons, including the fear of side effects, the fear of a negative impact on lifestyle, the pain of having to count and take a large number of pills every day, etc.

- The patient may develop complications that may have an adverse effect on the success of the treatment or the procedure.

**Doctor-linked factors**
- The surgeon may not be fully competent in the procedure or in managing the condition, thus making it difficult for him to deal with adverse consequences. This could be through lack of training/exposure or because the case is rare.

ISCMEDICAL
Interview Skills Consulting

# QUESTION 148

**What do you think would be the advantages, and difficulties, for a person with a major physical disability (e.g. blindness) wishing to become a doctor?**

This question is not difficult on the whole except for the fact that it asks about major disabilities in general without specifically focusing on one.

**Advantages**
- People whose disability has affected one of their senses severely often compensate by having another sense more developed. For example, a blind person may have developed better hearing and a stronger listening ability, which could help in a medical setting. Similarly, someone who is unable to walk may have developed a stronger dexterity which could be useful in carrying out procedures and surgery.

- Blind people have also often developed an ability to retain, analyse and information efficiently. This could prove very useful during their studies and later on during their medical career.

**Difficulties**
- Major disabilities could cause serious problems for day-to-day aspects of medical care. For example, someone who cannot walk would find it difficult to attend to a patient in an emergency. A blind person would not be able to examine a patient in depth and spot important clinical signs without help from other colleagues; they would also not be in a position to ensure that they are administering the correct drug at the right dosage to a patient.

- A blind student would find it difficult to learn as fast as his colleagues as he would need to transcribe all his notes in a readable format.

Interview Skills Consulting

**Discussion**

Ultimately, there is a place in Medicine for most people, even some of the more severely disabled. Although they will of course not be in a position to take on responsibilities where their disability would endanger patient safety, there are posts that offer real prospects, either because they can be carried out with the help of others (after all a blind person could perform well as a medic if he had a suitable assistant acting as his/her eyes) or because their work is of a more academic nature.

Do you think that the Hippocratic Oath is still relevant to modern day Medicine?

### A bit of history
Born in 460 BC, Hippocrates was a Greek physician regarded as the greatest of his time and is now commonly referred to as the "Father of Medicine". Hippocrates was the creator of clinical observation and believed that illness had a physical and a rational explanation. In particular, he rejected the views held at the time that illness could be caused by superstitions or the disbelief of the gods. He accurately described disease symptoms and was the first physician to accurately describe the symptoms of pneumonia and epilepsy in children. He promoted a natural healing process of rest, a good diet, fresh air and cleanliness. He was also the first physician that held the belief that thoughts, ideas and feelings come from the brain and not the heart. Although he often used imaginary entities, they drove him to a health and logical use of the art of curing. Hippocrates travelled throughout Greece practising his Medicine. He founded a medical school on the island of Cos, Greece and began teaching his ideas. His medical ethics are at the origin of the oath that doctors swear to before exercising their art.

### The Hippocratic Oath
Before you can even consider this question, you need to be familiar with the content of the Hippocratic Oath. Since you will need to sign at least a version of it, it makes sense to read up on the matter, notwithstanding the fact that there are a few questions that may be asked at interviews.

The original Oath can be summarised as follows (in today's language):
1. You undertake to respect the oath
2. You undertake to share your knowledge with others "without fee or contract", to those close to you and other doctors only.
3. You will help the sick to the best of your abilities and judgement and you will not harm anyone.

4.  You will not kill anyone if asked, nor will you suggest such thing. You will not perform abortions.
5.  You will be chaste and religious in life and in your practice.
6.  You will leave surgical procedures to those who are qualified.
7.  Whenever you go into a house, you will help the sick without any intention to harm or injure them. You will not have sexual contacts with anyone whether they are free men or slaves.
8.  You will maintain confidentiality of everything you hear or see whether in your profession or privately.

As you can see, despite the fact that the original Oath contains a number of items which could be described as belonging to the past, most of its content is still relevant. For example, you will have recognised:

- The duty of beneficence (point 3)
- The duty of non-maleficence (points 3, 4 and 7)
- The duty of confidentiality (point 8).

Other points such as not having sexual relationships with patients (point 7) are still applicable nowadays as they are regarded as an abuse of the doctor-patient relationship and therefore harm to the patient, though of course it would be a bit much to expect doctors to be totally chaste as point 5 suggests. Point 4 is particularly important because it refers to euthanasia and abortion, which are two controversial topics. To this day, euthanasia is still illegal in the UK although there are talks of possibly introducing assisted suicides. Abortion, however, has been legalised and therefore the Oath is slightly out of date in that respect but, having said that, doctors who do not want to perform abortions can abstain from doing it. Incidentally, the same is true of contraception.

Before your interview, you should make sure that you read the General Medical Council's website (www.gmc-uk.org) and particularly the section referred to as "Good Medical Practice", which contains the practical modern day application of the Hippocratic Oath.

Interview Skills Consulting

# QUESTION 150

**Do charities have a role in society or do you think that the government should decide where all the money should go?**

### Consequences of giving charities a role

☑ Individuals exercise personal responsibility by contributing directly to the advancement of causes that matter to them. Individuals can direct funds towards an area of their choice; for example a cause with personal significance (cancer, Multiple Sclerosis, etc.).

☑ Funds can be directed to causes which would not be necessarily of great interest on a nationwide basis (for example cures for rare conditions).

☑ Causes are handled by teams that are dedicated to that cause; this leads to more targeted advertising and awareness campaigns.

☑ Greater transparency as funds are handled by a team that has a single purpose as opposed to taxation proceeds which are all lumped before being redistributed.

☑ Charities are answerable to their donors and therefore have an incentive to minimise costs and wastage. This increases trust.

☑ Different charities may choose to concentrate on different aspects of a particular cause or may approach the same problems in different ways. Such diversity is more constructive than a single-handed governmental approach.

☑ Charities are better able to find innovative solutions to find new sources of funds and to address problems at local level.

☑ Charities may be better able to highlight important issues that need to be addressed and to raise government awareness.

☒ Small charities operating may spend a large proportion of their funds on overheads and therefore may allocate a small proportion of their revenue to the causes they deal with.

☒ Several charities may deal with the same cause, thus leading to duplication of effort and overheads.

## Consequences of leaving decisions to the government

- ☑ Funds would most likely be directed to areas which affect the greatest number of people. It could thus be argued that the money would be used in the best interest of society as a whole rather than small numbers of individuals.
- ☑ Government would be able to pool resources (e.g. advertising) thus reducing overheads and general costs.

- ☒ Government would collect funds through taxation rather than donations. This would effectively force every taxpayer to contribute towards all causes rather than leaving it to individual choice. Higher taxes may build resentment.
- ☒ Government may choose to allocate funds only to causes affecting large numbers of people or to causes that have a strong lobby group. This would act against the smaller causes.
- ☒ Government may choose to exploit the allocation of charitable funds to political aims. For example, increasing funding towards arthritis sufferers 6 months before an election would undoubtedly secure an important proportion of the elderly vote.

## Discussion

In practice, charities (particularly the bigger institutions) are partly funded by government and partly by the public. In particular, charities are often best placed to decide which research is needed to solve a particular problem and they are, in a sense, entrusted by the government to make the right decision. Such a system enables a good combination of general governmental intervention towards causes that are of national interest, while enabling individuals to contribute to causes that matter to them at a personal level. Therefore the answer to the question does not have to be black and white as both can cohabit quite happily.

# QUESTION 151

**What has been the most important discovery in the last 100 years?**

This question is tricky because it implies that there is a single answer to it. In reality, there are numerous discoveries that have made a real difference in their own way and which have all been very important. For example:

- Penicillin (in the 1940s) has revolutionised surgery by considerably lowering the risk of infection. It has been complemented by high-level advances in anaesthesia, which makes surgery what it is today.
- The invention of key-hole surgery, which has further reduced the need for invasive surgery, enabling patients to minimise the length of hospital stay and their chances for a quick recovery.
- Radiography in 1896. This has since been complemented by the invention of MRI scanning and other scans, which enable quick and non- or minimally-invasive diagnosis.
- Discovery of DNA by Watson and Crick in the early 1950s. Some important applications in Medicine, but also forensic science.
- Discovery of insulin that helps regulate the daily life of many diabetics.
- The discovery of new HIV medications or combinations which have helped transform HIV/AIDS into a chronic disease thus helping control an epidemic.

Ultimately, your choice is vast but make sure that you quote a discovery that has had a wide-ranging impact across society rather than something obscure. In addition, you would be well advised to ignore discoveries whose application has yet to be fully understood. For example, the Genome project has undoubtedly been an important step in Medicine but its practical applications have yet to be fully appreciated. Many candidates have been caught out by a hostile reception from interviewers at the mention of the Genome project, because so far it has not yet yielded great returns in terms of medical advancement. The same applies to stem cell research, another favourite of medical school applicants.

Interview Skills Consulting

# MEDICAL SCHOOL INTERVIEWS

# PREPARATION, TIPS & BODY LANGUAGE

Interview Skills Consulting

# PREPARING FOR YOUR INTERVIEW

There are different types of questions that you will be asked and the preparation will differ for each type. Although it is of course important to prepare, you should also avoid over-preparing, otherwise you will run the risk of sounding rehearsed on the day.

To strike the right compromise, we recommend that you prepare using a bullet point approach (using a presentation program such as Microsoft PowerPoint® or paper). For each question, you should first brainstorm your ideas and then organise them under 2-5 headings maximum. If you have too many headings, it will mean that your ideas are not as clear as they should be and you should think again. Once you have gathered your ideas under a handful of headings you can create your slide with a bullet point per heading and no more than a couple of lines per heading to summarise what you intend to talk about.

For example, for Q.7 "Tell me about your work experience", your slide could look as follows:

---

**Tell me about your work experience**

- **GP experience.** How I obtained the work. Observing communication skills, empathy and holistic approach. Gained understanding of the different roles of a doctor.

- **Oncology experience.** Discuss impact of working as a team, multidisciplinary approach, and real difference made to patients. Also discuss interest in research and teaching.

---

The advantage of preparing in this manner is that you only write down the essential aspects of your answer and, at the interview, you will not need to remember entire sentences by heart. Instead, once the question has been asked, you will be able to create a new slide within milliseconds in your mind. In turn, this will enable you to present a structured answer to more or less any question.

**Preparing for NHS issues, ethical scenarios and lateral thinking questions**

In order to produce a good performance on these questions, you will not only show that you are knowledgeable (this book should have given you a lot of answers in this respect) but also that you are able to discuss and debate the issue which is being addressed. Unfortunately, there is no secret. You must get into the habit of discussing issues and weighing arguments before formulating an opinion.

If you feel weak on your debating abilities, you should practise with friends and family. Simply take a topic every day and spend some time discussing it as a group. Even if you do this for 15 minutes every day, every little helps!

You should also read news websites on a daily basis. The BBC's website holds enough information for you to do well. Reading newspaper articles on important issues would also enhance your ability to see things from different perspectives and debate them.

**ISC**MEDICAL

Interview Skills Consulting

# TIPS & BODY LANGUAGE

- **Dress for business.** An interview is a business meeting. Although it may look like a chat in some cases, you should never approach it casually. Wear a suit. Be smart. They are not just recruiting you for a medical school interview. Subconsciously they will imagine you with a patient. If you wear a tie with Mickey Mouse on it, they might not take you too seriously.

- **No distracting features.** Make sure that you are dressed in such a way that nothing distracts the attention from you face. Keep the jewellery to a minimum and to the neck area (no brooches – they draw the eye to your shoulder). Wear simple colours (no pockets of colours all over the place), and do not wear a tie with big motives (like a big Pink Panther at the bottom).

- **No harsh colours.** For tie colours, stick to neutral colours but, if you can, avoid pure red (can be seen as aggressive) and pure yellow (the colour of power and of people who are in control – keep it for your consultant's interview. For now you want to show a more balanced picture of empathy and determination).

- **Dress comfortably.** What matters most is that you feel comfortable in your clothes. Do not turn up in your wedding outfit. You will not feel relaxed. Simple but smart is the key!

- **Be informed.** Make sure you know a lot about the school before you go. They should have sent you a prospectus but you can find information through other means: websites, internet forums, current students (open days are good for that) and work experience.

- **Be on time.** Turn up early. It is better to be 5 hours early than 3 minutes late. To avoid last minute stress, you may wish to stay overnight at a hotel near the school. That way, you won't have to worry about late trains, the wrong type of snow or a dodgy alarm clock. By going the day before, you will also have an opportunity to find out exactly where you need to go on the day.

- **Be prepared.** Make sure that you have prepared all your documents and that you have them with you on the day of the interview (passport, etc.).

- **Be humble.** If you have written reports or papers that you feel the interviewers may be interested in, do not impose these onto them. At the interview, you can talk about these reports and briefly summarise their content. You can tell the interviewers that if they are interested you have brought a copy with you but NEVER ever force it onto them. They are probably not interested anyway and you would only embarrass them. Focus your efforts on giving a sharp concise summary of your work.

- **Shake hands.** Many people wonder whether they should shake hands with their interviewers. The answer is: it depends. If the interviews are short (e.g. four stations of 5 minutes each), then you should consider the fact that they are probably not very interested in shaking hands every 5 minutes with people. The same applies if there are several people on the panel. You do not want to waste 1 minute giving five handshakes. So, as a rule, it is okay to shake hands if the panel is small (three or less) and the interviews are of a reasonable length. A good alternative is to shake the hand of the person who welcomes you at the door and to say good morning/afternoon to everyone else with a big smile before sitting down.

- **Sit properly.** When you sit down, make sure that your feet are firmly on the ground. It will stop you from fidgeting too much and from slipping down into an uncomfortable position. You should also adopt a straight-back position with your upper body being slightly slanted forward (so that you are leaning a little towards them). A good trick is to place your backside firmly against the back of the chair and keep both feet on the ground. It will lock you in that position for the duration and that will be one less problem to think about.

- **Beware the arms.** Never cross your arms; it will make you look defensive. If you feel nervous, you can interlock your fingers and place them on your lap (if there is no table) or on the table (if there is one). If there is a table, place both arms on the table but stop short of the elbow otherwise you will be invading their space. This will also be construed as aggressive.

**ISC**MEDICAL
Interview Skills Consulting

- **Beware the drink.** If there is a glass of water on the table or any other drink, do not touch it unless you are really desperate (tickly throat, etc.). Firstly, you are running the risk of falling victim to your nerves and ending up with coffee or water all over your shirt. Secondly, some interviewers use the glass of water as a trick to see how nervous you are (you might not be visibly shaking but the movement of the water will give you away!).

- **Maintain eye contact at all cost.** This interview is all about building a rapport with your interviewers. If you do not have that rapport, you will not be able to communicate effectively. If there are only two people on the panel, look at both equally. If there are more, then look mainly at the person who asked you the question and then, occasionally, glance at the others for a few seconds to involve them. Do not keep scanning the room to maintain eye contact with everyone at all times; you will get dizzy! And the interviewers will feel uncomfortable because they will not be able to find a suitable time to scratch their nose.

- **Don't make things up.** If they are asking you a question that you have absolutely no idea how to answer, it is always better to say that you don't know than to make things up. They might just about forgive you for not knowing something if you admit to it, but they won't forgive you for making things up or for pretending. Integrity and an ability to recognise your limitations are fundamental qualities of a doctor. Bear in mind that it probably means that you do not have such a great chance for success but you never know: few people may have an answer anyway (in which case you are all at the same level). If you feel that you kind of know the answer but are not sure then you can say that too. For example, if they asked you about Clinical Governance and you only have a vague idea of it, you could say: "I am not familiar with all the details but I believe that this is something to do with maintaining quality of care in the NHS". If you are confident enough when you say it, then you could sound very credible and if you are lucky they might actually lead you through the answer from then on. If you made something up, they may not bother.

# ASKING QUESTIONS AT THE END

At the end of the interview, they may ask you if you have any questions to ask. There are two ways in which this question can be interpreted. Having a good question to ask at the end could be a sign that you are keen and interested. However, it can also mean that you have not done your homework to find out the answer before you got to the interview. In our experience, we have rarely seen a candidate who had an intelligent question. We would therefore advise that you take a safe approach by saying that you have no questions. However, you should use the opportunity that this question offers to sell your enthusiasm and a short answer such as the following will do the trick:

> *No, I don't have any questions. I talked to a lot of students and tutors during the open day and I have also learnt a lot about the school through the internet site and by talking to people on forums. I am particularly excited about the fact that the school takes a PBL approach and also by the social environment that it provides, and I am really looking forward to studying here next year.*

The benefit of this answer is that it saves you asking a question to which you should probably already know the answer, it is short enough not to be too cheesy, it sells the homework that you have done and, delivered with an enthusiastic tone, it comes across very positively.